Merry Christmas to
Laura from Blaine

POETICAL FAVORITES

POETICAL FAVORITES

YOURS AND MINE

COMPILED BY

WARREN SNYDER

INDIANAPOLIS
THE BOBBS-MERRILL COMPANY
PUBLISHERS

PRESS OF
BRAUNWORTH & CO.
BOOKBINDERS AND PRINTERS
BROOKLYN. N. Y.

A PERSONAL WORD

IT can be said with truth that this compilation was begun thirty years ago, or more; for some of the poems were taken from the compiler's scrap-book, where they have been his good friends and companions for fully that length of time.

No effort has been made to make the collection exhaustive, for no one volume could possibly contain all the favorite poems.

It is hoped, however, that between the covers of this little book there will be found enough of your favorites to justify its title.

The compiler wishes to express his thanks to publishers and authors who have so kindly permitted him to include a number of poems subject to Copyright. Thanks are also due to my young friend and business associate, Herbert H. Fletcher, of Philadelphia, for suggestions and assistance. The title was given to the collection by him.

New York
    June, 1910.

COPYRIGHT NOTICE AND PUBLISHERS' ACKNOWLEDGMENT

[ix]

by O. W. Holmes; "Are the Children at Home," "Our Own," by M. E. Sangster.

By special permission of John Lane Company, "Leetla Joe," from *Carmina*, by T. A. Daly.

By special permission of Catholic Standard and Times Publishing Company, "The Song of the Thrush," from *Canzoni*, by T. A. Daly.

By special permission of Charles Scribner's Sons, "Christmas at Sea," "The Departed Friend," from *Poems*, by R. L. Stevenson; "The Questioner," by Carl Werner, from *Scribner's Magazine*, copyright 1910; "Fiddle-Dee-Dee," "Jes' fore Christmas," from *Love Songs of Childhood*, copyright 1894, by Eugene Field; "Little Boy Blue," "Wynken, Blynken, and Nod," from *With Trumpet and Drum*, copyright 1892, by Mary French Field.

By special permission of Little, Brown & Company, "Lines on the Death of his Son Charles," by Daniel Webster, from *Daniel Webster's Complete Works*.

By special permission of Longmans, Green & Company, "Outward," from *Poems*, by W. J. Cameron.

By special permission of Edwin Markham, "Lincoln, the Man of the People."

POETICAL FAVORITES

RECOMPENSE

BY EDWIN M. ABBOTT

What is the price of manhood?
  What sale does honor bring?
Does pure, untarnished character
  Count nought in lifetime's ring?
Do bauble scions rule us?
  Does riot, ruin reign
The purest soul to trample down
  To crush, destroy, rend twain?
Is there no truth or honor
  To cause mankind to stay
The all-consuming thirst for lust
  That lures them far away?
Does honest labor cheapen
  The mold wherein we're cast;
Is black, corrupt impurity
  The flag flung from life's mast?
Forget not. One is watching,
  Our actions, day by day,

[1]

And riches gained at such a cost
   He surely will repay.
For though mankind is judging
   Appearances, poor art,
The God, the just the righteous Judge.
   Inspects our inmost heart.
Condemn not, then, I pray thee,
   For thou, thyself, some day
May seek for mercy from thy Judge,
   Whose verdict none can sway.
And temper all thy judgments
   With love and common sense.
The end well merits all 'twill bring;
   It serves full recompense.

LEEDLE YAWCOB STRAUSS

BY CHARLES FOLLEN ADAMS

I haf got a leedle boy
   Vot gomes schust to my knee;
Der queerest schap, der greatest rogue
   As efer you dit see;
He runs and jumps, and smashes dings
   In all barts of der house —
But vot of dot? he vas mine son,
   Mine leedle Yawcob Strauss.

He get der measles und der mumbs,
   Unt eferyding dot's oud;
He sbills mine glass of lager beer,
   Poots schnuff indo mine kraut;

[2]

He fills my pipe mit Limburg cheese, —
  Dot vas der roughest chouse;
I'd dake dot vrom no oder boy
  But leedle Yawcob Strauss.

He dakes der milk ban for a dhrum,
  Und cuts mine cane in dwo
To make der schticks to beat it mit —
  Mine cracious, dot vas drue!
I dinks mine head vas schplit abart,
  He kicks oup sooch a touse —
But nefer mind, der poys vas few
  Like dot young Yawcob Strauss.

He asks me questions sooch as dese:
  Who baints mine nose so red?
Who vas it cut dot schmoot blace out
  Vrom der hair ubon mine head?
Und vhere der plaze goes vrom der lamp
  Vene'er der glim I douse —
How gan I all dose dings eggsblain
  To dot shmall Yawcob Strauss?

I somedimes dink I schall go vild
  Mit sooch a grazy poy,
Und vish vonce more I gould haf rest
  Und beaceful dimes enshoy;
But ven he was ashleep in ped
  So guiet as a mouse,
I brays der Lord, "Dake anydings,
  But leaf dot Yawcob Strauss."

[3]

MOTHER'S DOUGHNUTS

El Dorado, 1851

BY CHARLES FOLLEN ADAMS

I've just been down ter Thompson's, boys,
  'N feelin' kind o' blue,
I thought I'd look in at " The Ranch,"
  Ter find out what wuz new;
When I seed this sign a-hanging
  On a shanty by the lake:
" Here's whar yer get your doughnuts
  Like yer mother used ter make."

I've seen a grizzly show his teeth,
  I've seen Kentucky Pete
Draw out his shooter, 'n advise
  A " tenderfoot " ter treat;
But nuthin' ever tuk me down,
  'N made my benders shake,
Like that sign about the doughnuts
  That my mother used ter make.

A sort o' mist shut out the ranch,
  'N standin' thar instead,
I seen an old, white farm-house,
  With its doors all painted red.
A whiff came through the open door —
  Wuz I sleepin' or awake?
The smell wuz that of doughnuts
  Like my mother used ter make.

[4]

The bees wuz hummin' round the porch
   Whar honeysuckles grew;
A yellow dish of apple-sass
   Wuz settin' thar in view.
'N on the table, by the stove,
   An old-time " Johnny-cake,"
'N a platter full of doughnuts
   Like my mother used ter make.

A patient form I seemed ter see,
   In tidy dress of black,
I almost thought I heard the words,
   " When will my boy come back?"
'N then — the old sign creaked:
   But now it was the boss who spake:
"Here's whar yer gets yer doughnuts
   Like yer mother used ter make."

Well, boys, that kind o' broke me up,
   'N ez I've " struck pay gravel,"
I ruther think I'll pack my kit,
   Vamoose the ranch, 'n travel.
I'll make the old folks jubilant,
   'N if I don't mistake,
I'll try some o' them doughnuts
   Like my mother used ter make.

THE WANTS OF MAN

BY JOHN QUINCY ADAMS

" Man wants but little here below,
　　Nor wants that little long."
'T is not with *me* exactly so;
　　But 't is so in the song.
My wants are many and, if told,
　　Would muster many a score;
And were each wish a mint of gold,
　　I still should long for more.

What first I want is daily bread —
　　And canvas-backs — and wine —
And all the realms of nature spread
　　Before me, when I dine.
Four courses scarcely can provide
　　My appetite to quell;
With four choice cooks from France beside,
　　To dress my dinner well.

What next I want, at princely cost,
　　Is elegant attire:
Black sable furs for winter's frost,
　　And silks for summer's fire,
And Cashmere shawls, and Brussels lace
　　My bosom's front to deck, —
And diamond rings my hands to grace,
　　And rubies for my neck.

[6]

I want (who does not want?) a wife, —
    Affectionate and fair;
To solace all the woes of life,
    And all its joys to share.
Of temper sweet, of yielding will,
    Of firm, yet placid mind, —
With all my faults to love me still
    With sentiment refined.

And as Time's car incessant runs,
    And Fortune fills my store,
I want of daughters and of sons
    From eight to half a score.
I want (alas! can mortal dare
    Such bliss on earth to crave?)
That all the girls be chaste and fair,
    The boys all wise and brave.

I want a warm and faithful friend,
    To cheer the adverse hour;
Who ne'er to flatter will descend,
    Nor bend the knee to power, —
A friend to chide me when I'm wrong,
    My inmost soul to see;
And that my friendship prove as strong
    For him as his for me.

I want the seals of power and place,
    The ensigns of command;
Charged by the People's unbought grace
    To rule my native land.

[7]

Nor crown nor sceptre would I ask
    But from my country's will,
By day, by night, to ply the task
    Her cup of bliss to fill.

I want the voice of honest praise
    To follow me behind,
And to be thought in future days
    The friend of human kind,
That after ages, as they rise,
    Exulting may proclaim
In choral union to the skies
    Their blessings on my name.

These are the Wants of mortal Man, —
    I cannot want them long,
For life itself is but a span,
    And earthly bliss — a song.
My last great Want — absorbing all —
    Is, when beneath the sod,
And summoned to my final call,
    The *Mercy of my God.*

ROCK ME TO SLEEP

BY ELIZABETH ANN AKERS

Backward, turn backward, O Time, in your flight,
Make me a child again just for to-night!
Mother, come back from the echoless shore,
Take me again to your heart as of yore;

Kiss from my forehead the furrows of care,
Smooth the few silver threads out of my hair;
Over my slumbers your loving watch keep;—
Rock me to sleep, mother,— rock me to sleep!

Backward, flow backward, O tide of the years!
I am so weary of toil and of tears,—
Toil without recompense, tears all in vain,—
Take them, and give me my childhood again!
I have grown weary of dust and decay,—
Weary of flinging my soul-wealth away;
Weary of sowing for others to reap;—
Rock me to sleep, mother,— rock me to sleep!

Tired of the hollow, the base, the untrue,
Mother, O mother, my heart calls for you!
Many a summer the grass has grown green,
Blossomed, and faded our faces between,
Yet with strong yearning and passionate pain
Long I to-night for your presence again.
Come from the silence so long and so deep;—
Rock me to sleep, mother,— rock me to sleep!

Over my heart, in the days that are flown,
No love like mother-love ever has shone;
No other worship abides and endures,—
Faithful, unselfish, and patient like yours:
None like a mother can charm away pain
From the sick soul and the world-weary brain.
Slumber's soft calms o'er my heavy lids creep;—
Rock me to sleep, mother,— rock me to sleep!

[9]

Come, let your brown hair, just lighted with gold,
Fall on your shoulders again as of old;
Let it drop over my forehead to-night,
Shading my faint eyes away from the light;
For with its sunny-edged shadows once more
Haply will throng the sweet vision of yore;
Lovingly, softly, its bright billows sweep;—
Rock me to sleep, mother,— rock me to sleep!

Mother, dear mother, the years have been long
Since I last listened your lullaby song:
Sing, then, and unto my soul it shall seem
Womanhood's years have been only a dream.
Clasped to your heart in a loving embrace,
With your light lashes just sweeping my face,
Never hereafter to wake or to weep;—
Rock me to sleep, mother,— rock me to sleep!

SHE AND HE

BY EDWIN ARNOLD

" She is dead! " they said to him. " Come away;
Kiss her! and leave her! — thy love is clay! "

They smoothed her tresses of dark brown hair;
On her forehead of marble they laid it fair:

Over her eyes, which gazed too much,
They drew the lids with a gentle touch;

With a tender touch they closed up well
The sweet thin lips that had secrets to tell;

[10]

About her brows, and her dear, pale face
They tied her veil and her marriage-lace;

And drew on her white feet her white silk shoes;—
Which were the whiter no eye could choose!

And over her bosom they crossed her hands;
"Come away," they said,—"God understands!"

And then there was Silence;—and nothing there
But the Silence—and scents of eglantere,

And jasmine, and roses, and rosemary;
For they said, "As a lady should lie, lies she!"

And they held their breath as they left the room,
With a shudder to glance at its stillness and gloom.

But he—who loved her too well to dread
The sweet, the stately, the beautiful dead,—

He lit his lamp, and took the key,
And turn'd it!—Alone again—he and she!

He and she; but she would not speak,
Though he kiss'd, in the old place, the quiet cheek;

He and she; yet she would not smile,
Though he call'd her the name that was fondest erewhile.

He and she; and she did not move
To any one passionate whisper of love!

Then he said, "Cold lips! and breast without breath!
Is there no voice?—no language of death

[11]

" Dumb to the ear and still to the sense
But to heart and to soul distinct, — intense?

"See, now, — I listen with soul, not ear—
What was the secret of dying, Dear?

" Was it the infinite wonder of all,
That you ever could let life's flower fall?

" Or was it a greater marvel to feel
The perfect calm o'er the agony steal?

" Was the miracle greatest to find how deep,
Beyond all dreams, sank downward that sleep?

" Did life roll backward its record, Dear,
And show, as they say it does, past things clear?

"And was it the innermost heart of the bliss
To find out so what a wisdom love is?

" Oh, perfect Dead! oh, Dead most dear,
I hold the breath of my soul to hear;

" I listen — as deep as to horrible hell,
As high as to heaven! — and you do not tell!

" There must be pleasures in dying, Sweet,
To make you so placid from head to feet!

" I would tell *you*, Darling, if I were dead,
And 'twere your hot tears upon *my* brow shed.

" I would say though the angel of death had laid
His sword on my lips to keep it unsaid.

[12]

" *You* should not ask, vainly, with streaming eyes,
Which in Death's touch was the chiefest surprise;

" The very strangest and suddenest thing
Of all the surprises that dying must bring."

Ah! foolish world! Oh! most kind Dead!
Though he told me, who will believe it was said?

Who will believe that he heard her say,
With the soft rich voice, in the dear old way:—

" The utmost wonder is this, — I hear,
And see you, and love you, and kiss you, Dear;

" I can speak, now you listen with soul alone;
If your soul could see, it would all be shown.

" What a strange delicious amazement is Death,
To be without body and breathe without breath.

" I should laugh for joy if you did not cry;
Oh, listen! Love lasts! — Love never will die.

" I am only your Angel who was your Bride;
And I know, that though dead, I have never died."

WOMAN'S INCONSTANCY

BY SIR ROBERT AYTON

I loved thee once, I'll love no more,
    Thine be the grief as is the blame;
Thou art not what thou wast before,
    What reason I should be the same?

[13]

He that can love unloved again,
　Hath better store of love than brain:
God send me love my debts to pay,
While unthrifts fool their love away.

Nothing could have my love o'erthrown,
　If thou hadst still continued mine;
Yea, if thou hadst remain'd thy own,
　I might perchance have yet been thine.
　　But thou thy freedom did recall,
　　That if thou might elsewhere inthrall;
　And then how could I but disdain
　A captive's captive to remain?

When new desires had conquer'd thee,
　And changed the object of thy will,
It had been lethargy in me,
　Not constancy, to love thee still.
　　Yea, it had been a sin to go
　　And prostitute affection so,
　Since we are taught no prayers to say
　To such as must to others pray.

Yet do thou glory in thy choice,
　Thy choice of his good fortune boast;
I'll neither grieve nor yet rejoice,
　To see him gain what I have lost;
　　The height of my disdain shall be,
　　To laugh at him, to blush for thee;
　To love thee still, but go no more
　A begging to a beggar's door.

[14]

SCHOOL DAYS

BY THE REV. DR. MALTBIE D. BABCOCK

Lord, let me make this rule,
To think of life as school,
    And try my best
    To stand each test,
    And do my work
    And nothing shirk.

Should some one else outshine
This dullard head of mine,
    Should I be sad?
    I will be glad.
    To do my best
    Is Thy behest.

If weary with my book
I cast a wistful look
    Where posies grow
    O let me know
    That flowers within
    Are best to win.

Dost take my book away
Anon to let me play,
    And let me out
    To run about?
    I grateful bless
    Thee for recess.

Then recess past, alack,
I turn me slowly back.
  On my hard bench
  My hands to clench,
  And set my heart
  To learn my part.

These lessons Thou dost give
To teach me how to live,
  To do, to bear,
  To get and share,
  To work and pray
  And trust alway.

What though I may not ask
To choose my daily task?
  Thou hast decreed
  To meet my need.
  What pleases Thee,
  That shall please me.

Some day the bell will sound
Some day my heart will bound,
  As with a shout
  That school is out
  And lessons done,
  I homeward run!

LIFE

"Animula, vagula, blandula."— EMPEROR HADRIAN

BY ANNA LETITIA BARBAULD

Life! I know not what thou art,
But know that thou and I must part;
And when, or how, or where we met
I own to me's a secret yet.
But this I know, when thou art fled,
Where'er they lay these limbs, this head,
No clod so valueless shall be,
As all that then remains of me.
O, whither, whither dost thou fly,
Where bend unseen thy trackless course,
   And in this strange divorce,
Ah, tell where I must seek this compound I?

To the vast ocean of empyreal flame,
   From whence thy essence came,
   Dost thou thy flight pursue, when freed
   From matter's base encumbering weed?
      Or dost thou, hid from sight,
      Wait, like some spell-bound knight,
Through blank, oblivious years the appointed hour
To break thy trance and reassume thy power?
Yet canst thou, without thought or feeling be?
O, say what art thou, when no more thou 'rt thee?

Life! we've been long together
Through pleasant and through cloudy weather;
   'Tis hard to part when friends are dear, —

[17]

Perhaps 't will cost a sigh, a tear;
Then steal away, give little warning,
   Choose thine own time;
Say not Good Night, — but in some brighter clime
   Bid me Good Morning.

THE NEW YEAR LEDGER

BY AMELIA E. BARR

I said one year ago,
  " I wonder, if I truly kept
A list of days when life burnt low,
  Of days I smiled and days I wept,
If good or bad would highest mount
When I made up the year's account? "

I took a ledger fair and fine,
  " And now," I said, " when days are glad,
I'll write with bright red ink the line,
  And write with black when they are bad,
So that they'll stand before my sight
As clear apart as day and night.

" I will not heed the changing skies,
  Nor if it shine nor if it rain;
But if there comes some sweet surprise,
  Or friendship, love or honest gain,
Why, then it shall be understood
That day is written down as good.

" Or if to any one I love
  A blessing meets them on the way,

[18]

That will to me a pleasure prove:
  So it shall be a happy day;
And if some day, I've cause to dread
Pass harmless by, I'll write it red.

" When hands and brain stand labor's test,
    And I can do the thing I would
Those days when I am at my best
    Shall all be traced as very good.
And in ' red letter,' too, I'll write
Those rare, strong hours when right is might.

" When first I meet in some grand book
    A noble soul that touches mine,
And with this vision I can look
    Through some gate beautiful of time,
That day such happiness will shed
That golden-lined will seem the red.

" And when pure, holy thoughts have power
    To touch my heart and dim my eyes,
And I in some diviner hour
    Can hold sweet converse with the skies,
Ah! then my soul may safely write:
' This day has been most good and bright.' "

What do I see on looking back?
    A red-lined book before me lies,
With here and there a thread of black,
    That like a gloomy shadow flies, —
A shadow it must be confessed,
That often rose in my own breast.

[19]

And I have found it good to note
   The blessing that is mine each day;
For happiness is vainly sought
   In some dim future far away.
Just try my ledger for a year,
   Then look with grateful wonder back,
And you will find, there is no fear,
   The red days far exceed the black.

THE QUESTIONS

BY BYRON BEACH

Ah, Life, what art thou,
   With thy smiles, and with thy fears?
And what is Love,
   That kisses Youth, and lingers through the years?
And what is Death,
   That chills each heart, and stills all troubling fears?

Dost thou not know, thou wanderer of mine?
   Dost thou not harken to the breath of Spring
And hopes that thrill and pine?
   Dost thou know enough, that Life is good;
That Life is joy untold,
   As free and broad as sunset ray?
A clay it is, for thine own hand to mold;
   To make or mar it — as you may.

And what is Love?
Ah, foolish child, to ask it in thy mood.
What it is, thine own heart knows,

[20]

And strives to do its bidding.
It serves thee well and tenderly.
What else it is, thou canst not know.

And what is Death?
Ah, child of mine, seek far and well
    Before you turn from me.
    A dream is but a rose's breath — so pure and free;
And so is Death.   'Tis but a dream,
    A sleep — a tender kiss;
A pillow for thy care and tear; —
    It is not, then, amiss.

And what is Life?
And what is Love?
And what is Death?

Seek, child, no more, nor worry with thy queries,
    For Life is Love; and Love is Death,
    And Death is peace and sweet, —
Sweet rest for one who wearies.

DIRGE FOR A SOLDIER

On the death of General Philip Kearney at Chantilly, Va.

BY GEORGE HENRY BOKER

Close his eyes; his work is done!
    What to him is friend or foeman,
Rise of moon or set of sun,
    Hand of man or kiss of woman?

[21]

Lay him low, lay him low,
In the clover or the snow!
What cares he? he cannot know;
Lay him low!

As man may, he fought his fight,
Proved his truth by his endeavor;
Let him sleep in solemn night,
Sleep forever and forever.
Lay him low, lay him low,
In the clover or the snow!
What cares he? he cannot know;
Lay him low!

Fold him in his country's stars,
Roll the drum and fire the volley!
What to him are all our wars? —
What but death-bemocking folly?
Lay him low, lay him low,
In the clover or the snow!
What cares he? he cannot know;
Lay him low!

Leave him to God's watching eye;
Trust him to the hand that made him.
Mortal love weeps idly by;
God alone has power to aid him.
Lay him low, lay him low,
In the clover or the snow!
What care he? he cannot know;
Lay him low!

[22]

LIGHT

BY FRANCIS W. BOURDILLON

The night has a thousand eyes,
  And the day but one;
Yet the light of the bright world dies,
  With the dying sun.

The mind has a thousand eyes,
  And the heart but one;
Yet the light of a whole life dies,
  When love is done.

O LITTLE TOWN OF BETHLEHEM

BY THE REV. DR. PHILLIPS BROOKS

O little town of Bethlehem,
  How still we see thee lie!
Above thy deep and dreamless sleep
  The silent hours go by;
Yet in thy dark street shineth
  The everlasting Light;
The hopes and fears of all the years
  Are met in thee to-night.

For Christ is born of Mary,
  And, gathered all above,
While mortals sleep, the angels keep
  Their watch of wond'ring love;
O morning stars, together
  Proclaim the holy birth,

And praises sing to God the King,
  And peace to men on earth.

How silently, how silently,
  The wondrous gift is given!
So God imparts to human hearts
  The blessings of His heaven;
No ear may hear His coming,
  But in this world of sin,
Where meek souls will receive Him, still
  The dear Christ enters in.

O Holy Child of Bethlehem,
  Decend to us, we pray;
Cast out our sin and enter in;
  Be born in us to-day;
We hear the Christmas angels
  The great glad tidings tell;
O come to us, abide with us,
  Our Lord Immanuel.

A COURT LADY

BY ELIZABETH BARRETT BROWNING

Her hair was tawny with gold, her eyes with purple
    were dark,
Her cheeks' pale opal burnt with a red and restless
    spark.

Never was lady of Mílan nobler in name and in race;
Never was lady of Italy fairer to see in the face.

Never was lady on earth more true as woman and
      wife,
Larger in judgment and instinct, prouder in manners
      and life.

She stood in the early morning, and said to her maidens,
      " Bring
That silken robe made ready to wear at the court of
      the king.

" Bring me the clasps of diamond, lucid, clear of the
      mote,
Clasp me the large at the waist, and clasp me the
      small at the throat.

" Diamonds to fasten the hair, and diamonds to fasten
      the sleeves,
Laces to drop from their rays, like a powder of snow
      from the eaves."

Gorgeous she entered the sunlight which gathered
      her up in a flame,
While straight, in her open carriage, she to the hospi-
      tal came.

In she went at the door, and gazing, from end to end,
" Many and low are the pallets, but each is the place
      of a friend."

Up she passed through the wards, and stood at a
      young man's bed:

Bloody the band on his brow, and livid the droop of
 his head.

"Art thou a Lombard, my brother? Happy art
 thou!" she cried,
And smiled like Italy on him: he dreamed in her
 face and died.

Pale with his passing soul, she went on still to a second
He was a grave, hard man, whose years by dungeons
 were reckoned.

Wounds in his body were sore, wounds in his life
 were sorer.
"Art thou a Romagnole?" Her eyes drove lightnings before her.

"Austrian and priest had joined to double and tighten
 the cord
Able to bind thee, O strong one, — free by the stroke
 of a sword.

"Now be grave for the rest of us, using the life over-
 cast
To ripen our wine of the present (too new) in glooms
 of the past."

Down she stepped to a pallet where lay a face like
 a girl's,
Young, and pathetic with dying, — a deep black hole
 in the curls.

Art thou from Tuscany, brother? and seest thou,
    dreaming in pain,
Thy mother stand in the piazza, searching the list
    of the slain? "

Kind as a mother herself, she touched his cheeks
    with her hands:
" Blessed is she who has borne thee, although she
    should weep as she stands."

On she passed to a Frenchman, his arm carried off
    by a ball:
Kneeling, . . . " O more than my brother! how shall
    I thank thee for all?

' Each of the heroes around us has fought for his
    land and line,
But *thou* hast fought for a stranger, in hate of a wrong
    not thine.

" Happy are all free peoples, too strong to be dis-
    possessed;
But blesséd are those among nations who dare to be
    strong for the rest! "

Ever she passed on her way, and came to a couch
    where pined
One with a face from Venetia, white with a hope
    out of mind.

Long she stood and gazed, and twice she tried at
    the name,

[27]

But two great crystal tears were all that faltered
and came.

Only a tear for Venice? — she turned as in passion
and loss,
And stooped to his forehead and kissed it, as if she
were kissing the cross.

Faint with that strain of heart, she moved on then
to another,
Stern and strong in his death. "And dost thou
suffer, my brother?"

Holding his hands in hers: — "Out of the Piedmont
lion
Cometh the sweetness of freedom! sweetest to live
or to die on."

Holding his cold, rough hands, — "Well, O, well
have ye done
In noble, noble Piedmont, who would not be noble
alone."

Back he fell while she spoke. She rose to her feet
with a spring, —
"That was a Piedmontese! and this is the Court
of the King."

A WOMAN'S ANSWER

BY ELIZABETH BARRETT BROWNING

Do you know you have asked for the costliest thing
   Ever made by the Hand above —
A woman's heart and a woman's life,
   And a woman's most wonderful love?

Do you know you have asked for this priceless thing,
   As a child might ask for a toy?
Demanding what others have died to win,
   With a reckless dash of a boy?

You have written my lesson of duty out,
   Manlike you have questioned me —
Now stand at the bar of my woman's soul
   Until I question thee.

You require your mutton shall always be hot,
   Your socks and your shirts shall be whole;
I require your heart to be true as God's stars,
   And pure as heaven your soul.

You require a cook for your mutton and beef;
   I require a far better thing:
A seamstress you ask for stockings and shirt,
   I look for a man and a king.

A king for a beautiful realm called home,
   And a man that the Maker, God,
Shall look upon as he did the first,
   And say, " It is very good."

I am fair and young, but the rose will fade
  From my soft young cheek one day;
Will you love me then 'mid the falling leaves,
  As you did 'mid the bloom of May?

Is your heart an ocean so strong and deep
  I may launch my all on its tide?
A loving woman finds heaven or hell
  On the day she is made a bride.

I require all things that are grand and true,
  All things that man should be;
If you give this all I would stake my life
  To be all you demand of me.

If you cannot do this — a laundress and cook
  You can hire, with little to pay;
But a woman's heart and a woman's life
  Are not to be won that way.

EVELYN HOPE

BY ROBERT BROWNING

Beautiful Evelyn Hope is dead!
  Sit and watch by her side an hour.
That is her book-shelf, this her bed;
  She plucked that piece of geranium-flower,
Beginning to die too, in the glass.
  Little has yet been changed, I think;
The shutters are shut, — no light may pass
  Save two long rays through the hinge's chink.

[30]

Sixteen years old when she died!
　　Perhaps she had scarcely heard my name, —
It was not her time to love; beside,
　　Her life had many a hope and aim,
Duties enough and little cares;
　　And now was quiet, now astir, —
Till God's hand beckoned unawares,
　　And the sweet white brow is all of her.

Is it too late, then, Evelyn Hope?
　　What! your soul was pure and true;
The good stars met in your horoscope,
　　Made you of spirit, fire, and dew;
And just because I was thrice as old,
　　And our paths in the world diverged so wide,
Each was naught to each, must I be told?
　　We were fellow-mortals, — naught beside?

No, indeed! for God above
　　Is great to grant as mighty to make,
And creates the love to reward the love;
　　I claim you still, for my own love's sake!
Delayed, it may be, for more lives yet,
　　Through worlds I shall traverse, not a few;
Much is to learn and much to forget
　　Ere the time be come for taking you.

But the time will come — at last it will —
　　When, Evelyn Hope, what meant, I shall say,
In the lower earth, — in the years long still, —
　　That body and soul so pure and gay?

[31]

Why your hair was amber I shall divine,
   And your mouth of your own geranium's red,—
And what you would do with me, in fine,
   In the new life come in the old one's stead.

I have lived, I shall say, so much since then,
   Given up myself so many times,
Gained me the gains of various men,
   Ransacked the ages, spoiled the climes;
Yet one thing — one — in my soul's full scope,
   Either I missed or itself missed me, —
And I want and find you, Evelyn Hope!
   What is the issue? let us see!

I loved you, Evelyn, all the while;
   My heart seemed full as it could hold, —
There was place and to spare for the frank young
     smile,
   And the red young mouth, and the hair's young
     gold.
So, hush! I will give you this leaf to keep;
   See, I shut it inside the sweet, cold hand.
There, that is our secret! go to sleep;
   You will wake, and remember, and understand.

THE DEATH OF THE FLOWERS

BY WILLIAM CULLEN BRYANT

The melancholy days are come, the saddest of the
   year,
Of wailing winds, and naked woods, and meadows
   brown and sere.

[32]

Heap'd in the hollows of the grove, the autumn leaves
    lie dead;
They rustle to the eddying gust, and to the rabbit's
    tread.
The robin and the wren are flown, and from the shrubs
    the jay,
And from the wood-top calls the crow through all the
    gloomy days.

Where are the flowers, the fair young flowers, that
    lately sprang and stood
In brighter light and softer airs, a beauteous sister-
    hood?
Alas! they all are in their graves; the gentle race of
    flowers
Are lying in their lowly beds with the fair and good of
    ours.
The rain is falling where they lie; but the cold Novem-
    ber rain
Calls not from out the gloomy earth the lovely ones
    again.

The wind-flower and the violet, they perish'd long
    ago,
And the brier-rose and the orchis died amid the sum-
    mer glow;
But on the hill the golden-rod, and the aster in the
    wood,
And the yellow sunflower by the brook, in autumn
    beauty stood,
Till fell the frost from the clear cold heaven, as falls
    the plague on men,

And the brightness of their smile was gone from upland, glade, and glen.

And now, when comes the calm mild day, as still such
days will come,
To call the squirrel and the bee from out their winter
home;
When the sound of dropping nuts is heard, though all
the trees are still,
And twinkle in the smoky light the waters of the
rill,
The south wind searches for the flowers whose fragrance late he bore,
And sighs to find them in the wood and by the stream
no more.

And then I think of one who in her youthful beauty
died,
The fair meek blossom that grew up and faded by my
side.
In the cold moist earth we laid her when the forest
cast the leaf,
And we wept that one so lovely should have a life so
brief;
Yet not unmeet it was that one, like that young friend
of ours,
So gentle and so beautiful, should perish with the
flowers.

AMERICA

BY WILLIAM CULLEN BRYANT

O mother of a mighty race,
Yet lovely in thy youthful grace!
The elder dames, thy haughty peers,
Admire and hate thy blooming years;
   With words of shame
And taunts of scorn they join thy name.

For on thy cheeks the glow is spread
That tints thy morning hills with red;
Thy step, — the wild deer's rustling feet
Within thy woods are not more fleet;
   Thy hopeful eye
Is bright as thine own sunny sky.

Ay, let them rail, those haughty ones,
While safe thou dwellest with thy sons.
They do not know how loved thou art,
How many a fond and fearless heart
   Would rise to throw
Its life between thee and the foe.

They know not, in their hate and pride,
What virtues with thy children bide, —
How true, how good, thy graceful maids
Make bright, like flowers, the valley shades;
   What generous men
Spring, like thine oaks, by hill and glen;

What cordial welcomes greet the guest
By thy lone rivers of the west;
How faith is kept, and truth revered,
And man is loved, and God is feared,
　　　In woodland homes,
And where the ocean border foams.

There's freedom at thy gates, and rest
For earth's down-trodden and opprest,
A shelter for the hunted head,
For the starved laborer toil and bread.
　　　Power, at thy bounds,
Stops, and calls back his baffled hounds.

O fair young mother! on thy brow
Shall sit a nobler grace than now.
Deep in the brightness of thy skies,
The thronging years in glory rise,
　　　And, as they fleet,
Drop strength and riches at thy feet.

Thine eye, with every coming hour,
Shall brighten, and thy form shall tower;
And when thy sisters, elder born,
Would brand thy name with words of scorn,
　　　Before thine eye
Upon their lips the taunt shall die.

THE PLANTING OF THE APPLE–TREE
BY WILLIAM CULLEN BRYANT

Come, let us plant the apple-tree.
Cleave the tough greensward with the spade;
Wide let its hollow bed be made;
There gently lay the roots, and there
Sift the dark mould with kindly care,
   And press it o'er them tenderly,
As round the sleeping infant's feet
We softly fold the cradle-sheet;
   So plant we the apple-tree.

What plant we in this apple-tree?
Buds, which the breath of summer days
Shall lengthen into leafy sprays;
Boughs where the thrush with crimson breast
Shall haunt, and sing, and hide her nest;
   We plant, upon the sunny lea,
A shadow for the noontide hour,
A shelter from the summer shower,
   When we plant the apple-tree.

What plant we in this apple-tree?
Sweets for a hundred flowery springs
To load the May-wind's restless wings,
When, from the orchard row, he pours
Its fragrance through our open doors;
   A world of blossoms for the bee,
Flowers for the sick girl's silent room,
For the glad infant sprigs of bloom,
   We plant with the apple-tree.

[37]

What plant we in this apple-tree?
Fruits that shall swell in sunny June,
And redden in the August noon,
And drop, when gentle airs come by,
That fan the blue September sky,
　While children come, with cries of glee,
And seek them where the fragrant grass
Betrays their bed to those who pass,
　　At the foot of the apple-tree.

And when, above this apple-tree,
The winter stars are quivering bright,
And winds go howling through the night,
Girls, whose young eyes o'erflow with mirth,
Shall peel its fruit by cottage hearth,
　And guests in prouder homes shall see,
Heaped with the grape of Cintra's vine
And golden orange of the Line,
　　The fruit of the apple-tree.

The fruitage of this apple-tree
Winds and our flag of stripe and star
Shall bear to coasts that lie afar,
Where men shall wonder at the view,
And ask in what fair groves they grew;
　And sojourners beyond the sea
Shall think of childhood's careless day
And long, long hours of summer play,
　　In the shade of the apple-tree.

Each year shall give this apple-tree
A broader flush of roseate bloom,

A deeper maze of verdurous gloom,
And loosen, when the frost-clouds lower,
The crisp brown leaves in thicker shower.
  The years shall come and pass, but we
Shall hear no longer, where we lie,
The summer's songs, the autumn's sigh,
  In the boughs of the apple-tree.

And time shall waste this apple-tree.
O, when its aged branches throw
Thin shadows on the ground below,
Shall fraud and force and iron will
Oppress the weak and helpless still?
  What shall the tasks of mercy be,
Amid the toils, the strifes, the tears
Of those who live when length of years
  Is wasting this apple-tree?

" Who planted this old apple-tree? "
The children of that distant day
Thus to some aged man shall say;
And, gazing on its mossy stem,
The gray-haired man shall answer them:
  " A poet of the land was he,
Born in the rude but good old times;
'Tis said he made some quaint old rhymes
  On planting the apple-tree."

THANATOPSIS

BY WILLIAM CULLEN BRYANT

"'Thanatopsis' appeared in the September number of the *North American Review* for 1817 [Bryant wrote it in 1812 at the age of 18], and proved to be not only the finest poem which had yet been produced on this continent, but one of the most remarkable poems ever produced at such an early age. From the day this poem appeared, the name of its author was classed among the most cherished literary assets of the nation." —JOHN BIGELOW.

To him who, in the love of Nature, holds
Communion with her visible forms, she speaks
A various language: for his gayer hours
She has a voice of gladness, and a smile
And eloquence of beauty; and she glides
Into his darker musings with a mild
And healing sympathy, that steals away
Their sharpness, ere he is aware. When thoughts
Of the last bitter hour come like a blight
Over thy spirit, and sad images
Of the stern agony, and shroud, and pall,
And breathless darkness, and the narrow house,
Make thee to shudder, and grow sick at heart,
Go forth under the open sky, and list
To Nature's teachings, while from all around —
Earth and her waters, and the depths of air —
Comes a still voice: — Yet a few days, and thee
The all-beholding sun shall see no more
In all his course; nor yet in the cold ground,
Where thy pale form was laid, with many tears,
Nor in the embrace of ocean, shall exist
Thy image. Earth, that nourished thee, shall claim

Thy growth, to be resolved to earth again;
And, lost each human trace, surrendering up
Thine individual being, shalt thou go
To mix forever with the elements;
To be a brother to the insensible rock,
And to the sluggish clod, which the rude swain
Turns with his share, and treads upon. The oak
Shall send his roots abroad, and pierce thy mould.
    Yet not to thine eternal resting-place
Shalt thou retire alone, — nor couldst thou wish
Couch more magnificent. Thou shalt lie down
With patriarchs of the infant world, — with kings,
The powerful of the earth, — the wise, the good,
Fair forms, and hoary seers of ages past,
All in one mighty sepulchre. The hills,
Rock-ribbed, and ancient as the sun; the vales
Stretching in pensive quietness between;
The venerable woods; rivers that move
In majesty, and the complaining brooks,
That make the meadows green; and, poured round all,
Old ocean's gray and melancholy waste, —
Are but the solemn decorations all
Of the great tomb of man! The golden sun,
The planets, all the infinite host of heaven,
Are shining on the sad abodes of death,
Through the still lapse of ages. All that tread
The globe are but a handful to the tribes
That slumber in its bosom. Take the wings
Of morning, pierce the Barcan wilderness,
Or lose thyself in the continuous woods
Where rolls the Oregon, and hears no sound

Save his own dashings, — yet the dead are there!
And millions in those solitudes, since first
The flight of years began, have laid them down
In their last sleep, — the dead reign there alone!
So shalt thou rest; and what if thou withdraw
In silence from the living, and no friend
Take note of thy departure? All that breathe
Will share thy destiny. The gay will laugh
When thou art gone, the solemn brood of care
Plod on, and each one, as before, will chase
His favorite phantom; yet all these shall leave
Their mirth and their employments, and shall come
And make their bed with thee. As the long train
Of ages glide away, the sons of men —
The youth in life's green spring, and he who goes
In the full strength of years, matron and maid,
And the sweet babe, and the gray-headed man —
Shall, one by one, be gathered to thy side
By those who in their turn shall follow them.

So live, that when thy summons comes to join
The innumerable caravan that moves
To the pale realms of shade, where each shall take
His chamber in the silent halls of death,
Thou go not, like the quarry-slave at night,
Scourged to his dungeon, but, sustained and soothed
By an unfaltering trust, approach thy grave
Like one who wraps the drapery of his couch
About him, and lies down to pleasant dreams.

WASHINGTON'S BIRTHDAY

BY WILLIAM CULLEN BRYANT

Yet has no month a prouder day,
　　Not even when the summer broods
O'er meadows in their fresh array,
　　Or autumn tints the glowing woods.

For this chill season now again
　　Brings in its annual rounds the morn
When greatest of the sons of men,
　　Our glorious Washington, was born.

AULD LANG SYNE

BY ROBERT BURNS

Should auld acquaintance be forgot,
　　And never brought to min'?
Should auld acquaintance be forgot,
　　And days o' lang syne?

CHORUS

For auld lang syne, my dear,
　　For auld lang syne,
We'll tak a cup o' kindness yet,
　　For auld lang syne.

We twa hae run about the braes,
　　And pu'd the gowans fine;
But we've wandered mony a weary foot
　　Sin' auld lang syne.
　　　　　For auld, etc.

[43]

We twa hae paidl't i' the burn,
   Frae mornin' sun till dine;
But seas between us braid hae roared
   Sin' auld lang syne.
         For auld, etc.

And here's a hand, my trusty fiere,
   And gie's a hand o' thine;
And we'll tak a right guid-willie waught
   For auld lang syne.
         For auld, etc.

And surely ye'll be your pint-stowp,
   And surely I'll be mine;
And we'll tak a cup o' kindness yet
   For auld lang syne.
         For auld, etc.

HIGHLAND MARY

BY ROBERT BURNS

Ye banks, and braes, and streams around
   The castle o' Montgomery,
Green be your woods, and fair your flowers,
   Your waters never drumlie!
There simmer first unfauld her robes,
   And there the langest tarry;
For there I took the last fareweel
   O' my sweet Highland Mary.

How sweetly bloom'd the gay green birk,
   How rich the hawthorn's blossom,

As, underneath their fragrant shade,
   I clasp'd her to my bosom!
The golden hours, on angel wings,
   Flew o'er me and my dearie;
For dear to me as light and life
   Was my sweet Highland Mary!

Wi' mony a vow, and lock'd embrace,
   Our parting was fu' tender;
And, pledging aft to meet again,
   We tore oursels asunder;
But, oh, fell death's untimely frost,
   That nipp'd flower sae early!
Now green's the sod, and cauld's the clay,
   That wraps my Highland Mary!

Oh, pale, pale now, those rosy lips
   I aft ha'e kiss'd sae fondly!
And closed for aye the sparkling glance
   That dwalt on me sae kindly!
And mouldering now in silent dust
   That heart that lo'ed me dearly;
But still within my bosom's core
   Shall live my Highland Mary!

MAN WAS MADE TO MOURN

BY ROBERT BURNS

Gilbert Burns, the brother of the poet, says: "He (Burns) used to remark to me that he could not well conceive a more mortifying picture of human life than a man seeking work. In casting about in his mind how this sentiment might be brought forward, the elegy, ' Man was Made to Mourn' was composed."

When chill November's surly blast
    Made fields and forests bare,
One evening, as I wandered forth
    Along the banks of Ayr,
I spied a man whose aged step
    Seemed weary, worn with care;
His face was furrowed o'er with years,
    And hoary was his hair.

" Young stranger, whither wanderest thou? "
    Began the reverend sage;
" Does thirst of wealth thy step constrain,
    Or youthful pleasures rage?
Or haply, prest with cares and woes,
    Too soon thou hast began
To wander forth, with me, to mourn
    The miseries of man!

" The sun that overhangs yon moors,
    Outspreading far and wide,
Where hundreds labor to support
    A haughty lordling's pride, —
I've seen yon weary winter sun
    Twice forty times return;

[46]

And every time has added proofs
   That man was made to mourn.

" O man, while in thy early years,
   How prodigal of time!
Misspending all thy precious hours,
   Thy glorious youthful prime!
Alternate follies take the sway:
   Licentious passions burn;
Which tenfold force gives Nature's law,
   That man was made to mourn.

" Look not alone on youthful prime,
   Or manhood's active might;
Man then is useful to his kind,
   Supported in his right;
But see him on the edge of life,
   With cares and sorrows worn,
Then age and want, O ill-matched pair!
   Show man was made to mourn.

" A few seem favorites of fate,
   In pleasure's lap carest;
Yet think not all the rich and great
   Are likewise truly blest.
But, O, what crowds in every land
   Are wretched and forlorn!
Through weary life this lesson learn, —
   That man was made to mourn.

" Many and sharp the numerous ills,
   Inwoven with our frame!

[47]

More pointed still we make ourselves,
    Regret, remorse, and shame!
And man, whose heaven-erected face
    The smiles of love adorn,
Man's inhumanity to man
    Makes countless thousands mourn!

" See yonder poor, o'erlabored wight,
    So abject, mean, and vile,
Who begs a brother of the earth
    To give him leave to toil;
And see his lordly fellow-worm
    The poor petition spurn,
Unmindful, 'though a weeping wife
    And helpless offspring mourn.

" If I'm designed yon lordling's slave,
    By Nature's law designed, —
Why was an independent wish
    E'er planted in my mind?
If not, why am I subject to
    His cruelty or scorn?
Or why has man the will and power
    To make his fellow mourn?

" Yet let not this too much, my son,
    Disturb thy youthful breast:
This partial view of humankind
    Is surely not the last!
The poor, oppressèd, honest man
    Had never, sure, been born,

Had there not been some recompense
  To comfort those that mourn!

" O Death! the poor man's dearest friend,
  The kindest and the best!
Welcome the hour my aged limbs
  Are laid with thee at rest!
The great, the wealthy, fear thy blow,
  From pomp and pleasure torn;
But O, a blest relief to those
  That weary-laden mourn! "

FARE THEE WELL

BY LORD BYRON

Fare thee well! and if for ever,
  Still for ever, fare thee well:
Even though unforgiving, never
  'Gainst thee shall my heart rebel.

Would that breast were bared before thee
  Where thy head so oft hath lain,
While that placid sleep came o'er thee
  Which thou ne'er canst know again!

Would that breast, by thee glanced over,
  Every inmost thought could show!
Then thou wouldst at last discover
  'Twas not well to spurn it so.

Though the world for this commend thee,—
  Though it smile upon the blow,

Even its praises must offend thee,
　　Founded on another's woe:

Though my many faults defaced me,
　　Could no other arm be found,
Than the one which once embraced me,
　　To inflict a cureless wound?

Yet, oh yet, thyself deceive not:
　　Love may sink by slow decay,
But by sudden wrench, believe not
　　Hearts can thus be torn away:

Still thine own its life retaineth,—
　　Still must mine, though bleeding, beat;
And the undying thought which paineth
　　Is — that we no more may meet.

These are words of deeper sorrow
　　Than the wail above the dead;
Both shall live, but every morrow
　　Wake us from a widowed bed.

And when thou wouldst solace gather,
　　When our child's first accents flow,
Wilt thou teach her to say "Father!"
　　Though his care she must forego?

When her little hands shall press thee,
　　When her lip to thine is pressed,

[50]

Think of him whose prayer shall bless thee,
  Think of him thy love had blessed!

Should her lineaments resemble
  Those thou nevermore mayst see,
Then thy heart will softly tremble
  With a pulse yet true to me.

All my faults perchance thou knowest,
  All my madness none can know;
All my hopes, where'er thou goest,
  Wither, yet with *thee* they go.

Every feeling hath been shaken;
  Pride, which not a world could bow,
Bows to thee,— by thee forsaken,
  Even my soul forsakes me now:

But 'tis done: all words are idle,—
  Words from me are vainer still;
But the thoughts we cannot bridle
  Force their way without the will.

Fare thee well! — thus disunited,
  Torn from every nearer tie,
Seared in heart, and lone, and blighted,
  More than this I scarce can die.

THE TEAR

BY LORD BYRON

"O lachrymarum fons, tenero sacros
Ducentium ortus ex animo; quater
Felix! in imo qui scatentem
Pectore te, pia Nympha, sensit." — GRAY.

When Friendship or Love our sympathies move,
    When Truth in a glance should appear,
The lips may beguile with a dimple or smile,
    But the test of affection's a Tear.

Too oft is a smile but the hypocrite's wile,
    To mask detestation or fear;
Give me the soft sigh, whilst the soul-telling eye
    Is dimm'd for a time with a Tear.

Mild Charity's glow, to us mortals below,
    Shows the soul from barbarity clear;
Compassion will melt where this virtue is felt,
    And its dew is diffused in a Tear.

The man doom'd to sail with the blast of the gale,
    Through billows Atlantic to steer,
As he bends o'er the wave which may soon be his
    grave,
    The green sparkles bright with a Tear.

The soldier braves death for a fanciful wreath
    In Glory's romantic career;
But he raises the foe when in battle laid low,
    And bathes every sound with a Tear.

[52]

If with high-bounding pride he return to his bride,
   Renouncing the gore-crimson'd spear,
All his toils are repaid when, embracing the maid,
   From her eyelid he kisses the Tear.

Sweet scene of my youth! seat of Friendship and Truth,
   Where love chased each fast-fleeting year,
Loth to leave thee, I mourn'd, for a last look I turn'd,
   But thy spire was scarce seen through a Tear.

Though my vows I can pour to my Mary no more,
   My Mary to Love once so dear,
In the shade of her bower I remember the hour
   She rewarded those vows with a Tear.

By another possesst, may she live ever blest!
   Her name still my heart must revere:
With a sigh I resign what I once thought was mine,
   And forgive her deceit with a Tear.

Ye friends of my heart, ere from you I depart,
   This hope to my breast is most near;
If again we shall meet in this rural retreat,
   May we meet, as we part, with a Tear.

When my soul wings her flight to the regions of night,
   And my corse shall recline on its bier,
As ye pass by the tomb where my ashes consume,
   Oh! moisten their dust with a Tear.

May no marble bestow the splendor of woe
   Which the children of vanity rear;
No fiction of fame shall blazon my name,
   All I ask — all I wish — is a Tear.

[53]

OUTWARD

BY W. J. CAMERON

The sun's high and the moon's high;
  The bay's a crescent of blue.
The ships of the world go by without,
But the great hill-gates stand round about,
  And only the waves come through.

The town sleeps and the bay sleeps.
  Tangled and golden brown,
The seaweed drifts on a dreaming sea,
Where anchored boats rock lazily,
  As the waves lap, up and down.

The night comes and the wind comes;
  Landward the white crests ride.
Hark to the voice in the wind that cries,
As it drifts like a bird 'twixt the sea and the skies,
  " There is one that will go with the tide! "

The dawn's here and the day's here!
  The wind ebbs out, and the sea.
The mists roll back and the hills are plain,
But the great sea-gates are narrow in vain,
  For the sea-bird's out to the sea.

LORD ULLIN'S DAUGHTER
BY THOMAS CAMPBELL

A chieftain, to the Highlands bound,
   Cries, " Boatman, do not tarry!
And I'll give thee a silver pound,
   To row us o'er the ferry."

" Now who be ye, would cross Lochgyle,
   This dark and stormy water? "
" O, I'm the chief of Ulva's isle,
   And this Lord Ullin's daughter.

" And fast before her father's men
   Three days we've fled together,
For should he find us in the glen,
   My blood would stain the heather.

" His horsemen hard behind us ride;
   Should they our steps discover,
Then who will cheer my bonny bride
   When they have slain her lover? "

Out spoke the hardy Highland wight,
   " I'll go, my chief, — I'm ready: —
It is not for your silver bright;
   But for your winsome lady:

" And by my word! the bonny bird
   In danger shall not tarry:
So, though the waves are raging white,
   I'll row you o'er the ferry."

[55]

By this the storm grew loud apace,
   The water-wraith was shrieking;
And in the scowl of heaven each face
   Grew dark as they were speaking.

But still as wilder blew the wind,
   And as the night grew drearer,
Adown the glen rode armèd men,
   Their trampling sounded nearer.

" O, haste thee, haste! " the lady cries,
   " Though tempests round us gather;
I'll meet the raging of the skies,
   But not an angry father."

The boat has left a stormy land,
   A stormy sea before her, —
When, O, too strong for human hand,
   The tempest gathered o'er her.

And still they rowed amidst the roar
   Of waters fast prevailing:
Lord Ullin reached that fatal shore,
   His wrath was changed to wailing.

For sore dismayed, through storm and shade,
   His child he did discover:
One lovely hand she stretched for aid,
   And one was round her lover.

" Come back! come back! " he cried in grief,
   " Across this stormy water:

And I'll forgive your Highland chief,
   My daughter! — O my daughter! "

'T was vain; — the loud waves lashed the shore,
   Return or aid preventing;
The waters wild went o'er his child,
   And he was left lamenting.

SALLY IN OUR ALLEY

BY HENRY CAREY

Of all the girls that are so smart
   There's none like pretty Sally;
She is the darling of my heart,
   And she lives in our alley.
There is no lady in the land
   Is half so sweet as Sally;
She is the darling of my heart,
   And she lives in our alley.

Her father he makes cabbage-nets,
   And through the streets does cry 'em;
Her mother she sells laces long
   To such as please to buy 'em;
But sure such folks could ne'er beget
   So sweet a girl as Sally!
She is the darling of my heart,
   And she lives in our alley.

When she is by I leave my work,
   I love her so sincerely;

[57]

My master comes like any Turk,
   And bangs me most severely.
But let him bang his bellyful,
   I'll bear it all for Sally;
For she's the darling of my heart,
   And she lives in our alley.

Of all the days that's in the week
   I dearly love but one day,
And that's the day that comes betwixt
   The Saturday and Monday;
For then I'm drest all in my best
   To walk abroad with Sally;
She is the darling of my heart,
   And she lives in our alley.

My master carries me to church,
   And often am I blamed
Because I leave him in the lurch
   As soon as text is named:
I leave the church in sermon-time,
   And slink away to Sally;
She is the darling of my heart,
   And she lives in our alley.

When Christmas comes about again,
   O, then I shall have money!
I'll hoard it up, and box it all,
   And give it to my honey;
I would it were ten thousand pound!
   I'd give it all to Sally;

She is the darling of my heart,
   And she lives in our alley.

My master and the neighbors all
   Make game of me and Sally,
And, but for her, I'd better be
   A slave, and row a galley;
But when my seven long years are out,
   O, then I'll marry Sally!
And when we're wed, we'll blithesome be,
   But not in our alley!

ELIZABETH BARRETT BROWNING

BY NORMA BRIGHT CARSON

Though frail of form, thou wert of spirit large and
   free,
A living, burning flame, that spirit seemed to be,
Enkindled from a spark of holy fire;
To glorious expression did thy soul aspire;
Close to the border-land of Heav'n, thou dwelt'st
   through life,
Yet actively could stand for right in the world's
   strife.
Great was the suffering set to be thy lot,
But suffering, in Love's compensation was forgot;
The Valley of the Shadow round thee grew,
When valiant Love, the spectre Death o'erthrew.
Ah! Life for fifteen years was the proud prize;
Yes, so it is that Love all unkind force defies.
Thy greatest gift to man does lie in this—

The poet thou didst inspire; the bliss
Thou perfected. No verse whate'er of thine
Can bounds of mankind's gratitude to thee define,
As does this fact of thy sweet woman's heart
Which had in poet's growth so large a part.
Yet, we must cherish thee for thy sweet song,
Which has with nobler thoughts enriched the world
　　for long;
Let us not fail a tribute large to bring,
For that thou from a pure and perfect heart didst
　　sing.

THE EYES OF THE CHRIST

BY NORMA BRIGHT CARSON

Pause now and let a lightsome world go by;
Heed not the laughter frivolous, the sinwrought sigh;
The music and the dance, the pride, the sham, the
　　boast;
What have you kin with all this selfish and this fool-
　　ish host?

Parade of affectation; self-sought joy;
And sorrow, more self-seeking, false sympathies decoy.
Turn from this tinselled army, in extravagance be-
　　decked;
Turn to where Calvary's Cross the ages long has
　　becked.

See where the Christ sits by Samaria's well,
And gently rolls the sealing stone across the mouth
　　of hell.

[60]

See how his eyes in pity's tenderness do rest
Where sin hath fixed its mark — the mark of passion's
    zest.

No smile of grieved condoling — but a pardon full
    gives he,
Though the great heart bleeds because of that the
    shadowed eyes did see.
Down future years those eyes go travelling — pained,
    distressed,
The while a prayer for mercy's kindness is addressed
The Father's ear.

That was the sacrifice of Christ,
To see, to know the future and the past —
To hear the voice of martyr loudly shrieking;
To hear the ribald laughter, the rude speaking
Of ungodly tongues.

To see the crimson blood go flowing,
Of these and all earth's sorrows always knowing.
A torture this, not Dante even could portray
With truth's reality; oh, brother, turn and pray.

AN ORDER FOR A PICTURE
BY ALICE CARY

Oh, good painter, tell me true,
    Has your hand the cunning to draw
    Shapes of things that you never saw?
Aye? Well, here is an order for you.

[61]

Woods and corn fields, a little brown,—
  The picture must not be over-bright,—
  Yet all in the golden and gracious light
Of a cloud, when the summer sun is down.
  Alway and alway, night and morn,
  Woods upon woods, with field of corn
    Lying between them, not quite sere,
And not in the full, thick, leafy bloom,
When the wind can hardly find breathing-room
    Under their tassels,— cattle near,
Biting shorter the short green grass,
And a hedge of sumach and sassafras,
With bluebirds twittering all around,—
(Ah, good painter, you can't paint sound !) —
  These, and the house where I was born,
Low and little, and black and old,
With children, many as it can hold,
All at the windows, open wide,—
Heads and shoulders clear outside,
And fair young faces all ablush:
  Perhaps you may have seen, some day,
  Roses crowding the self-same way,
Out of a wilding, wayside bush.

  Listen closer.   When you have done
    With woods and corn fields and grazing herds,
  A lady, the loveliest ever the sun
Looked down upon you must paint for me:
Oh, if I only could make you see
  The clear blue eyes, the tender smile,
The sovereign sweetness, the gentle grace,

[62]

The woman's soul, and the angel's face
   That are beaming on me all the while,
      I need not speak these foolish words:
      Yet one word tells you all I would say, —
She is my mother: you will agree
   That all the rest may be thrown away.

Two little urchins at her knee
You must paint, sir: one like me, —
      The other with a clearer brow,
      And the light of his adventurous eyes
      Flashing with boldest enterprise:
At ten years old he went to sea, —
      God knoweth if he be living now, —
      He sailed in the good ship Commodore,
Nobody ever crossed her track
To bring us news, and she never came back.
   Ah, it is twenty long years and more
Since that old ship went out of the bay
   With my great-hearted brother on her deck:
   I watched him till he shrank to a speck
And his face was toward me all the way.
Bright his hair was, a golden brown,
   The time we stood at our mother's knee:
That beauteous head, if it did go down,
   Carried sunshine into the sea!

Out in the fields one summer night
   We were together, half afraid
      Of the corn-leaves' rustling, and of the shade
      Of the high hills stretching so still and far, —

[63]

Loitering till after the low little light
  Of the candle shone through the open door,
And over the hay-stack's pointed top,
All of a tremble and ready to drop
    The first half-hour, the great yellow star,
  That we, with staring, ignorant eyes,
Had often and often watched to see
  Propped and held in its place in the skies
By the fork of a tall red mulberry-tree,
    Which close in the edge of our flax field grew, —
Dead at the top, — just one branch full
Of leaves, notched round, lined with wool,
  From which it tenderly shook the dew
Over our heads, when we came to play
In its hand-breadth of shadow, day after day.
    Afraid to go home, sir; for one of us bore
A nest full of speckled and thin-shelled eggs, —
The other, a bird, held fast by the legs,
Not so big as a straw of wheat:
The berries we gave her she wouldn't eat,
But cried and cried, till we held her bill,
So slim and shining, to keep her still.

At last we stood at our mother's knee.
  Do you think, sir, if you try,
  You can paint the look of a lie?
  If you can, pray have the grace
  To put it solely in the face
Of the urchin that is likest me:
    I think 't was solely mine, indeed:
  But that's no matter, — paint it so;

[64]

The eyes of our mother —(take good heed) —
Looking not on the nestful of eggs,
Nor the fluttering bird, held so fast by the legs,
But straight through our faces down to our lies,
And, oh, with such injured, reproachful surprise!
  I felt my heart bleed where that glance went,
      as though
  A sharp blade struck through it.

                      You sir, know
That you on the canvas are to repeat
Things that are fairest, things most sweet, —
Woods and corn fields and mulberry-tree, —
The mother,— the lads, with their bird, at her
      knee:
  But, oh, that look of reproachful woe!
High as the heavens your name I'll shout,
If you paint me the picture, and leave that out.

PICTURES OF MEMORY

BY ALICE CARY

Among the beautiful pictures
  . That hang on Memory's wall
Is one of a dim old forest,
  That seemeth best of all;
Not for its gnarled oaks olden,
  Dark with the mistletoe;
Not for the violets golden
  That sprinkle the vale below;
Not for the milk-white lilies
  That lean from the fragrant ledge,

[65]

Coquetting all day with the sunbeams,
  And stealing their golden edge;
Not for the vines on the upland,
  Where the bright red berries rest,
Nor the pinks, nor the pale sweet cowslip,
  It seemeth to me the best.

I once had a little brother,
  With eyes that were dark and deep;
In the lap of that old dim forest
  He lieth in peace asleep:
Light as the down of the thistle,
  Free as the winds that blow,
We roved there the beautiful summers,
  The summers of long ago;
But his feet on the hills grew weary,
  And, one of the autumn eves,
I made for my little brother
  A bed of the yellow leaves.
Sweetly his pale arms folded
  My neck in a meek embrace,
As the light of immortal beauty
  Silently covered his face;
And when the arrows of sunset
  Lodged in the tree-tops bright,
He fell, in his saint-like beauty,
  Asleep by the gates of light.
Therefore, of all the pictures
  That hang on Memory's wall,
The one of the dim old forest
  Seemeth the best of all.

[66]

NEARER HOME

BY PHŒBE CARY

One sweetly solemn thought
  Comes to me o'er and o'er;
I'm nearer my home to-day
  Than I ever have been before;

Nearer my Father's house,
  Where the many mansions be;
Nearer the great white throne,
  Nearer the crystal sea;

Nearer the bound of life,
  Where we lay our burdens down;
Nearer leaving the cross,
  Nearer gaining the crown!

But the waves of that silent sea
  Roll dark before my sight
That brightly the other side
  Break on a shore of light.

O, if my mortal feet
  Have almost gained the brink;
If it be I am nearer home
  Even to-day than I think, —

Father, perfect my trust!
  Let my spirit feel, in death,
That her feet are firmly set
  On the Rock of a living faith!

THE MUSINGS OF ARROYO AL

BY ARTHUR CHAPMAN

It seems to me this life we lead
   Is jest like that in Cattle Land;
A few wild critters will stampede
   A quiet and contented band;
And find out what the trouble was! —
And can't, because there ain't no cause.

One bawlin' critter in the herd
   Kin do much damage on a drive;
His locoed doin's is absurd.
   And at the market — man alive! —
That critter that has scairt the bunch
Don't fetch enough to buy a lunch.

They has to be, it seems to me,
   These locoed steers and locoed men.
But think how easy life'd be
   If, when they bawl and bawl again,
The herd'd stand there, as it shud,
And jest take fresh holt on its cud!

SUNSET THOUGHTS

BY MINNIE CONWAY

To-night, as I sat by my window,
   As the west was all agleam
With that strange and wonderful splendor
   That is fleeting as a dream,

[68]

I thought that the hands of angels
    Had swung heaven's gateway wide,
And I caught some glimpse of the glory
    From the hills on the other side.

Is it not a beautiful fancy,
    This sunset thought of mine,
That the gates of heaven are always
    Swung open at day's decline
That those whose day is ended
    Of earthly woes and ills
May pass to the morning of gladness
    That dwells on the heavenly hills?

Perhaps while I sat there dreaming
    Of the gateway in the west,
Some poor soul went through the portals
    To a long and endless rest.
Went in through the sunset gateway
    To the city paved with gold,
Passed in to the new life's gladness,
    To be no longer old.

When for me the sunset gateway
    Shall at day's decline unclose,
And I enter through its portals
    To a long and sweet repose,
I know I shall remember
    In that land so fair and far
My strange and beautiful fancy
    Of the sunset gates ajar.

THE OLD ARM–CHAIR

BY ELIZA COOK

I love it, I love it! and who shall dare
To chide me for loving that old arm-chair?
I've treasured it long as a sainted prize,
I've bedewed it with tears, I've embalmed it with
    sighs.
'T is bound by a thousand bands to my heart;
Not a tie will break, not a link will start;
Would you know the spell? — a mother sat there!
And a sacred thing is that old arm-chair.

In childhood's hour I lingered near
The hallowed seat with listening ear;
And gentle words that mother would give
To fit me to die, and teach me to live.
She told me that shame would never betide
With Truth for my creed, and God for my guide;
She taught me to lisp my earliest prayer,
As I knelt beside that old arm-chair.

I sat, and watched her many a day,
When her eye grew dim, and her locks were gray;
And I almost worshipped her when she smiled,
And turned from her Bible to bless her child.
Years rolled on, but the last one sped, —
My idol was shattered, my earth-star fled!
I learnt how much the heart can bear,
When I saw her die in her old arm-chair.

'T is past, 't is past! but I gaze on it now,
With quivering breath and throbbing brow:
'Twas there she nursed me, 'twas there she died,
And memory flows with lava tide.
Say it is folly, and deem me weak,
Whilst scalding drops start down my cheek;
But I love it, I love it, and cannot tear
My soul from a mother's old arm-chair.

ROSES UNDERNEATH THE SNOW

BY GEORGE COOPER

Summer groves may lose their gladness,
   Wintry winds may wander by;
Cares may come and weary sadness,
   Must we then forever sigh?
Brave the storm with firm endeavor,
   Let your vain repinings go!
Hopeful hearts will find forever
   Roses underneath the snow.

One by one the links that bind us
   May be severed here on earth;
But the sun will surely find us,
   Through the winter's gloomy dearth!
Cheerful hearts around us beating,
   Wearing ever summer's glow,
Ah! we know you're always meeting
   Roses underneath the snow.

Never joy that earth can send us,
   Can forever leave us here;

Every flower that spring can lend us
    Bloom again another year.
Cares may come, but never mind them;
    Joys may come and joys may go;
Look around and you will find them,
    Roses underneath the snow.

Brave the storm with firm endeavor,
    Let your vain repining go;
Hopeful hearts will find forever
    Roses underneath the snow.

VERSES

SUPPOSED TO BE WRITTEN BY ALEXANDER SELKIRK
DURING HIS SOLITARY ABODE IN THE ISLAND OF
JUAN FERNANDEZ.

BY WILLIAM COWPER

I am monarch of all I survey;
    My right there is none to dispute;
From the centre all round to the sea
    I am lord of the fowl and the brute.
O Solitude! where are the charms
    That sages have seen in thy face?
Better dwell in the midst of alarms
    Than reign in this horrible place.

I am out of humanity's reach;
    I must finish my journey alone;
Never hear the sweet music of speech —
    I start at the sound of my own.

[72]

The beasts that roam over the plain,
  My form with indifference see;
They are so unacquainted with man,
  Their tameness is shocking to me.

Society, Friendship, and Love,
  Divinely bestow'd upon man,
Oh, had I the wings of a dove,
  How soon would I taste you again!
My sorrows I then might assuage
  In the ways of religion and truth,
Might learn from the wisdom of age,
  And be cheer'd by the sallies of youth.

Religion! what treasure untold
  Resides in that heavenly word!
More precious than silver and gold,
  Or all that this earth can afford.
But the sound of the church-going bell
  These valleys and rocks never heard;
Never sigh'd at the sound of a knell,
  Or smiled when a Sabbath appear'd.

Ye winds that have made me your sport,
  Convey to this desolate shore
Some cordial endearing report
  Of a land I shall visit no more:
My friends, do they now and then send
  A wish or a thought after me?
Oh, tell me I yet have a friend,
  Though a friend I am never to see.

[73]

How fleet is the glance of the mind!
  Compared with the speed of its flight,
The tempest itself lags behind,
  And the swift-wingèd arrows of light.
When I think of my own native land,
  In a moment I seem to be there;
But, alas! recollection at hand
  Soon hurries me back to despair.

But the sea-fowl is gone to her nest,
  The beast is laid down in his lair;
Even here is a season of rest,
  And I to my cabin repair.
There's mercy in every place,
  And mercy — encouraging thought! —
Gives even affliction a grace,
  And reconciles man to his lot.

THE DIVERTING HISTORY OF JOHN GILPIN

SHOWING HOW HE WENT FARTHER THAN HE INTENDED
AND CAME SAFE HOME AGAIN.

BY WILLIAM COWPER

John Gilpin was a citizen
  Of credit and renown;
A trainband captain eke was he
  Of famous London town.

John Gilpin's spouse said to her dear —
  " Tho' wedded we have been

[74]

These twice ten tedious years, yet we
   No holiday have seen.

" To-morrow is our wedding-day,
   And we will then repair
Unto the Bell at Edmonton
   All in a chaise and pair.

" My sister and my sister's child,
   Myself and children three,
Will fill the chaise; so you must ride
   On horseback after we."

He soon replied, " I do admire
   Of womankind but one,
And you are she, my dearest dear:
   Therefore it shall be done.

" I am a linendraper bold,
   As all the world doth know;
And my good friend, the calender,
   Will lend his horse to go."

Quoth Mrs. Gilpin, " That's well said;
   And, for that wine is dear,
We will be furnish'd with our own,
   Which is both bright and clear."

John Gilpin kiss'd his loving wife;
   O'erjoyed was he to find
That, though on pleasure she was bent,
   She had a frugal mind.

The morning came, the chaise was brought,
 But yet was not allow'd
To drive up to the door, lest all
 Should say that she was proud.

So three doors off the chaise was stay'd,
 Where they did all get in —
Six precious souls, and all agog
 To dash through thick and thin.

Smack went the whip, round went the wheel —
 Were never folks so glad;
The stones did rattle underneath,
 As if Cheapside were mad.

John Gilpin at his horse's side
 Seized fast the flowing mane,
And up he got, in haste to ride —
 But soon came down again:

For saddletree scarce reach'd had he,
 His journey to begin,
When, turning round his head, he saw
 Three customers come in.

So down he came: for loss of time,
 Although it grieved him sore,
Yet loss of pence, full well he knew,
 Would trouble him much more.

'Twas long before the customers
 Were suited to their mind;

When Betty, screaming, came down stairs —
  " The wine is left behind! "

" Good lack! " quoth he — " yet bring it me,
  My leathern belt likewise,
In which I bear my trusty sword
  When I do exercise."

Now Mistress Gilpin (careful soul!)
  Had two stone bottles found,
To hold the liquor that she loved,
  And keep it safe and sound.

Each bottle had a curling ear,
  Through which the belt he drew,
And hung a bottle on each side,
  To make his balance true.

Then over all, that he might be
  Equipp'd from top to toe,
His long red cloak, well brush'd and neat,
  He manfully did throw.

Now see him mounted once again
  Upon his nimble steed,
Full slowly pacing o'er the stones,
  With caution and good heed.

But finding soon a smoother road
  Beneath his well-shod feet,
The snorting beast began to trot,
  Which gall'd him in his seat.

[77]

So, " Fair and softly," John he cried,
    But John he cried in vain;
That trot became a gallop soon,
    In spite of curb and rein.

So stooping down, as needs he must
    Who cannot sit upright,
He grasp'd the mane with both his hands,
    And eke with all his might.

His horse, who never in that sort
    Had handled been before,
What thing upon his back had got
    Did wonder more and more.

Away went Gilpin, neck or naught;
    Away went hat and wig;
He little dreamt, when he set out,
    Of running such a rig.

The wind did blow — the cloak did fly,
    Like streamer long and gay;
Till, loop and button failing both,
    At last it flew away.

Then might all people well discern
    The bottles he had slung —
A bottle swinging at each side,
    As hath been said or sung.

The dogs did bark, the children scream'd,
    Up flew the windows all;

[78]

And every soul cried out, " Well done! "
　　As loud as he could bawl.

Away went Gilpin — who but he?
　　His fame soon spread around —
" He carries weight! he rides a race!
　　'Tis for a thousand pound! "

And still as fast as he drew near,
　　'Twas wonderful to view
How in a trice the turnpike men
　　Their gates wide open threw.

And now, as he went bowing down
　　His reeking head full low,
The bottles twain behind his back
　　Were shatter'd at a blow.

Down ran the wine into the road,
　　Most piteous to be seen,
Which made his horse's flanks to smoke
　　As they had basted been.

But still he seem'd to carry weight,
　　With leathern girdle braced;
For all might see the bottle-necks
　　Still dangling at his waist.

Thus all through merry Islington
　　These gambols he did play,
Until he came unto the Wash
　　Of Edmonton so gay;

[79]

And there he threw the wash about
  On both sides of the way,
Just like unto a trundling mop,
  Or a wild goose at play.

At Edmonton his loving wife
  From the balcony spied
Her tender husband, wondering much
  To see how he did ride.

" Stop, stop, John Gilpin! here's the house,"
  They all at once did cry;
" The dinner waits, and we are tired: "
  Said Gilpin — " So am I! "

But yet his horse was not a whit
  Inclined to tarry there;
For why? — his owner had a house
  Full ten miles off, at Ware.

So like an arrow swift he flew,
  Shot by an archer strong;
So did he fly — which brings me to
  The middle of my song.

Away went Gilpin out of breath,
  And sore against his will,
Till at his friend's the calender's
  His horse at last stood still.

The calender, amazed to see
  His neighbor in such trim,

Laid down his pipe, flew to the gate,
  And thus accosted him:

" What news? what news? your tidings tell;
  Tell me you must and shall —
Say why bareheaded you are come,
  Or why you come at all? "

Now Gilpin had a pleasant wit,
  And loved a timely joke;
And thus unto the calender
  In merry guise he spoke:

" I came because your horse would come;
  And, if I well forbode,
My hat and wig will soon be here,
  They are upon the road."

The calender, right glad to find
  His friend in merry pin,
Return'd him not a single word,
  But to the house went in;

Whence straight he came with hat and wig,
  A wig that flow'd behind,
A hat not much the worse for wear —
  Each comely in its kind.

He held them up, and in his turn
  Thus show'd his ready wit —
" My head is twice as big as yours,
  They therefore needs must fit.

[81]

" But let me scrape the dirt away
   That hangs upon your face;
And stop and eat, for well you may
   Be in a hungry case."

Said John, " It is my wedding-day,
   And all the world would stare
If wife should dine at Edmonton,
   And I should dine at Ware."

So turning to his horse, he said,
   " I am in haste to dine;
'Twas for your pleasure you came here —
   You shall go back for mine."

Ah, luckless speech and bootless boast,
   For which he paid full dear!
For, while he spake, a braying ass
   Did sing most loud and clear;

Whereat his horse did snort, as he
   Had heard a lion roar,
And gallop'd off with all his might,
   As he had done before.

Away went Gilpin, and away
   Went Gilpin's hat and wig:
He lost them sooner than at first,
   For why? — they were too big.

Now Mistress Gilpin, when she saw
   Her husband posting down

Into the country far away,
  She pull'd out half a crown;

And thus unto the youth she said
  That drove them to the Bell,
" This shall be yours when you bring back
  My husband safe and well."

The youth did ride, and soon did meet
  John coming back amain —
Whom in a trice he tried to stop,
  By catching at his rein;

But not performing what he meant,
  And gladly would have done,
The frighted steed he frighted more,
  And made him faster run.

Away went Gilpin, and away
  Went post-boy at his heels,
The post-boy's horse right glad to miss
  The lumbering of the wheels.

Six gentlemen upon the road,
  Thus seeing Gilpin fly,
With post-boy scampering in the rear,
  They raised the hue and cry:

" Stop thief! stop thief — a highwayman! "
  Not one of them was mute;
And all and each that pass'd that way
  Did join in the pursuit.

[83]

And now the turnpike-gates again
  Flew open in short space:
The toll-men thinking as before,
  That Gilpin rode a race.

And so he did, and won it too,
  For he got first to town;
Nor stopp'd till where he had got up
  He did again get down.

Now let us sing, Long live the king!
  And Gilpin, long live he;
And when he next doth ride abroad,
  May I be there to see!

AN EXPERIENCE AND A MORAL

BY FREDERICK SWARTWOUT COZZENS

I lent my love a book one day;
  She brought it back; I laid it by:
'T was little either had to say, —
  She was so strange, and I so shy.

But yet we loved indifferent things, —
  The sprouting buds, the birds in tune, —
And Time stood still and wreathed his wings
  With rosy links from June to June.

For her, what task to dare or do?
  What peril tempt? what hardship bear?
But with her — ah! she never knew
  My heart, and what was hidden there!

[84]

And she, with me, so cold and coy,
    Seemed a little maid bereft of sense;
But in the crowd, all life and joy,
    And full of blushful impudence.

She married, — well, — a woman needs
    A mate, her life and love to share, —
And little cares sprang up like weeds
    And played around her elbow-chair.

And years rolled by, — but I, content,
    Trimmed my own lamp, and kept it bright,
Till age's touch my hair besprent
    With rays and gleams of silver light.

And then it chanced I took the book
    Which she perused in days gone by;
And as I read, such passion shook
    My soul, — I needs must curse or cry.

For, here and there, her love was writ,
    In old, half-faded pencil-signs,
As if she yielded — bit by bit —
    Her heart in dots and underlines.

Ah, silvered fool, too late you look!
    I know it; let me here record
This maxim: *Lend no girl a book*
    Unless you read it afterward!

[85]

LEETLA JOE

BY T. A. DALY

Leetla Joe he always say:
"W'en I am beeg man som' day,
   Eef so be I gona grow
Strong an' fat so like my Pop,
I weell go for be a cop,
   Mebbe so."
Soocha talk for four-year-old!
Dough he brag so beeg an' bold
Een wan handa you could hold
   Leetla Joe.

Leetla Joe he lay hees cheek
On my breast w'en he ees seeck,
   Squeeze my arm an' tal me: "Oh!
Pretta soon I gona gat
Granda muscle lika dat.
   W'en I grow
Like my Pop how proud I be!
Justa wait an' you weell see."
Ah! so sweet to hug to me
   Leetla Joe!

But, baycause I'm 'fraid dat he
Wan day would be 'shame' of me, —
   'Shame' for call me " Pop " an' know,
W'en he's fina 'Merican,
I'm so poor old Dagoman —
   W'en I go

Where hees grave ees on da heell,
Dere ees joy for me to feel
Dat my heart can keep heem steell
    Leetla Joe.

THE SONG OF THE THRUSH

BY T. A. DALY

Ah! the May was grand this mornin'!
Sure, how could I feel forlorn in
Such a land, when tree and flower tossed their kisses
    to the breeze?
Could an Irish heart be quiet
While the Spring was runnin' riot,
An' the birds of free America were singin' in the
    trees?

In the songs that they were singin'
No familiar note was ringin',
But I strove to imitate them an' I whistled like a
    lad.
O! my heart was warm to love them
For the very newness of them —
For the ould songs that they helped me to forget —
    an' I was glad.

So I mocked the feathered choir
To my hungry heart's desire,
An' I gloried in the comradeship that made their joy
    my own,
    Till a new note sounded, stillin'

All the rest. A thrush was trillin'!
Ah! the thrush I left behind me in the fields about
    Athlone!

Where, upon the whitethorn swayin',
He was minstrel of the Mayin',
In my days of love an' laughter that the years have
    laid at rest;
Here again his notes were ringin'!
But I'd lost the heart for singin' —
Ah! the song I could not answer was the one I knew
    the best.

BURIED TREASURE

BY EVA DEAN

God buried in a woman's soul
A treasure rare
  For His safekeeping, till the day
That he to whom it was bequeathed
Should, by some look, or whisper breathed,
  Beseech his birthright hid away.

She kept it long, for safety locked
Deep in her heart,
  And there it grew more fair, more bright;
But no one brought the magic key
That claimed the treasure held in fee:
  So, deeper still, she buried it from sight.

[88]

At last the donor spoke and said:
" Give lavishly
  To all you meet from out your store;
A heart of love, like purse of gold,
Unspent, but curses those who hold."
  Yet as she gave, the hoard but grew the more!

THE IVY GREEN

BY CHARLES DICKENS

O, a dainty plant is the ivy green,
  That creepeth o'er ruins old!
Of right choice food are his meals, I ween,
  In his cell so lone and cold.
The walls must be crumbled, the stones decayed,
  To pleasure his dainty whim;
And the mouldering dust that years have made,
  Is a merry meal for him.
      Creeping where no life is seen,
      A rare old plant is the Ivy green.

Fast he stealeth on, though he wears no wings,
  And a staunch old heart has he!
How closely he twineth, how tight he clings
  To his friend, the huge oak-tree!
And slyly he traileth along the ground,
  And his leaves he gently waves,
And he joyously twines and hugs around
  The rich mould of dead men's graves.
      Creeping where grim death has been,
      A rare old plant is the Ivy green.

[89]

Whole ages have fled, and their works decayed,
    And nations have scattered been;
But the stout old ivy shall never fade
    From its hale and hearty green.
The brave old plant in its lonely days
    Shall fatten upon the past;
For the stateliest building man can raise
    Is the ivy's food at last.
        Creeping on where Time has been,
        A rare old plant is the Ivy green.

THE LEGEND OF THE ORGAN–BUILDER

BY JULIA C. R. DORR

Day by day the Organ-Builder in his lonely chamber
    wrought;
Day by day the soft air trembled to the music of his
    thought;
Till at last the work was ended, and no organ voice
    so grand
Ever yet had soared responsive to the master's magic
    hand.

Ay, so rarely was it builded that whenever groom or
    bride
Who in God's sight were well-pleasing in the church
    stood side by side,
Without touch or breath the organ of itself began to
    play,
And the very airs of heaven through the soft gloom
    seemed to stray.

[90]

He was young, the Organ-Builder, and o'er all the
    land his fame
Ran with fleet and eager footsteps, like a swiftly
    rushing flame.
All the maidens heard the story; all the maidens
    blushed and smiled,
By his youth and wondrous beauty and his great
    renown beguiled.

So he sought and won the fairest, and the wedding
    day was set:
Happy day — the brightest jewel in the glad year's
    coronet!
But when they the portal entered, he forgot his lovely
    bride —
Forgot his love, forgot his God, and his heart swelled
    high with pride.

" Ah! " thought he, " how great a master am I! When
    the organ plays,
How the vast cathedral arches will re-echo with my
    praise!
Up the aisle the gay procession moved. The altar
    shone afar,
With its every candle gleaming through soft shadows
    like a star.

But he listened, listened, listened, with no thought
    of love or prayer,
For the swelling notes of triumph from the organ
    standing there.

[91]

All was silent. Nothing heard he save the priest's
　　low monotone,
And the bride's robe trailing softly o'er the floor of
　　fretted stone.

Then his lips grew white with anger. Surely God was
　　pleased with him
Who had built the wondrous organ for His temple
　　vast and dim?
Whose the fault, then? Hers — the maiden stand-
　　ing meekly at his side!
Flamed his jealous rage, maintaining she was false
　　to him — his bride.

Vain were all her protestations, vain her innocence
　　and truth;
On that very night he left her to her anguish and
　　her ruth.

．　．　．　．　．　．　．　．　．　．　．　．　．　．　．　．　．　．

Far he wandered to a country wherein no man knew
　　his name.
For ten weary years he dwelt there, nursing still his
　　wrath and shame.

Then his haughty heart grew softer, and he thought
　　by night and day
Of the bride he had deserted till he hardly dared to
　　pray —

Thought of her, a spotless maiden, fair and beautiful
　　and good;

Thought of his relentless anger that had cursed her
womanhood;

Till his yearning grief and penitence at last were all
complete,
And he longed, with bitter longing, just to fall down
at her feet.

. . . .

Ah! how throbbed his heart when, after many a weary
day and night,
Rose his native towers before him, with the sunset
glow alight!

Through the gates into the city on he pressed with
eager tread;
There he met a long procession — mourners following
the dead.

" Now why weep ye so, good people? and whom bury
ye to-day?
Why do yonder sorrowing maidens scatter flowers
along the way?

" Has some saint gone up to Heaven? " " Yes, "
they answered, weeping sore:
" For the Organ-Builder's saintly wife our eyes shall
see no more;

" And because her days were given to the service of
God's poor,

From His church we mean to bury her. See! yonder
    is the door."

No one knew him; no one wondered when he cried
    out, white with pain;
No one questioned when, with pallid lips, he poured
    his tears like rain.

" 'Tis some one whom she has comforted who mourns
    with us," they said,
As he made his way unchallenged, and bore the coffin's
    head.

Bore it through the open portal, bore it up the echoing
    aisle,
Set it down before the altar, where the lights burned
    clear the while:

When, oh, hark! the wondrous organ of itself began
    to play,
Strains of rare, unearthly sweetness never heard until
    that day!

All the vaulted arches rang with the music sweet and
    clear;
All the air was filled with glory, as of angels hovering
    near;

And ere yet the strain was ended, he who bore the
    coffin's head,

[94]

With the smile of one forgiven, gently sank beside
    it — dead.

They who raised the body knew him, and they laid
    him by his bride;
Down the aisle and o'er the threshold they were
    carried side by side;

While the organ played a dirge that no man ever
    heard before,
And then softly sank to silence — silence kept for
    evermore.

ANNIE LAURIE

BY WILLIAM DOUGLAS

Maxwelton banks are bonnie,
    Where early fa's the dew;
Where me and Annie Laurie
    Made up the promise true;
Made up the promise true,
    And never forget will I;
And for bonnie Annie Laurie
    I'll lay me down and die.

She's backit like the peacock,
    She's breistit like the swan,
She's jimp about the middle,
    Her waist ye weel micht span;
Her waist ye weel micht span,
    And she has a rolling eye;
And for bonnie Annie Laurie
    I'll lay me down and die.

[95]

THE OLD STORY

BY FANNY DOWNING

It chanced that once a Persian maid
Into a sacred forest strayed,
And roving on in restless mood,
Half frightened at the solitude,
Within the greenwood's depths profound,
Awestruck, a marble idol found.

So well the chiselled stone was wrought,
So truly Nature's features caught,
That, as the girl in wonder gazed,
In glorious majesty it blazed,
And grandly glistened on the sod, —
No image, but an actual god.

Bold by degrees, she faltering stepped,
Close and more closely still up crept,
And as one sees in Eastern land,
An instant into bloom expand
The buds by tropic sunshine nursed,
So in her heart love full blown burst.

She tears the clinging vines away
That hide her treasure from the day,
Of lotos flowers and campac leaves,
With jasmine buds rich garlands weaves,
And makes their dewy splendors climb
About the brow she calls sublime.

Her snowy arms around it pressed,
With glowing cheeks and heaving breast,
To warm the marble into life
And wake it up to passion's strife
By every artless art she strove,
Till it should give her love for love.

But strove in vain! No answering tone
Sends back an echo to her own,
Until at last with footsteps slow
And tear-blind eyes and voice of woe,
The young life chilled with bitter pain,
She hastens to her home again.

'Tis thus with women! We enshrine
A human love we deem divine,
To it in admiration cling,
Round it our heart's best treasures fling,
Exalt our idol on its throne,
And find it but a senseless stone.

THE AMERICAN FLAG

BY JOSEPH RODMAN DRAKE

When Freedom, from her mountain height,
    Unfurled her standard to the air,
She tore the azure robe of night,
    And set the stars of glory there!
She mingled with its gorgeous dyes
The milky baldric of the skies,

And striped its pure, celestial white
With streakings of the morning light;
Then, from his mansion in the sun,
She called her eagle-bearer down,
And gave into his mighty hand
The symbol of her chosen land!

Majestic monarch of the cloud!
    Who rear'st aloft thy regal form,
To hear the tempest trumping loud,
And see the lightning lances driven,
    When strive the warriors of the storm,
And rolls the thunder-drum of heaven, —
Child of the Sun! to thee 't is given
    To guard the banner of the free,
To hover in the sulphur smoke,
To ward away the battle-stroke,
And bid its blendings shine afar,
Like rainbows on the cloud of war,
    The harbingers of victory!

Flag of the brave! thy folds shall fly,
The sign of hope and triumph high!
When speaks the signal-trumpet tone,
And the long line comes gleaming on,
Ere yet the life-blood, warm and wet,
Has dimmed the glistening bayonet,
Each soldier's eye shall brightly turn
To where thy sky-born glories burn,
And, as his springing steps advance,
Catch war and vengeance from the glance.

And when the cannon-mouthings loud
Heave in wild wreaths the battle shroud,
And gory sabres rise and fall
Like shoots of flame on midnight's pall,
Then shall thy meteor glances glow,
   And cowering foes shall shrink beneath
Each gallant arm that strikes below
   That lovely messenger of death.

Flag of the seas! on ocean wave
Thy stars shall glitter o'er the brave;
When death, careering on the gale,
Sweeps darkly round the bellied sail,
And frighted waves rush wildly back
Before the broadside's reeling rack,
Each dying wanderer of the sea
Shall look at once to heaven and thee,
And smile to see thy splendors fly
In triumph o'er his closing eye.

Flag of the free heart's hope and home,
   By angel hands to valor given!
Thy stars have lit the welkin dome,
   And all thy hues were born in heaven.
Forever float that standard sheet!
   Where breathes the foe but falls before us,
With Freedom's soil beneath our feet,
   And Freedom's banner streaming o'er us!

LAMENT OF THE IRISH EMIGRANT

BY HELEN SELINA SHERIDAN, LADY DUFFERIN

I'm sittin' on the stile, Mary,
　Where we sat side by side
On a bright May mornin' long ago,
　When first you were my bride;
The corn was springin' fresh and green,
　And the lark sang loud and high;
And the red was on your lip, Mary,
　And the love-light in your eye.

The place is little changed, Mary;
　The day is bright as then;
The lark's loud song is in my ear,
　And the corn is green again;
But I miss the soft clasp of your hand,
　And your breath, warm on my cheek;
And I still keep list'nin' for the words
　You nevermore will speak.

'Tis but a step down yonder lane,
　And the little church stands near, —
The church where we were wed, Mary;
　I see the spire from here.
But the graveyard lies between, Mary,
　And my step might break your rest, —
For I've laid you, darling, down to sleep,
　With your baby on your breast.

[100]

I'm very lonely now, Mary,
  For the poor make no new friends;
But, O, they love the better still
  The few our Father sends!
And you were all I had, Mary, —
  My blessin' and my pride;
There's nothing left to care for now,
  Since my poor Mary died.

Yours was the good, brave heart, Mary,
  That still kept hoping on,
When the trust in God had left my soul,
  And my arm's young strength was gone;
There was comfort ever on your lip,
  And the kind look on your brow, —
I bless you, Mary, for that same,
  Though you cannot hear me now.

I thank you for the patient smile
  When your heart was fit to break, —
When the hunger-pain was gnawin' there,
  And you hid it for my sake;
I bless you for the pleasant word,
  When your heart was sad and sore, —
O, I'm thankful you are gone, Mary,
  Where grief can't reach you more!

I'm biddin' you a long farewell,
  My Mary — kind and true!
But I'll not forget you, darling,
  In the land I'm goin' to;

[101]

They say there's bread and work for all,
   And the sun shines always there, —
But I'll not forget old Ireland,
   Were it fifty times as fair!

And often in those grand old woods
   I'll sit, and shut my eyes,
And my heart will travel back again
   To the place where Mary lies;
And I'll think I see the little stile
   Where we sat side by side,
And the springin' corn, and the bright May morn,
   When first you were my bride.

TRUE REST

BY JOHN SULLIVAN DWIGHT

Sweet is the pleasure
   Itself cannot spoil!
Is not true leisure
   One with true toil?

Thou that wouldst taste it,
   Still do thy best;
Use it, not waste it, —
   Else 't is no rest.

Wouldst behold beauty
   Near thee? all round?
Only hath duty
   Such a sight found.

[102]

Rest is not quitting
　　The busy career;
Rest is the fitting
　　Of self to its sphere.

'T is the brook's motion,
　　Clear without strife,
Fleeing to ocean
　　After its life.

Deeper devotion
　　Nowhere hath knelt;
Fuller emotion
　　Heart never felt.

'T is loving and serving
　　The highest and best;
'T is onwards! unswerving, —
　　And that is true rest.

O, MAY I JOIN THE CHOIR INVISIBLE!

BY GEORGE ELIOT

O, may I join the choir invisible
Of those immortal dead who live again
In minds made better by their presence; live
In pulses stirred to generosity,
In deeds of daring rectitude, in scorn
Of miserable aims that end with self,
In thoughts sublime that pierce the night like stars,
And with their mild persistence urge men's minds

[103]

To vaster issues.
        So to live is heaven:
To make undying music in the world,
Breathing a beauteous order, that controls
With growing sway the growing life of man.
So we inherit that sweet purity
For which we struggled, failed, and agonized
With widening retrospect that bred despair.
Rebellious flesh that would not be subdued,
A vicious parent shaming still its child,
Poor anxious penitence, is quick dissolved;
Its discords quenched by meeting harmonies,
Die in the large and charitable air.
And all our rarer, better, truer self,
That sobbed religiously in yearning song,
That watched to ease the burden of the world,
Laboriously tracing what must be,
And what may yet be better, — saw within
A worthier image for the sanctuary,
And shaped it forth before the multitude,
Divinely human, raising worship so
To higher reverence more mixed with love,
That better self shall live till human Time
Shall fold its eyelids, and the human sky
Be gathered like a scroll within the tomb,
Unread forever.
        This is life to come,
Which martyred men have made more glorious
For us, who strive to follow.
        May I reach
That purest heaven, — be to other souls

[104]

The cup of strength in some great agony,
Enkindle generous ardor, feed pure love,
Beget the smiles that have no cruelty,
Be the sweet presence of a good diffused,
And in diffusion ever more intense!
So shall I join the choir invisible,
Whose music is the gladness of the world.

TO THE HUMBLEBEE

BY RALPH WALDO EMERSON

Burly, dozing humblebee!
Where thou art is clime for me;
Let them sail for Porto Rique,
Far-off heats through seas to seek,
I will follow thee alone,
Thou animated torrid zone!
Zigzag steerer, desert cheerer,
Let me chase thy waving lines;
Keep me nearer, me thy hearer,
Singing over shrubs and vines.

Insect lover of the sun,
Joy of thy dominion!
Sailor of the atmosphere;
Swimmer through the waves of air,
Voyager of light and noon,
Epicurean of June!
Wait, I prithee, till I come
Within earshot of thy hum, —
All without is martyrdom.

When the south-wind, in May days,
With a net of shining haze
Silvers the horizon wall;
And, with softness touching all,
Tints the human countenance
With the color of romance;
And infusing subtle heats
Turns the sod to violets, —
Thou in sunny solitudes,
Rover of the underwoods,
The green silence dost displace
With thy mellow breezy bass.

Hot midsummer's petted crone,
Sweet to me thy drowsy tone
Tells of countless sunny hours,
Long days, and solid banks of flowers;
Of gulfs of sweetness without bound,
In Indian wildernesses found;
Of Syrian peace, immortal leisure,
Firmest cheer, and birdlike pleasure.

Aught unsavory or unclean
Hath my insect never seen;
But violets, and bilberry bells,
Maple sap, and daffodels,
Grass with green flag half-mast high,
Succory to match the sky,
Columbine with horn of honey,
Scented fern, and agrimony,
Clover, catchfly, adder's-tongue,

[106]

And brier-roses, dwelt among:
All beside was unknown waste,
All was picture as he passed.
Wiser far than human seer,
Yellow-breeched philosopher,
Seeing only what is fair,
   Sipping only what is sweet,
Thou dost mock at fate and care,
   Leave the chaff and take the wheat.
When the fierce northwestern blast
Cools sea and land so far and fast,—
Thou already slumberest deep;
Woe and want thou canst outsleep;
Want and woe, which torture us,
Thy sleep makes ridiculous.

ODE

BY RALPH WALDO EMERSON

[Sung in the Town Hall, Concord, July 4, 1857]

O tenderly the haughty day
   Fills his blue urn with fire;
One morn is in the mighty heaven,
   And one in our desire.

The cannon booms from town to town,
   Our pulses beat not less,
The joy-bells chime their tidings down,
   Which children's voices bless.

[107]

For He that flung the broad blue fold
  O'er-mantling land and sea,
One-third part of the sky unrolled
  For the banner of the free.

The men are ripe of Saxon kind
  To build an equal state, —
To take the statute from the mind
  And make of duty fate.

United States! the ages plead, —
  Present and Past in under-song, —
Go put your creed into your deed,
  Nor speak with double tongue.

For sea and land don't understand
  Nor skies without a frown
See rights for which the one hand fights
  By the other cloven down.

Be just at home; then write your scroll
  Of honor o'er the sea,
And bid the broad Atlantic roll
  A ferry of the free.

And henceforth there shall be no chain,
  Save underneath the sea
The wires shall murmur through the main
  Sweet songs of liberty.

The conscious stars accord above,
  The waters wild below,

And under, through the cable wove,
   Her fiery errands go.

For He that worketh high and wise,
   Nor pauses in his plan,
Will take the sun out of the skies
   Ere freedom out of man.

PEACE

BY CORA FABRI

God spoke to her, and so she fell asleep,
   I laid a white fair lily on her heart,
And when I saw her face I could not weep.

It had the peace Death only understands;
   And when I knew she would not wake on earth
I laid my heart between her folded hands.

God spoke to her so softly, saying " Rest! "
   And when she wakes in Heaven she will find
My lily and my heart upon her breast.

THE LAST HYMN

BY MARIANNE FARNINGHAM

The Sabbath day was ending, in a village by the sea,
The uttered benediction touched the people tenderly,
And they rose to face the sunset in the glowing, lighted
    west,
And then hastened to their dwellings for God's blessed
    boon of rest.

[109]

But they looked across the waters, and a storm was
    raging there:
A fierce spirit moved above them — the wild spirit
    of the air —
And it lashed, and shook, and tore them, till they
    thundered, groaned, and boomed.
And, alas! for any vessel in their yawning gulfs en-
    tombed.

Very anxious were the people on that rocky coast of
    Wales
Lest the dawns of coming morrows should be telling
    awful tales,
When the sea had spent its passion, and should cast
    upon the shore
Bits of wreck, and swollen victims, as it had done
    heretofore.

With the rough winds blowing round her, a brave
    woman strained her eyes,
And she saw along the billows a large vessel fall and
    rise.
Oh! it did not need a prophet to tell what the end
    must be,
For no ship could ride in safety near that shore on
    such a sea.

Then the pitying people hurried from their homes and
    thronged the beach.
Oh! for the power to cross the waters and the perish-
    ing to reach!

Helpless hands were wrung for sorrow, tender hearts
    grew cold with dread,
And the ship, urged by the tempest, to the fatal rock-
    shore sped.

" She has parted in the middle! Oh! the half of her
    goes down!
God have mercy! Is His heaven far to seek for those
    who drown? "
Lo, when next the white, shocked faces looked with
    terror on the sea,
Only one last clinging figure on the spar was seen to be.

Nearer the trembling watchers came the wreck tossed
    by the wave,
And the man still clung and floated, though no power
    on earth could save.
" Could we send him a short message? Here's a trum-
    pet. Shout away! "
'Twas the preacher's hand that took it, and he won-
    dered what to say.

Any memory of his sermon? Firstly? Secondly?
    Ah, no!
There was but one thing to utter in the awful hour of
    woe;
So he shouted through the trumpet, " Look to Jesus!
    Can you hear? "
And " Ay, ay, sir! " rang the answer o'er the waters
    loud and clear.

[111]

Then they listened. He is singing! "Jesus, lover of
    my soul";
And the winds brought back the echo, "while the
    nearer waters roll";
Strange, indeed, it was to hear him, "till the storm of
    life is past,"
Singing bravely from the waters, "Oh, receive my
    soul at last."

He could have no other refuge! "Hangs my helpless
    soul on Thee;
Leave, oh, leave me not." — The singer dropped at
    last into the sea,
And the watchers, looking homeward, through their
    eyes with tears made dim,
Said, "He passed to be with Jesus in the singing of
    the hymn."

FIDDLE-DEE-DEE

BY EUGENE FIELD

There once was a bird that lived up in a tree
And all he could whistle was Fiddle-dee-dee —
A very provoking, unmusical song
For one to be whistling the Summer day long!
Yet always contented and busy was he
With that vocal recurrence of Fiddle-dee-dee!

Hard by lived a brave little soldier of four,
That weird iteration repented him sore;

" I pri'thee, Dear-Mother-Mine! fetch me my gun,
For, by our St. Didy, the deed must be done
That shall presently rid all creation and me
Of that ominous bird and his Fiddle-dee-dee! "

Then out came Dear-Mother-Mine, bringing her son
His awfully truculent little red gun,
The stock was of pine and the barrel of tin,
The " bang " it came out where the bullet went in —
The right kind of weapon, I think you'll agree,
For slaying all fowl that go Fiddle-dee-dee!

The brave little soldier quoth never a word,
But he up and he drew a straight bead on that bird;
And, while that vain creature provokingly sang,
The gun went off with a terrible bang!
Then loud laughed the youth — " By my Bottle,"
    cried he,
" I've put a quietus on Fiddle-dee-dee! "

Out then came Dear-Mother-Mine, saying: " My son,
Right well have you wrought with your little red
    gun!
Hereafter no evil at all need I fear,
With such a brave soldier as You-My-Love here! "
She kissed the dear boy. (The bird in the tree
Continued to whistle his Fiddle-dee-dee!)

JES' FORE CHRISTMAS

BY EUGENE FIELD

Father calls me William, sister calls me Will,
Mother calls me Willie — but the fellers call me Bill!
Mighty glad I ain't a girl — ruther be a boy
Without them sashes, curls, an' things that's worn
    by Fauntleroy!
Love to chawnk green apples an' go swimmin' in the
    lake —
Hate to take the castor-oil they give f'r stomach-ache!
Most all the time the hull year roun' there ain't no
    flies on me,
But jes' fore Christmas I'm as good as I kin be!

Got a yaller dog named Sport — sick 'im on the cat;
Fust thing *she* knows she doesn't know where she's at!
Got a clipper-sled, an' when us boys goes out to slide
'Long comes the grocery cart, an' we all hook a ride!
But, sometimes, when the grocery man is worrited an'
    cross,
He reaches at me with his whip an' larrups up his
    hoss;
An' then I laff an' holler: "Oh, you never teched
    me!"
But jes' 'fore Christmas I'm as good as I kin be!

Gran'ma says she hopes that when I git to be a man
I'll be a missionerer like her oldes' brother Dan
As wuz et up by the cannib'ls that lives in Ceylon's
    isle!

Where ev'ry prospeck pleases an' only man is vile.
But gran'ma she had never been to see a Wild West
    show,
Or read the life uv Daniel Boone, or else I guess she'd
    know
That Buffalo Bill an' cowboys is good enough f'r
    me —
Excep' jes' 'fore Christmas, when I'm good as I kin be!

Then ol' Sport, he hangs around, so sollum-like an'
    still —
His eyes they seem a-sayin' : " What's the matter,
    little Bill? "
The cat she sneaks down off her perch, a-wonderin'
    what's become
Uv them two enemies uv hern that uster make things
    hum!
But I am so perlite an' stick so earnest-like to biz
That mother says to father: " How improved our
    Willie is! "
But father, havin' been a boy hisself, suspicions me
When, jes' 'fore Christmas, I'm as good as I kin be!

For Christmas, with its lots and lots uv candies, cakes,
    an' toys,
Wuz made, they say, f'r proper kids, an' *not* f'r naughty
    boys!
So wash yer face, an' bresh yer hair, an' mind yer p's
    and q's,
An' don't bust out yer pantaloons, an' don't wear out
    yer shoes;

[115]

Say " yessum " to the ladies, an' " yessir " to the
    men,
An' when they's company don't pass yer plate f'r pie
    again;
But, thinkin' uv the things you'd like to see upon *that*
    tree,
Jes' 'fore Christmas be as good as you kin be!

LITTLE BOY BLUE

BY EUGENE FIELD

The little toy dog is covered with dust,
    But sturdy and stanch he stands;
And the little toy soldier is red with rust,
    And his musket moulds in his hands.
Time was when the little toy dog was new,
    And the soldier was passing fair;
And that was the time when our Little Boy Blue
    Kissed them and put them there.

." Now, don't you go till I come," he said,
    " And don't you make any noise! "
So, toddling off to his trundle-bed,
    He dreamt of his pretty toys;
And, as he was dreaming, an angel song
    Awakened our Little Boy Blue —
Oh! the years are many, the years are long,
    But the little toy friends are true!

Ay, faithful to Little Boy Blue they stand,
    Each in the same old place —

[116]

Awaiting the touch of a little hand,
  The smile of a little face;
And they wonder, as waiting the long years through
  In the dust of that little chair,
What has become of our Little Boy Blue,
  Since he kissed them and put them there.

WYNKEN, BLYNKEN, AND NOD

BY EUGENE FIELD

Wynken, Blynken, and Nod, one night,
  Sailed off in a wooden shoe,
Sailed on a river of misty light
  Into a sea of dew;
"Where are you going and what do you wish?"
  The old man asked the three.
"We have come to fish for the herring fish,
  That live in this beautiful sea;
  Nets of gold and silver have we,"
      Said Wynken, Blynken, and Nod.

The old man laughed and sung a song,
  As they rock'd in the wooden shoe,
The wind that sped them all night along
  Ruffled the waves of dew;
The little stars were the herring fish
  That lived in the beautiful sea.
"Now cast your nets where'ver you wish,
  But never afeared are we";
  So cried the stars to the fishermen three,
      Wynken, Blynken, and Nod.

[117]

All night long their nets they threw,
　　For the fish in the twinkling foam;
Down from the sky came the wooden shoe,
　　Bringing the fishermen home.
'T was all so pretty; a sail, it seemed
　　As if it could not be;
And some folks tho't 't was a dream they dream'd,
　　Of sailing that beautiful sea;
　　But I shall name you the fishermen three,
　　　　Wynken, Blynken, and Nod.

Wynken and Blynken are two eyes,
　　And Nod is a little head,
The wooden shoe that sail'd the skies
　　Is a wee one's trundle bed;
So shut your eyes while mother sings
　　Of wonderful sights that be;
And you shall see the beautiful things,
　　As you rock on the misty sea,
　　Where the old shoe rock'd the fishermen three,
　　　　Wynken, Blynken, and Nod.

THE TEMPEST

BY JAMES THOMAS FIELDS

We were crowded in the cabin,
　　Not a soul would dare to sleep,—
It was midnight on the waters
　　And a storm was on the deep.

'T is a fearful thing in winter
　　To be shattered by the blast,

[118]

And to hear the rattling trumpet
    Thunder, " Cut away the mast! "

So we shuddered there in silence, —
    For the stoutest held his breath,
While the hungry sea was roaring,
    And the breakers talked with Death.

As thus we sat in darkness,
    Each one busy in his prayers,
" We are lost! " the captain shouted
    As he staggered down the stairs.

But his little daughter whispered,
    As she took his icy hand,
" Is n't God upon the ocean
    Just the same as on the land? "

Then we kissed the little maiden,
    And we spoke in better cheer,
And we anchored safe in harbor
    When the morn was shining clear.

THE BLUE AND THE GRAY

BY FRANCIS MILES FINCH

[Written in honor of women of Columbus, Mississippi, who, in 1867, when decorating soldiers' graves, strewed flowers "alike for the friend and the foe." Northern soldiers' graves were as lovingly decorated as were Southern soldiers' graves — blossoms bloomed for all.]

By the flow of the inland river,
  Whence the fleets of iron have fled,
Where the blades of the grave-grass quiver,
  Asleep are the ranks of the dead: —
    Under the sod and the dew,
      Waiting the judgment-day;
    Under the one, the Blue,
      Under the other, the Gray.

These in the robings of glory,
  Those in the gloom of defeat,
All with the battle-blood gory,
  In the dusk of eternity meet: —
    Under the sod and the dew,
      Waiting the judgment-day;
    Under the laurel, the Blue,
      Under the willow, the Gray.

From the silence of sorrowful hours,
  The desolate mourners go,
Lovingly laden with flowers,
  Alike for the friend and the foe: —
    Under the sod and the dew,
      Waiting the judgment-day;
    Under the roses, the Blue,
      Under the lilies, the Gray.

[120]

So, with an equal splendor,
  The morning sun-rays fall,
With a touch impartially tender,
  On the blossoms blooming for all; —
     Under the sod and the dew,
       Waiting the judgment-day;
     Broidered with gold, the Blue,
       Mellowed with gold, the Gray.

So, when the summer calleth
  On forest and field of grain,
With equal murmur falleth
  The cooling drip of the rain: —
     Under the sod and the dew,
       Waiting the judgment-day;
     Wet with the rain, the Blue,
       Wet with the rain, the Gray.

Sadly, but not with upbraiding,
  The generous deed was done;
In the storm of the years that are fading,
  No braver battle was won: —
     Under the sod and the dew,
       Waiting the judgment-day;
     Under the blossoms, the Blue,
       Under the garlands, the Gray.

No more shall the war-cry sever,
  Or the winding rivers be red;
They banish our anger forever
  When they laurel the graves of our dead: —

[121] ·

Under the sod and the dew,
  Waiting the judgment-day;
Love and tears for the Blue,
  Tears and love for the Gray.

THE CALF-PATH

BY SAM WALTER FOSS

I

One day through the primeval wood
A calf walked home as good calves should,

But made a trail all bent askew,
A crooked trail as all calves do.

Since then two hundred years have fled,
And, I infer, the calf is dead.

II

But still he left behind his trail,
And thereby hangs my moral tale.

The trail was taken up next day
By a lone dog that passed that way;

And then a wise bell-wether sheep
Pursued the trail o'er vale and steep,

And drew the flock behind him, too,
As good bell-wethers always do.

[122]

And from that day o'er hill and glade
Through those old woods a path was made.

III

And many men wound in and out,
And dodged and turned and bent about,

And uttered words of righteous wrath
Because 'twas such a crooked path;

But still they followed — do not laugh —
The first migrations of that calf,

And through this winding wood-way stalked
Because he wobbled when he walked.

IV

This forest path became a lane
That bent and turned and turned again:

This crooked lane became a road
Where many a poor horse with his load,

Toiled on beneath the burning sun,
And travelled some three miles in one.

And thus a century and a half
They trod the footsteps of that calf.

V

The years passed on in swiftness fleet,
The road became a village street,

And this, before men were aware,
A city's crowded thoroughfare.

And soon the central street was this
Of a renowned metropolis;

And men two centuries and a half
Trod in the footsteps of that calf.

VI

Each day a hundred thousand rout
Followed this zigzag calf about;

And o'er his crooked journey went
The traffic of a continent.

A hundred thousand men were led
By one calf near three centuries dead.

They followed still his crooked way
And lost one hundred years a day.

For thus such reverence is lent
To well-established precedent.

VII

A moral lesson this might teach
Were I ordained and called to preach.

For men are prone to go it blind
Along the calf paths of the mind;

And work away from sun to sun
To do what other men have done.

They follow in the beaten track,
And out and in, and forth and back,

And still their devious course pursue
To keep the path that others do.

They keep the path a sacred groove
Along which all their lives they move;

But how the wise old wood-gods laugh,
Who saw the first primeval calf.

Ah, many things this tale might teach —
But I am not ordained to preach.

THE VOLUNTEER ORGANIST

BY SAM WALTER FOSS

The gret big church wuz crowded full uv broadcloth
    and uv silk,
An' satins rich as cream thet grows on our ol' brindle's
    milk;
Shined boots, biled shirts, stiff dickeys, an' stovepipe
    hats were there,
An' doods 'ith trouserloons so tight they couldn't
    kneel down in prayer.
The elder in his poolpit high said, as he slowly riz:
" Our organist is kep' to hum, laid up 'ith roomatiz,

An' as we hev no substitoot, as Brother Moore ain'
here,
Will some 'un in the congregation be so kind's to volun-
teer? "

An' then a red-nosed, drunken tramp of low-toned
rowdy style
Give an interductory hiccup, an' then staggered up
the aisle;
Then thro' thet holy atmosphere there crep' a sense
er sin,
An' thro' thet air of sanctity the odor uv ol' gin.

Then Deacon Purington he yelled, his teeth all sot on
edge:
" This man purfanes the house of God! W'y, this is
sacrilege! "
The tramp didn' hear a word he said, but slouched 'ith
stumblin' feet,
An' sprawled an' staggered up the steps, an' gained
the organ seat.

He then went pawin' through the keys, an' soon there
rose a strain
Thet seemed to jest bulge out the heart, an' 'lectrify
the brain;
An' then he slapped down on the thing 'ith hands an'
head an' knees,
He slam-dashed his hull body down 'kerflop upon the
keys.
The organ roared, the music flood went sweepin' high
and dry,

It swelled into the rafters and bulged out into the sky.
The ol' church shook an' staggered, an' seemed to reel
    an' sway,
An' the elder shouted "Glory!" an' I yelled out
    "Hooray!"

An' then he tried a tender strain that melted in our
    ears,
Thet brought up blessed memories an' drenched 'em
    down 'ith tears;
An' we dreamed of ol' time kitchens, 'ith Tabby on
    the mat,
Uv home an' luv an' baby days, an' mother an' all
    that!

An' then he struck a streak uv hope — a song from
    souls forgiven —
Thet burst from prison bars uv sin, an' stormed the
    gates of heaven;
The mornin' stars they sung together — no soul was
    left alone —
We felt the universe wuz safe, an' God wuz on his
    throne!

An' then a wail uv deep despair an' darkness come
    again,
An' long black crape hung on the doors uv all the
    homes uv men;
No luv, no light, no joy, no hope, no songs uv glad
    delight,
An' then — the tramp he staggered down an' reeled
    into the night!

But we knew he'd tol' his story, tho' he never spoke a
    word
An' it wuz the saddest story thet our ears had ever
    heard!
He hed tol' his own life history, an' no eye wuz dry
    thet day,
W'en the elder rose and simply said: "My brethren,
    let us pray."

MY OLD KENTUCKY HOME

STEPHEN COLLINS FOSTER

The sun shines bright in our old Kentucky home;
    'Tis summer, the darkeys are gay;
The corn top's ripe and the meadows in the bloom,
    While the birds make music all the day;
The young folks roll on the little cabin floor,
    All merry, all happy, all bright;
By'm by hard times comes a-knockin' at the door,—
    Then, my old Kentucky home, good-night!
Weep no more, my lady; O, weep no more to-day!
We'll sing one song for the old Kentucky home,
    For our old Kentucky home far away.

They hunt no more for the possum and the coon
    On the meadow, the hill, and the shore;
They sing no more by the glimmer of the moon
    On the bench by the old cabin door;
The day goes by, like a shadow o'er the heart,
    With sorrow where all was delight;
The time has come when the darkeys have to part,

Then my old Kentucky home, good-night!
Weep no more, my lady; O, weep no more to-day!
We'll sing one song for the old Kentucky home,
    For our old Kentucky home far away.

The head must bow, and the back will have to bend,
    Wherever the darkey may go;
A few more days, and the troubles all will end,
    In the field where the sugar-canes grow;
A few more days to tote the weary load,
    No matter, it will never be light;
A few more days till we totter on the road,
    Then, my old Kentucky home, good-night!
Weep no more my lady; O, weep no more to-day!
We'll sing one song for the old Kentucky home,
    For our old Kentucky home far away.

PALMETTO AND PINE

BY L. VIRGINIA FRENCH

After reading the debate on amnesty in the United States Congress, an accomplished Tennessee lady, Mrs. L. Virginia French, wrote this poem for the *Nashville American*. It is an impassioned plea for peace, and more than peace, for affectionate brotherhood and the revival of friendly memories older than the late civil strife.

They planted them together — our gallant sires of
    old —
Though one was crowned with crystal snow, and one
    with solar gold;
They planted them together — on the world's majestic height,

[129]

At Saratoga's deathless charge, at Eutaw's stubborn
fight.

At midnight on the dark redoubt, 'mid plunging shot
and shell —

At noontide gasping in the crush of battle's bloody
swell —

With gory hands and reeking brows, amid the mighty
fray,

Which surged and swelled around them on that memorable day,

When they planted Independence, as a symbol and
a sign,

They struck deep soil and planted the Palmetto and
the Pine!

They planted them together — by the river of the
Years —

Watered with our fathers' hearts' blood, watered with
our mothers' tears;

In the strong, rich soil of Freedom, with a bounteous
benison

From their Prophet, Priest, and Pioneer — our Father,
Washington!

Above them floated echoes of the ruin and the
wreck,

Like " drums that beat at Louisburg and thundered
at Quebec; "

But the old lights sank in darkness as the new stars
rose to shine

O'er those emblems of the sections — the Palmetto
and the Pine.

And we'll plant them still together — for 'tis yet the
    selfsame soil
Our fathers' valor won for us by victory and toil;
In Florida's fair everglades, by bold Ontario's flood,
And thro' them send electric life as leaps the kindred
    blood!
For thus it is they taught us, who for Freedom lived
    and died,
The Eternal law of justice must and shall be justi-
    fied —
That God has joined together by a fiat all divine
The destinies of dwellers 'neath the Palm tree and the
    Pine.

Aye! we'll plant them yet together — though the
    cloud is on their brows,
And winds antagonistic writhe and wrench the stal-
    wart boughs;
Driving winds that drift the nations into gaping gulfs
    of gloom,
Sweeping ages, cycles, systems, into vortices of doom;
Though the waves of faction rolling in triumphant
    to the shore,
Are breaking down our bulwarks with their sullen
    rage and roar;
Serried armaments of ocean filing in line after line,
Washing up the deep foundations of Palmetto and of
    Pine.

Shall this, the soil of Freedom, from their roots be
    washed away

By the changing of the billows and the breaking of
the spray?
No! the Hand which rules the vortex which is surging
now before us,
Above its " hell of waters " sets the bow of promise
o'er us —
And the time will come when Discord shall be buried
in the past.
The oriflamme of Love shall wave above the breach
at last,
And beneath that starry banner — type of unity
divine —
Shall stand those stately signals — the Palmetto and
the Pine.

Shall the old victorious Eagle from their boughs be
wrenched away
By the double-headed Vulture of Disunion and De-
cay?
Forbid it, Heaven! Columbia, guard thine emblems
gathered here,
To grace the brilliant dawning of this grand Cen-
tennial year,
And bear them as thou marchest on with gonfalons
unfurled,
With thy foot upon the fetter, for the freeing of the
world!
And guard thy Holy Sepulchre — Mount Vernon's
sacred shrine —
For this is Freedom's Holy Land — her promised
Palestine.

Oh! thou voice of God outflowing from the lips of
    holy Peace,
Soothe the turmoil and the tumult — bid this strife
    and sorrow cease!
O'er savannahs steeped in sunshine, over mountains
    dark with rain,
Send the glad and thrilling tidings in thy sweetly
    solemn strain —
Let snowy North and sunny South send up the shout,
    " All's well! "
And the music of thy coming strike our heartstrings
    with its swell,
(As to Jessie Brown at Lucknow struck the air of
    " Auld Lang Syne,"
From the Highland pipes of Havelock) — Save the
    Palm and save the Pine!

God plant them still together! let them flourish side
    by side.
In the halls of our Centennial — mailed in more than
    marble pride;
With kindly deeds and noble names we'll grave them
    o'er and o'er,
With brave historic legends of the glorious days of
    yore;
While the clear, exultant chorus, rising from united
    bands,
The echo of our triumph peals to earth's remotest
    lands —
While " Faith, Fraternity and Love " shall joyfully
    entwine

[133]

Around our chosen Emblems — the Palmetto and the
    Pine.

" Together! " shouts Niagara his thunder-toned de-
    cree —
" Together! " echo back the waves upon the Mexic
    Sea —
" Together! " sing the sylvan hills where old Atlantic
    roars —
" Together! " boom the breakers on the wild Pacific
    shores —
" Together! " cry the People and " together " it
    shall be,
An everlasting charter-bond forever for the free;
Of Liberty the signet-seal — the one eternal sign
Be those united emblems — the Palmetto and the
    Pine!

ELEGY ON THE DEATH OF A MAD DOG

BY OLIVER GOLDSMITH

Good people all, of every sort,
    Give ear unto my song;
And if you find it wondrous short,
    It cannot hold you long.

In Islington there was a man
    Of whom the world might say,
That still a godly race he ran —
    Whene'er he went to pray.

[134]

A kind and gentle heart he had,
   To comfort friends and foes:
The naked every day he clad —
   When he put on his clothes.

And in that town a dog was found,
   As many dogs there be,
Both mongrel, puppy, whelp, and hound,
   And curs of low degree.

This dog and man at first were friends;
   But when a pique began,
The dog, to gain his private ends,
   Went mad, and bit the man.

Around from all the neighboring streets
   The wondering neighbors ran,
And swore the dog had lost his wits,
   To bite so good a man!

The wound it seemed both sore and sad
   To every Christian eye:
And while they swore the dog was mad,
   They swore the man would die.

But soon a wonder came to light,
   That showed the rogues they lied: —
The man recovered of the bite,
   The dog it was that died!

ELEGY ON MADAM BLAIZE

BY OLIVER GOLDSMITH

Good people all, with one accord,
  Lament for Madam Blaize;
Who never wanted a good word —
  From those who spoke her praise.

The needy seldom passed her door,
  And always found her kind;
She freely lent to all the poor —
  Who left a pledge behind.

She strove the neighborhood to please,
  With manner wondrous winning;
She never followed wicked ways —
  Unless when she was sinning.

At church, in silk and satins new,
  With hoop of monstrous size,
She never slumbered in her pew —
  But when she shut her eyes.

Her love was sought, I do aver,
  By twenty beaux, or more;
The king himself has followed her —
  When she has walked before.

But now, her wealth and finery fled,
  Her hangers-on cut short all,

Her doctors found, when she was dead —
   Her last disorder mortal.

Let us lament, in sorrow sore;
   For Kent Street well may say,
That, had she lived a twelvemonth more —
   She had not died to-day.

THE PHILOSOPHIC BEGGAR

BY BLAKENEY GRAY

In a city stamped with plenty,
   Full of dolce far niente,
I observed a beggarman upon the way;
   And, by Jove, the chap was smiling
   In a fashion most beguiling,
And he seemed the happiest man I'd seen that day.

I had little time for chinning,
   But I asked him: " Why this grinning?
Are your rags and tatters then a merry joke?
   Is this hunger you've been vaunting,
   And these pennies you've been wanting,
Just a sort of passing whim that ends in smoke? "

" Not a bit! " he said, instanter.
   " My hard luck is far from banter;
But the thought has just now flashed across my mind
   That I really should not hanker
   For to be a worried banker
Who must find the cash he gives his womenkind.

[137]

"I don't have to buy rich sables,
  Motor-cars, and pearls in cables,
For to keep my wife a-smiling all the while;
  And I do not have to worry,
  Nor to hurry, or to scurry,
For the cash to dress my daughters up in style.

"I can win a smiling dimple
  With a present that is simple,
And a dollar's all I need to meet the call,
  So I think upon the whole, sir —
  Yes, I do, upon my soul, sir —
That I'm better off than others, after all!"

And that is how it came to be
He got a dollar out of me!

ELEGY

WRITTEN IN A COUNTRY CHURCHYARD

BY THOMAS GRAY

The curfew tolls the knell of parting day,
  The lowing herd winds slowly o'er the lea,
The ploughman homeward plods his weary way,
  And leaves the world to darkness and to me.

Now fades the glimmering landscape on the sight,
  And all the air a solemn stillness holds,
Save where the beetle wheels his droning flight,
  And drowsy tinklings lull the distant folds:

[138]

Save that from yonder ivy-mantled tower
   The moping owl does to the moon complain
Of such as, wandering near her secret bower,
   Molest her ancient solitary reign.

Beneath those rugged elms, that yew tree's shade,
   Where heaves the turf in many a mouldering heap,
Each in his narrow cell for ever laid,
   The rude forefathers of the hamlet sleep.

The breezy call of incense-breathing morn,
   The swallow twittering from the straw-built shed,
The cock's shrill clarion, or the echoing horn,
   No more shall rouse them from their lowly bed.

For them no more the blazing hearth shall burn
   Or busy housewife ply her evening care:
No children run to lisp their sire's return,
   Or climb his knees the envied kiss to share.

Oft did the harvest to their sickle yield,
   Their furrow oft the stubborn glebe has broke;
How jocund did they drive their team afield!
   How bow'd the woods beneath their sturdy stroke!

Let not Ambition mock their useful toil,
   Their homely joys, and destiny obscure;
Nor Grandeur hear with a disdainful smile
   The short and simple annals of the poor.

The boast of heraldry, the pomp of power,
   And all that beauty, all that wealth e'er gave,

Await alike th' inevitable hour:—
  The paths of glory lead but to the grave.

Nor you, ye proud, impute to these the fault
  If Memory o'er their tomb no trophies raise,
Where through the long-drawn aisle and fretted vault
  The pealing anthem swells the note of praise.

Can storied urn or animated bust
  Back to its mansion call the fleeting breath?
Can Honor's voice provoke the silent dust,
  Or Flattery soothe the dull cold ear of Death?

Perhaps in this neglected spot is laid
  Some heart once pregnant with celestial fire;
Hands, that the rod of empire might have sway'd,
  Or waked to ecstasy the living lyre:

But Knowledge to their eyes her ample page
  Rich with the spoils of time did ne'er unroll;
Chill Penury repress'd their noble rage,
  And froze the genial current of the soul.

Full many a gem of purest ray serene
  The dark unfathom'd caves of ocean bear:
Full many a flower is born to blush unseen,
  And waste its sweetness on the desert air.

Some village Hampden, that with dauntless breast
  The little tyrant of his fields withstood,
Some mute inglorious Milton here may rest,
  Some Cromwell, guiltless of his country's blood.

Th' applause of list'ning senates to command,
  The threats of pain and ruin to despise,
To scatter plenty o'er a smiling land
  And read their history in a nation's eyes,

Their lot forbade: nor circumscribed alone
  Their growing virtues, but their crimes confined;
Forbade to wade through slaughter to a throne,
  And shut the gates of mercy on mankind;

The struggling pangs of conscious truth to hide,
  To quench the blushes of ingenuous shame,
Or heap the shrine of Luxury and Pride
  With incense kindled at the Muse's flame.

Far from the madding crowd's ignoble strife
  Their sober wishes never learn'd to stray;
Along the cool sequester'd vale of life
  They kept the noiseless tenor of their way.

Yet e'en these bones from insult to protect
  Some frail memorial still erected nigh,
With uncouth rhymes and shapeless sculpture deck'd,
  Implores the passing tribute of a sigh.

Their name, their years, spelt by th' unletter'd Muse,
  The place of fame and elegy supply:
And many a holy text around she strews
  That teach the rustic moralist to die.

For who, to dumb forgetfulness a prey,
  This pleasing anxious being e'er resign'd,

[141]

Left the warm precincts of the cheerful day,
  Nor cast one longing lingering look behind?

On some fond breast the parting soul relies,
  Some pious drops the closing eye requires;
E'en from the tomb the voice of Nature cries,
  E'en in our ashes live their wonted fires.

For thee, who, mindful of th' unhonor'd dead,
  Dost in these lines their artless tale relate,
If chance, by lonely Contemplation led,
  Some kindred spirit shall inquire thy fate,—

Haply some hoary-headed swain may say,
  "Oft have we seen him at the peep of dawn
Brushing with hasty steps the dews away,
  To meet the sun upon the upland lawn;

"There at the foot of yonder nodding beech
  That wreathes its old fantastic roots so high,
His listless length at noontide would he stretch,
  And pore upon the brook that babbles by.

"Hard by yon wood, now smiling as in scorn,
  Muttering his wayward fancies he would rove;
Now drooping, woeful-wan, like one forlorn,
  Or crazed with care, or cross'd in hopeless love.

"One morn I miss'd him on the 'custom'd hill,
  Along the heath, and near his favorite tree;
Another came, nor yet beside the rill,
  Nor up the lawn, nor at the wood was he;

"The next with dirges due in sad array
  Slow through the churchway path we saw him borne;
Approach and read (for thou canst read) the lay
  Graved on the stone beneath yon aged thorn."

THE EPITAPH

Here rests his head upon the lap of Earth
  A youth, to fortune and to fame unknown;
Fair Science frown'd not on his humble birth,
  And Melancholy mark'd him for her own.

Large was his bounty, and his soul sincere;
  Heaven did a recompense as largely send:
He gave to Misery all he had, — a tear,
  He gain'd from Heaven — 'twas all he wish'd — a
    friend.

No farther seek his merits to disclose,
  Or draw his frailties from their dread abode
(There they alike in trembling hope repose),
  The bosom of his Father and his God.

THE BARON'S LAST BANQUET

BY ALBERT G. GREENE

O'er a low couch the setting sun
  Had thrown its latest ray,
Where in his last strong agony
  A dying warrior lay,—

[143]

The stern old Baron Rudiger,
   Whose frame had ne'er been bent
By wasting pain, till time and toil
   Its iron strength had spent.

" They come around me here, and say
   My days of life are o'er,
That I shall mount my noble steed
   And lead my band no more;
They come, and to my beard they dare
   To tell me now, that I,
Their own liege lord and master born, —
   That I — ha! ha! — must die.

" And what is Death? I've dared him oft
   Before the Paynim spear, —
Think ye he's entered at my gate,
   Has come to seek me here?
I've met him, faced him, scorned him,
   When the fight was raging hot, —
I'll try his might — I'll brave his power;
   Defy, and fear him not.

" Ho! sound the tocsin from my tower, —
   And fire the culverin, —
Bid each retainer arm with speed, —
   Call every vassal in;
Up with my banner on the wall, —
   The banquet-board prepare, —
Throw wide the portal of my hall,
   And bring my armor there! "

A hundred hands were busy then, —
  The banquet forth was spread, —
And rung the heavy oaken floor
  With many a martial tread,
While from the rich, dark tracery
  Along the vaulted wall,
Lights gleamed on harness, plume, and spear,
  O'er the proud old Gothic hall.

Fast hurrying through the outer gate,
  The mailed retainers poured,
On through the portal's frowning arch,
  And thronged around the board.
While at its head, within his dark,
  Carved oaken chair of state,
Armed cap-a-pie, stern Rudiger,
  With girded falchion, sate.

" Fill every beaker up, my men,
  Pour forth the cheering wine;
There's life and strength in every drop, —
  Thanksgiving to the vine!
Are ye all there, my vassals true? —
  Mine eyes are waxing dim; —
Fill round, my tried and fearless ones,
  Each goblet to the brim.

" Ye're there, but yet I see ye not.
  Draw forth each trusty sword, —
And let me hear your faithful steel
  Clash once around my board:

[145]

I hear it faintly: — Louder yet! —
  What clogs my heavy breath?
Up, all, — and shout for Rudiger,
  'Defiance unto Death!' "

Bowl rang to bowl, steel clanged to steel,
  And rose a deafening cry
That made the torches flare around,
  And shook the flags on high: —
" Ho! cravens, do ye fear him? —
  Slaves, traitors! have ye flown?
Ho! cowards, have ye left me
  To meet him here alone?

" But *I* defy him: — let him come! "
  Down rang the massy cup,
While from its sheath the ready blade
  Came flashing half-way up;
And, with the black and heavy plumes
  Scarce trembling on his head,
There, in his dark, carved, oaken chair,
  Old Rudiger sat, *dead*.

OLD GRIMES

BY ALBERT G. GREENE

Old Grimes is dead, that good old man, —
  We ne'er shall see him more;
He used to wear a long black coat,
  All buttoned down before.

His heart was open as the day,
   His feelings all were true;
His hair was some inclined to gray,—
   He wore it in a queue.

Whene'er he heard the voice of pain,
   His breast with pity burned;
The large round head upon his cane
   From ivory was turned.

Kind words he ever had for all;
   He knew no base design;
His eyes were dark and rather small,
   His nose was aquiline.

He lived at peace with all mankind,
   In friendship he was true;
His coat had pocket-holes behind,
   His pantaloons were blue.

Unharmed, the sin which earth pollutes
   He passed securely o'er, —
And never wore a pair of boots
   For thirty years or more.

But good Old Grimes is now at rest,
   Nor fears misfortune's frown;
He wore a double-breasted vest, —
   The stripes ran up and down.

He modest merit sought to find,
   And pay it its desert;

He had no malice in his mind,
　No ruffles on his shirt.

His neighbors he did not abuse, —
　Was sociable and gay;
He wore large buckles on his shoes,
　And changed them every day.

His knowledge, hid from public gaze
　He did not bring to view,
Nor make a noise, town-meeting days,
　As many people do.

His worldly goods he never threw
　In trust to fortune's chances,
But lived (as all his brothers do)
　In easy circumstances.

Thus undisturbed by anxious cares
　His peaceful moments ran;
And everybody said he was
　A fine old gentleman.

THE KINGS

BY LOUISE IMOGEN GUINEY

A man said unto his Angel:
　" My spirits are fallen low,
And I cannot carry this battle:
　O brother! where might I go?

" The terrible Kings are on me
  With spears that are deadly bright,
Against me so from the cradle
  Do fate and my fathers fight."

Then said to the man his Angel:
  " Thou wavering, witless soul,
Back to the ranks! What matter
  To win or to lose the whole,

" As judged by the little judges
  Who hearken not well, nor see?
Not thus, by the outer issue,
  The Wise shall interpret thee.

" Thy will is the sovereign measure
  And only event of things:
The puniest heart, defying,
  Were stronger than all these Kings.

" Though out of the past they gather,
  Mind's Doubt, and Bodily Pain,
And pallid Thirst of the Spirit
  That is kin to the other twain;

" And Grief, in a cloud of banners,
  And ringletted Vain Desires,
And Vice, with spoils upon him
  Of thee and thy beaten sires,—

" While Kings of eternal evil
  Yet darken the hills about,

[149]

Thy part is with broken sabre
  To rise on the last redoubt;

" To fear not sensible failure,
  Nor covet the game at all,
But fighting, fighting, fighting,
  Die, driven against the wall."

JOSEPH RODMAN DRAKE

DIED IN NEW YORK, SEPTEMBER, 1820

BY FITZ-GREENE HALLECK

Green be the turf above thee,
  Friend of my better days!
None knew thee but to love thee,
  Nor named thee but to praise.

Tears fell, when thou wert dying,
  From eyes unused to weep,
And long, where thou art lying,
  Will tears the cold turf steep.

When hearts, whose truth was proven,
  Like thine, are laid in earth,
There should a wreath be woven
  To tell the world their worth;

And I, who woke each morrow
  To clasp thy hand in mine,

Who shared thy joy and sorrow,
 Whose weal and woe were thine,

It should be mine to braid it
 Around thy faded brow,
But I've in vain essayed it,
 And feel I cannot now.

While memory bids me weep thee,
 Nor thoughts nor words are free,
The grief is fixed too deeply
 That mourns a man like thee.

MARCO BOZZARIS

BY FITZ-GREENE HALLECK

Marco Bozzaris, the Epaminondas of modern Greece, fell in a night attack upon the Turkish camp at Laspi, the site of the ancient Platæa, August 20, 1823, and expired in the moment of victory. His last words were: "To die for liberty is a pleasure, and not a pain."

At midnight, in his guarded tent,
 The Turk was dreaming of the hour
When Greece, her knee in suppliance bent,
 Should tremble at his power.
In dreams, through camp and court, he bore
The trophies of a conqueror;
 In dreams his song of triumph heard;
Then wore his monarch's signet-ring,
Then pressed that monarch's throne — a king;
As wild his thoughts, and gay of wing,
 As Eden's garden bird.

[151]

At midnight, in the forest shades,
   Bozzaris ranged his Suliote band, —
True as the steel of their tried blades,
   Heroes in heart and hand.
There had the Persian's thousands stood,
There had the glad earth drunk their blood,
   On old Platæa's day;
And now there breathed that haunted air
The sons of sires who conquered there,
With arm to strike, and soul to dare,
   As quick, as far, as they.

An hour passed on, the Turk awoke:
   That bright dream was his last;
He woke — to hear his sentries shriek,
   "To arms! they come! the Greek! the Greek!"
He woke — to die midst flame, and smoke,
And shout, and groan, and sabre-stroke,
   And death-shots falling thick and fast
As lightnings from the mountain-cloud;
And heard, with voice as trumpet loud,
   Bozzaris cheer his band:
"Strike — till the last armed foe expires;
Strike — for your altars and your fires;
Strike — for the green graves of your sires,
   God, and your native land!"

They fought — like brave men, long and well;
   They piled that ground with Moslem slain:
They conquered — but Bozzaris fell,
   Bleeding at every vein.

[152]

His few surviving comrades saw
His smile when rang their proud hurrah,
  And the red field was won;
Then saw in death his eyelids close
Calmly, as to a night's repose,
  Like flowers at set of sun.

Come to the bridal chamber, Death,
  Come to the mother, when she feels,
For the first time, her first-born's breath;
  Come when the blessed seals
That close the pestilence are broke,
And crowded cities wail its stroke;
Come in consumption's ghastly form,
The earthquake shock, the ocean storm;
Come when the heart beats high and warm,
  With banquet song and dance and wine,—
And thou art terrible; the tear,
The groan, the knell, the pall, the bier,
And all we know, or dream, or fear
  Of agony, are thine.

But to the hero, when his sword
  Has won the battle for the free,
Thy voice sounds like a prophet's word,
And in its hollow tones are heard
  The thanks of millions yet to be.
Come when his task of fame is wrought;
Come with her laurel-leaf, blood-bought;
  Come in her crowning hour, — and then
Thy sunken eye's unearthly light

[153]

To him is welcome as the sight
  Of sky and stars to prisoned men;
Thy grasp is welcome as the hand
Of brother in a foreign land;
Thy summons welcome as the cry
That told the Indian isles were nigh
  To the world-seeking Genoese,
When the land-wind, from woods of palm,
And orange-groves, and fields of balm,
  Blew o'er the Haytian seas.

Bozzaris! with the storied brave
  Greece nurtured in her glory's time,
Rest thee; there is no prouder grave,
  Even in her own proud clime.
She wore no funeral weeds for thee,
  Nor bade the dark hearse wave its plume,
Like torn branch from death's leafless tree,
In sorrow's pomp and pageantry,
  The heartless luxury of the tomb.
But she remembers thee as one
Long loved, and for a season gone.
For thee her poet's lyre is wreathed,
Her marble wrought, her music breathed;
For thee she rings the birthday bells;
Of thee her babes' first lisping tells;
For thine her evening prayer is said
At palace couch and cottage bed.
Her soldier, closing with the foe,
Gives for thy sake a deadlier blow;
His plighted maiden, when she fears

[154]

For him, the joy of her young years,
Thinks of thy fate, and checks her tears.
   And she, the mother of thy boys,
Though in her eye and faded cheek
Is read the grief she will not speak,
   The memory of her buried joys, —
And even she who gave thee birth, —
Will, by her pilgrim-circled hearth,
   Talk of thy doom without a sigh;
For thou art freedom's now, and fame's, —
One of the few, the immortal names
   That were not born to die.

PLAIN LANGUAGE FROM TRUTHFUL JAMES

POPULARLY KNOWN AS "THE HEATHEN CHINEE"

BY FRANCIS BRET HARTE

Which I wish to remark —
   And my language is plain —
That for ways that are dark
   And for tricks that are vain,
The heathen Chinee is peculiar:
   Which the same I would rise to explain.

Ah Sin was his name;
   And I shall not deny
In regard to the same
   What that name might imply;
But his smile it was pensive and childlike,
   As I frequent remarked to Bill Nye.

[155]

It was August the third,
   And quite soft was the skies,
Which it might be inferred
   That Ah Sin was likewise;
Yet he played it that day upon William
   And me in a way I despise.

Which we had a small game,
   And Ah Sin took a hand:
It was euchre. The same
   He did not understand,
But he smiled, as he sat by the table,
   With the smile that was childlike and bland.

Yet the cards they were stocked
   In a way that I grieve,
And my feelings were shocked
   At the state of Nye's sleeve,
Which was stuffed full of aces and bowers,
   And the same with intent to deceive.

But the hands that were played
   By that heathen Chinee,
And the points that he made,
   Were quite frightful to see, —
Till at last he put down a right bower,
   Which the same Nye had dealt unto me.

Then I looked up at Nye,
   And he gazed upon me;
And he rose with a sigh,

[156]

And said, " Can this be?
We are ruined by Chinese cheap labor,"—
   And he went for that heathen Chinee.

In the scene that ensued
   I did not take a hand,
But the floor it was strewed,
   Like the leaves on the strand,
With the cards that Ah Sin had been hiding
   In the game " he did not understand."

In his sleeves, which were long,
   He had twenty-four jacks, —
Which was coming it strong,
   Yet I state but the facts.
And we found on his nails, which were taper, —
   What is frequent in tapers, — that's wax.

Which is why I remark,
   And my language is plain,
That for ways that are dark,
   And for tricks that are vain,
The heathen Chinee is peculiar, —
   Which the same I am free to maintain.

MISS EDITH HELPS THINGS ALONG WITH HER ELDER SISTER'S BEAU

BY FRANCIS BRET HARTE

" My sister'll be down in a minute, and says for you
    to wait if you please.
  And says I might stay till she came, if I'd promise
    never to tease,
Nor speak till you spoke to me first. But that's
    nonsense; for how would you know
  What she told me to say if I didn't? Don't you
    really and truly think so?

" And then you'd feel strange here alone. And you
    wouldn't know where to sit,
  For that chair isn't strong on its legs, and we never
    use it a bit.
We keep it to match with the scfa; but Jack says
    it would be like you
  To flop yourself right down on it and knock out
    the very last screw.

Suppose you try? I won't tell. You're afraid to!
    Oh! you're afraid they would think it was mean.
  Well, then, there's the album; that's pretty, if
    you're sure that your fingers are clean,
For sister says, sometimes I daub it; but she only
    says that when she's cross.
  There's her picture, you know it? It's like her;
    but she ain't as good looking, of course.

[158]

" This is ME. It's the best of 'em all. Now, tell me
    you'd never have thought
  That once I was little as that. It's the only one
    that could be bought;
For that was the message to pa from the photograph
    man where I sat —
  That he wouldn't print off any more till he first
    got the money for that.

" What? Maybe you're tired of waiting. Why, often
    she's longer than this.
  There's all her back hair to do up, and all her front
    curls to friz.
But it's nice to be sitting here and talking like grown
    people, just you and me!
  Do you think you'll be coming here often? Oh,
    do! But don't come like Tom Lee. —

" Tom Lee's her last beau. Why, my gracious he
    used to be here day and night,
  Till the folks thought he'd be her husband; and
    Jack says that gave him a fright.
You won't run away then as he did; for you're not
    a rich man they say.
  Pa says you're poor as a church mouse. Now are
    you? And how poor are they?

" Ain't you glad that you met me? Well, I am, for
    I know now your hair isn't red.
  But what there is left of it's mousy, and not what
    that naughty Jack said.

But there, I must go; sister's coming; But I wish
    I could wait, just to see
  If she ran up to you, and kissed you in the way
    she used to kiss Tom Lee! ''

THE ENCHANTED SHIRT

BY JOHN HAY

The king was sick. His cheek was red.
    And his eye was clear and bright;
He ate and drank with a kingly zest,
    And peacefully snored at night.

But he said he was sick — and a king should know;
    And doctors came by the score;
They did not cure him. He cut off their heads,
    And sent to the schools for more.

At last two famous doctors came,
    And one was poor as a rat;
He had passed his life in studious toil
    And never found time to grow fat.

The other had never looked in a book;
    His patients gave him no trouble;
If they recovered, they paid him well,
    If they died, their heirs paid double.

Together they looked at the royal tongue,
    As the king on his couch reclined;
In succession they thumped his august chest,
    But no trace of disease could find.

[160]

The old sage said, " You're as sound as a nut."
  " Hang him up! " roared the king, in a gale,—
In a ten-knot gale of royal rage;
  The other grew a shadow pale;

But he pensively rubbed his sagacious nose,
  And thus his prescription ran:
" The king will be well if he sleeps one night
  In the shirt of a happy man."

Wide o'er the realm the couriers rode,
  And fast their horses ran,
And many they saw, and to many they spake,
  But they found no happy man.

They found poor men who would fain be rich
  And rich who thought they were poor;
And men who twisted their waists in stays
  And women that short hose wore.

They saw two men by the roadside sit,
  And both bemoaned their lot;
For one had buried his wife he said,
  And the other one had not.

At last they came to a village gate;
  A beggar lay whistling there;
He whistled and sang and laughed, and rolled
  On the grass in the soft June air.

The weary couriers paused and looked
  At the scamp so blithe and gay,

[161]

And one of them said, " Heaven save you, friend,
  You seem to be happy to-day."

" Oh yes, fair sirs," the rascal laughed,
  And his voice rang free and glad;
" An idle man has so much to do
  That he never has time to be sad."

" This is our man," the courier said,
  " Our luck has led us aright.
I will give you a hundred ducats, friend,
  For the loan of your shirt to-night."

The merry blackguard lay back on the grass
  And laughed till his face was black;
" I would do it, God wot," and he roared with fun,
  " But I haven't a shirt to my back."

Each day to the king the reports came in
  Of his unsuccessful spies,
And the sad panorama of human woes
  Passed daily under his eyes.

And he grew ashamed of his useless life,
  And his maladies hatched in gloom;
He opened the windows, and let in the air
  Of the free heaven into his room;

And out he went in the world, and toiled
  In his own appointed way,
And the people blessed him, the land was glad,
  And the king was well and gay.

INVOCATION

BY JOHN HAY

Lord, from far several climes we come,
  To meet at last in Thee, our home.
Thou who hast been our guide and guard,
  Be still our hope, our rich reward.

Defend us, Lord, from every ill,
  Strengthen our hearts to do Thy will,
In all we plan, and all we do,
  Still keep us to Thy service true.

O let us hear the inspiring word
  Which they of old at Horeb heard;
Breathe to our hearts the high command,
  " Go onward and possess the land! "

Thou who art light, shine on each soul,
  Thou who art truth, each mind control.
Open our eyes, and make us see
  The path which leads to Heaven and Thee.

JIM BLUDSO

BY JOHN HAY

Wall, no, I can't tell whar he lives,
  Because he don't live, you see;
Leastways, he's got out of the habit
  Of livin' like you and me.

[163]

Whar have you been for the last three year,
  That you haven't heard folks tell
How Jimmy Bludso passed in his checks
  The night of the *Prairie Belle?*

He weren't no saint — them engineers
  Is all pretty much alike —
One wife in Natchez-under-the-Hill,
  And another one here in Pike.
A keerless man in his talk was Jim,
  And an awkward hand in a row;
But he never flunked and he never lied —
  I reckon he never knowed how.

And this was all the religion he had —
  To treat his engine well;
Never be passed on the river;
  To mind the pilot's bell;
And if ever the *Prairie Belle* took fire —
  A thousand times he swore
He'd hold her nozzle ag'in' the bank
  Till the last soul got ashore.

All boats has their day on the Mississip',
  And her day come at last.
The *Movastar* was a better boat,
  But the *Belle* she wouldn't be passed.
And so she came tearin' along that night —
  The oldest craft on the line —
With a nigger squat on her safety-valve,
  And her furnace crammed — rosin and pine.

[164]

The fire burst out as she cl'ared the bar,
   And burnt a hole in the night,
And, quick as a flash, she turned and made
   For that willer bank on the right.
There was runnin' and cussin', but Jim yelled out,
   Over all the infernal roar:
" I'll hold the nozzle ag'in the bank
   Till the last galoot's ashore! "

Through the hot, black breath of the burnin' boat
   Jim Bludso's voice was heard,
And they all had trust in his cussedness,
   And knowed he would keep his word.
And, sure's you're born, they all got off
   Afore the smoke-stack fell;
And Bludso's ghost went up alone
   In the smoke of the *Prairie Belle*.

He weren't no saint, but at Jedgment
   I'd run my chance with Jim
'Longside of some pious gentlemen
   That wouldn't shook hands with him.
He seen his duty — a dead sure thing —
   And went for it thar and then;
And Christ ain't a-goin' to be too hard
   On a man that died for men.

THE LANDING OF THE PILGRIM FATHERS IN NEW ENGLAND

BY FELICIA HEMANS

The breaking waves dashed high
  On a stern and rock-bound coast,
And the woods against a stormy sky
  Their giant branches tossed;

And the heavy night hung dark
  The hills and waters o'er,
When a band of exiles moored their bark
  On the wild New England shore.

Not as the conquerer comes,
  They, the true-hearted, came;
Not with the roll of the stirring drums,
  And the trumpet that sings of fame:

Not as the flying come,
  In silence and in fear; —
They shook the depths of the desert gloom
  With their hymns of lofty cheer.

Amidst the storm they sang,
  And the stars heard, and the sea;
And the sounding aisles of the dim woods rang
  To the anthem of the tree,

The ocean eagle soared
  From his nest by the white wave's foam,

And the rocking pines of the forest roared,—
   This was their welcome home.

There were men with hoary hair
   Amidst that pilgrim-band:
Why had they come to wither there,
   Away from their childhood's land?

There was woman's fearless eye,
   Lit by her deep love's truth;
There was manhood's brow serenely high,
   And the fiery heart of youth.

What sought they thus afar?
   Bright jewels of the mine?
The wealth of seas, the spoils of war? —
   They sought a faith's pure shrine!

Ay, call it holy ground,
   The soil where first they trod;
They have left unstained what there they found,—
   Freedom to worship God.

THE BOYS

BY OLIVER WENDELL HOLMES

Has there any old fellow got mixed with the boys?
If there has, take him out, without making a noise.
Hang the Almanac's cheat and the Catalogue's spite!
Old Time is a liar! We're twenty to-night!

We're twenty! We're twenty! Who says we are more?
He's tipsy, — young jackanapes! — show him the
    door!
"Gray temples at twenty?" — Yes! *white*, if we
    please;
Where the snow-flakes fall thickest there's nothing
    can freeze!

Was it snowing I spoke of? Excuse the mistake!
Look close, — you will see not a sign of a flake!
We want some new garlands for those we have shed, —
And these are white roses in place of the red.

We've a trick, we young fellows, you may have been
    told,
Of talking (in public) as if we were old:
That boy we call "Doctor," and this we call
    "Judge;" —
It's a neat little fiction, — of course it's all fudge.

That fellow's the "Speaker," — the one on the right;
"Mr. Mayor," my young one, how are you to-night?
That's our "Member of Congress," we say when we
    chaff;
There's the "Reverend" What's his name? — don't
    make me laugh!

That boy with the grave mathematical look
Made believe he had written a wonderful book,
And the ROYAL SOCIETY thought it was *true!*
So they chose him right in, — a good joke it was too!

There's a boy, we pretend, with a three-decker brain,
That could harness a team with a logical chain;
When he spoke for our manhood in syllabled fire,
We called him " The Justice," but now he's " The
    Squire."

And there's a nice youngster of excellent pith,—
Fate tried to conceal him by naming him Smith,
But he shouted a song for the brave and the free,—
Just read on his medal, " My country," " of thee! "

You hear that boy laughing? — You think he's all
    fun;
But the angels laugh, too, at the good he has done;
The children laugh loud as they troop to his call,
And the poor man that knows him laughs loudest of
    all!

Yes, we're boys,— always playing with tongue or
    with pen;
And I sometimes have asked, Shall we ever be men?
Shall we always be youthful, and laughing, and gay,
Till the last dear companion drop smiling away?

Then here's to our boyhood, its gold and its gray!
The stars of its winter, the dews of its May!
And when we have done with our life-lasting toys,
Dear Father, take care of thy children, THE BOYS.

[169]

"OLD IRONSIDES"

[Written with reference to the proposed breaking up of the famous U. S. frigate "Constitution."]

BY OLIVER WENDELL HOLMES

Ay, tear her tattered ensign down!
　　Long has it waved on high,
And many an eye has danced to see
　　That banner in the sky;
Beneath it rung the battle-shout,
　　And burst the cannon's roar:
The meteor of the ocean air
　　Shall sweep the clouds no more!

Her deck, once red with heroes' blood,
　　Where knelt the vanquished foe,
When winds were hurrying o'er the flood
　　And waves were white below,
No more shall feel the victor's tread,
　　Or know the conquered knee:
The harpies of the shore shall pluck
　　The eagle of the sea!

O better that her shattered hulk
　　Should sink beneath the wave!
Her thunders shook the mighty deep,
　　And there should be her grave:
Nail to the mast her holy flag,
　　Set every threadbare sail,
And give her to the god of storms,
　　The lightning and the gale!

THE HEIGHT OF THE RIDICULOUS

BY OLIVER WENDELL HOLMES

I wrote some lines once on a time
  In wondrous merry mood,
And thought, as usual, men would say
  They were exceeding good.

They were so queer, so very queer,
  I laughed as I would die;
Albeit, in the general way,
  A sober man am I.

I called my servant, and he came;
  How kind it was of him,
To mind a slender man like me,
  He of the mighty limb!

" These to the printer," I exclaimed,
  And, in my humorous way,
I added (as a trifling jest),
  " There'll be the devil to pay."

He took the paper, and I watched,
  And saw him peep within;
At the first line he read, his face
  Was all upon the grin.

He read the next; the grin grew broad,
  And shot from ear to ear;
He read the third; a chuckling noise
  I now began to hear.

The fourth; he broke into a roar;
　The fifth; his waistband split;
The sixth; he burst five buttons off,
　And tumbled in a fit.

Ten days and nights, with sleepless eye,
　I watched that wretched man,
And since, I never dare to write
　As funny as I can.

THE LAST LEAF

BY OLIVER WENDELL HOLMES

I saw him once before,
As he passed by the door;
　And again
The pavement-stones resound
As he totters o'er the ground
　With his cane.

They say that in his prime,
Ere the pruning-knife of time
　Cut him down,
Not a better man was found
By the crier on his round
　Through the town.

But now he walks the streets,
And he looks at all he meets
　So forlorn;

And he shakes his feeble head,
That it seems as if he said,
   "They are gone."

The mossy marbles rest
On the lips that he has pressed
   In their bloom;
And the names he loved to hear
Have been carved for many a year
   On the tomb.

My grandmamma has said —
Poor old lady! she is dead
   Long ago —
That he had a Roman nose,
And his cheek was like a rose
   In the snow.

But now his nose is thin,
And it rests upon his chin
   Like a staff;
And a crook is in his back,
And a melancholy crack
   In his laugh.

I know it is a sin
For me to sit and grin
   At him here,
But the old three-cornered hat,
And the breeches, — and all that,
   Are so queer!

And if I should live to be
The last leaf upon the tree
    In the spring,
Let them smile, as I do now,
At the old forsaken bough
    Where I cling.

THE VOICELESS

BY OLIVER WENDELL HOLMES

We count the broken lyres that rest
    Where the sweet wailing singers slumber,
But o'er their silent sister's breast
    The wild-flowers who will stoop to number?
A few can touch the magic string,
    And noisy Fame is proud to win them: —
Alas for those that never sing,
    But die with all their music in them!

Nay, grieve not for the dead alone
    Whose song has told their hearts' sad story,—
Weep for the voiceless, who have known
    The cross without the crown of glory!
Not where Leucadian breezes sweep
    O'er Sappho's memory-haunted billow,
But where the glistening night-dews weep
    On nameless sorrow's churchyard pillow.

O hearts that break and give no sign
    Save whitening lip and fading tresses,
Till Death pours out his cordial wine
    Slow-dropp'd from Misery's crushing presses,—

[174]

If singing breath or echoing chord
  To every hidden pang were given,
What endless melodies were pour'd,
  As sad as earth, as sweet as heaven!

THE BRIDGE OF SIGHS

BY THOMAS HOOD

"Drowned! Drowned!" — HAMLET.

One more unfortunate,
Weary of breath,
Rashly importunate,
Gone to her death!

Take her up tenderly,
Lift her with care!
Fashioned so slenderly,
Young, and so fair!

Look at her garments
Clinging like cerements,
Whilst the wave constantly
Drips from her clothing;
Take her up instantly,
Loving, not loathing!

Touch her not scornfully!
Think of her mournfully,
Gently and humanly, —
Not of the stains of her;
All that remains of her
Now is pure womanly.

[175]

Make no deep scrutiny
Into her mutiny,
Rash and undutiful;
Past all dishonor,
Death has left on her
Only the beautiful.

Still, for all slips of hers,—
One of Eve's family,—
Wipe those poor lips of hers,
Oozing so clammily.
Loop up her tresses
Escaped from the comb,—
Her fair auburn tresses,—
Whilst wonderment guesses
Where was her home?

Who was her father?
Who was her mother?
Had she a sister?
Had she a brother?
Or was there a dearer one
Still, and a nearer one
Yet, than all other?

Alas! for the rarity
Of Christian charity
Under the sun!
O, it was pitiful!
Near a whole city full,
Home she had none.

Sisterly, brotherly,
Fatherly, motherly
Feelings had changed, —
Love, by harsh evidence,
Thrown from its eminence;
Even God's providence
Seeming estranged.

Where the lamps quiver
So far in the river,
With many a light
From window and casement,
From garret to basement,
She stood, with amazement,
Houseless by night.

The bleak wind of March
Made her tremble and shiver;
But not the dark arch,
Or the black flowing river;
Mad from life's history,
Glad to death's mystery,
Swift to be hurled —
Anywhere, anywhere
Out of the world!

In she plunged boldly,—
No matter how coldly
The rough river ran —
Over the brink of it!
Picture it — think of it,
Dissolute man!

[177]

Lave in it, drink of it,
Then, if you can!

Take her up tenderly,
Lift her with care!
Fashioned so slenderly,
Young, and so fair!

Ere her limbs, frigidly,
Stiffen too rigidly,
Decently, kindly,
Smooth and compose them!
And her eyes, close them,
Staring so blindly!
Dreadfully staring
Through muddy impurity,
As when with the daring
Last look of despairing
Fixed on futurity.

Perishing gloomily,
Spurred by contumely,
Cold inhumanity,
Burning insanity,
Into her rest!
Cross her hands humbly,
As if praying dumbly,
Over her breast!

Owing her weakness,
Her evil behavior,
And leaving, with meekness,
Her sins to her Saviour!

[178]

FAITHLESS NELLY GRAY

A PATHETIC BALLAD

BY THOMAS HOOD

Ben Battle was a soldier bold,
  And used to war's alarms;
But a cannon-ball took off his legs,
  So he laid down his arms.

Now as they bore him off the field,
  Said he, " Let others shoot;
For here I leave my second leg,
  And the Forty-second Foot."

The army-surgeons made him limbs:
  Said he, " They're only pegs;
But there's as wooden members quite,
  As represent my legs."

Now Ben he loved a pretty maid,—
  Her name was Nellie Gray;
So he went to pay her his devours,
  When he devoured his pay.

But when he called on Nelly Gray,
  She made him quite a scoff;
And when she saw his wooden legs,
  Began to take them off.

" O Nelly Gray! O Nelly Gray!
  Is this your love so warm?

The love that loves a scarlet coat
   Should be more uniform."

Said she, " I loved a soldier once,
   For he was blithe and brave;
But I will never have a man
   With both legs in the grave.

" Before you had those timber toes
   Your love I did allow;
But then, you know, you stand upon
   Another footing now."

" O Nelly Gray! O Nelly Gray!
   For all your jeering speeches,
At duty's call I left my legs
   In Badajos's breaches."

" Why, then," said she, " you've lost the feet
   Of legs in war's alarms,
And now you cannot wear your shoes
   Upon your feats of arms! "

" O false and fickle Nelly Gray!
   I know why you refuse:
Though I've no feet, some other man
   Is standing in my shoes.

" I wish I ne'er had seen your face;
   But, now, a long farewell!
For you will be my death; — alas!
   You will not be my Nell! "

Now when he went from Nelly Gray
  His heart so heavy got,
And life was such a burden grown,
  It made him take a knot.

So round his melancholy neck
  A rope he did entwine,
And, for his second time in life,
  Enlisted in the Line.

One end he tied around a beam,
  And then removed his pegs;
And, as his legs were off, — of course
  He soon was off his legs.

And there he hung till he was dead
  As any nail in town;
For, though distress had cut him up,
  It could not cut him down.

A dozen men sat on his corpse,
  To find out why he died,—
And they buried Ben in four cross-roads,
  With a stake in his inside.

I REMEMBER, I REMEMBER

BY THOMAS HOOD

I remember, I remember
  The house where I was born,
The little window where the sun
  Came peeping in at morn.

[181]

He never came a wink too soon,
  Nor brought too long a day;
But now I often wish the night
  Had borne my breath away!

I remember, I remember
  The roses, red and white,
The violets, and the lily-cups, —
  Those flowers made of light!
The lilacs where the robin built,
  And where my brother set
The laburnum on his birthday, —
  The tree is living yet!

I remember, I remember
  Where I was used to swing,
And thought the air must rush as fresh
  To swallows on the wing;
My spirit flew in feathers then,
  That is so heavy now,
And summer pools could hardly cool
  The fever on my brow!

I remember, I remember
  The fir-trees dark and high;
I used to think their slender tops
  Were close against the sky.
It was a childish ignorance,
  But now 't is little joy
To know I'm farther off from heaven
  Than when I was a boy.

THE SONG OF THE SHIRT

BY THOMAS HOOD

With fingers weary and worn,
   With eyelids heavy and red,
A woman sat, in unwomanly rags,
   Plying her needle and thread,—
     Stitch! stitch! stitch!
In poverty, hunger, and dirt;
   And still with a voice of dolorous pitch
She sang the " Song of the Shirt "!

"Work! work! work
   While the cock is crowing aloof!
And work — work — work
   Till the stars shine through the roof.
It's, O, to be a slave
   Along with the barbarous Turk,
Where woman has never a soul to save,
   If this is Christian work!

"Work — work — work
   Till the brain begins to swim!
Work — work — work
   Till the eyes are heavy and dim!
Seam, and gusset, and band,
   Band, and gusset, and seam,—
Till over the buttons I fall asleep,
   And sew them on in a dream!

"O men with sisters dear!
    O men with mothers and wives!
It is not linen you're wearing out,
    But human creatures' lives!
        Stitch — stitch — stitch,
    In poverty, hunger, and dirt,—
Sewing at once, with a double thread,
    A shroud as well as a shirt!

"But why do I talk of death,—
    That phantom of grisly bone?
I hardly fear his terrible shape,
    It seems so like my own,—
It seems so like my own
    Because of the fasts I keep;
O God! that bread should be so dear,
    And flesh and blood so cheap!

"Work — work — work!
    My labor never flags;
And what are its wages? A bed of straw,
    A crust of bread — and rags,
That shattered roof — and this naked floor —
    A table — a broken chair —
And a wall so blank my shadow I thank
    For sometimes falling there!

"Work — work — work
    From weary chime to chime!
Work — work — work
    As prisoners work for crime!

[184]

Band, and gusset, and seam,
  Seam, and gusset, and band, —
Till the heart is sick and the brain benumbed,
  As well as the weary hand.

"Work — work — work
  In the dull December light!
And work — work — work
  When the weather is warm and bright!
While underneath the eaves
  The brooding swallows cling,
As if to show me their sunny backs,
  And twit me with the Spring.

"O, but to breathe the breath
  Of the cowslip and primrose sweet, —
With the sky above my head,
  And the grass beneath my feet!
For only one short hour
  To feel as I used to feel,
Before I knew the woes of want
  And the walk that costs a meal!

"O, but for one short hour, —
  A respite, however brief!
No blessèd leisure for love or hope,
  But only time for grief!
A little weeping would ease my heart;
  But in their briny bed
My tears must stop, for every drop
  Hinders needle and thread!"

[185]

With fingers weary and worn,
    With eyelids heavy and red,
A woman sat, in unwomanly rags,
    Plying her needle and thread, —
        Stitch! stitch! stitch!
        In poverty, hunger, and dirt;
And still with a voice of dolorous pitch —
Would that its tone could reach the rich! —
    She sang this " Song of the Shirt! "

FROM "THE WATER-BABIES"

BY CHARLES KINGSLEY

" When all the world is young, lad, and all the trees
        are green,
    And ev'ry goose a swan, lad, and ev'ry lass a queen;
    Then hey for boot and horse, lad, and ride the world
        away,
    Young blood must have its course, lad, and ev'ry
        dog his day.

" When all the world is old, lad, and all the trees are
        brown,
    And all the sport is stale, lad, and all the wheels
        run down;
    Creep home, and take thy place there, thy early
        friends among,
    God grant you find one face there, you loved when
        all was young."

BATTLE–HYMN OF THE REPUBLIC

BY JULIA WARD HOWE

Mine eyes have seen the glory of the coming of the
    Lord:
He is trampling out the vintage where the grapes of
    wrath are stored;
He hath loosed the fateful lightning of his terrible
    swift sword.
        His truth is marching on.

I have seen him in the watch-fires of a hundred circling
    camps;
They have builded him an altar in the evening dews
    and damps;
I can read his righteous sentence by the dim and flaring
    lamps.
        His day is marching on.

I have read a fiery gospel, writ in burnished rows of
    steel:
"As ye deal with my contemners, so with you my
    grace shall deal;
Let the Hero, born of woman, crush the serpent with
    his heel,
        Since God is marching on."

He has sounded forth the trumpet that shall never
    call retreat;
He is sifting out the hearts of men before his judgment
    seat:

O, be swift, my soul, to answer him! be jubilant my
feet!
Our God is marching on.

In the beauty of the lilies Christ was born across the
sea,
With a glory in his bosom that transfigures you and
me;
As he died to make men holy, let us die to make men
free,
While God is marching on.

ABOU BEN ADHEM

BY LEIGH HUNT

Abou Ben Adhem (may his tribe increase!)
Awoke one night from a deep dream of peace,
And saw within the moonlight in his room,
Making it rich and like a lily in bloom,
An angel writing in a book of gold:
Exceeding peace had made Ben Adhem bold,
And to the presence in the room he said,
" What writest thou? " The vision raised its head,
And, with a look made of all sweet accord,
Answered, " The names of those who love the Lord."
" And is mine one? " said Abou. " Nay, not so,"
Replied the angel. Abou spoke more low,
But cheerly still; and said, " I pray thee, then,
Write me as one that loves his fellow-men."

[188]

The angel wrote, and vanished. The next night
It came again, with a great wakening light,
And showed the names whom love of God had blessed, —
And, lo! Ben Adhem's name led all the rest!

OUR FAME

BY JOHN A. JOYCE

A thousand years of glory
   Shall immortalize our fame —
With a tale in song and story
   To keep green the hallowed name,
Of the victor and the vanquished
   On the land and on the sea,
A band of noble brothers
   Led by gallant Grant and Lee.
And the tears of beaming beauty
   Shall freshen every flower —
In the May-time of our duty,
   Through the sunlit, fleeting hour.
Then we'll strew the rarest roses
   O'er the graves we bless to-day,
And we'll pluck the purest posies
   To enwreath the " Blue " and " Gray."
And down the circling ages,
   From the father to the son,
We'll tell on golden pages
   How the field was lost and won;
And how a band of brothers
   Fought each other hard and true
To bind the Union arches

[189]

O'er the " Gray " and o'er the " Blue,"
And rearing a lasting temple
  So complete in every plan,
To justice, truth, and mercy
  And the liberty of man!

FANCY

BY JOHN KEATS

Ever let the Fancy roam,
Pleasure never is at home:
At a touch sweet Pleasure melteth,
Like to bubbles when rain pelteth;
Then let wingèd Fancy wander
Through the thought still spread beyond her:
Open wide the mind's cage-door,
She'll dart forth, and cloudward soar.

O sweet Fancy! let her loose;
Summer's joys are spoilt by use,
And the enjoying of the Spring
Fades as does its blossoming.
Autumn's red-lipped fruitage too,
Blushing through the mist and dew,
Cloys with tasting.   What do then?
Sit thee by the ingle, when
The sear fagot blazes bright,
Spirit of a winter's night;
When the soundless earth is muffled,
And the cakèd snow is shuffled
From the ploughboy's heavy shoon;

When the Night doth meet the Noon
In a dark conspiracy
To banish Even from her sky.
— Sit thee there, and send abroad
With a mind self-overawed
Fancy, high-commissioned: — send her!
She has vassals to attend her;
She will bring, in spite of frost,
Beauties that the earth hath lost;
She will bring thee, all together,
All delights of summer weather;
All the buds and bells of May
From dewy sward or thorny spray;

All the heapèd Autumn's wealth,
With a still, mysterious stealth;
She will mix these pleasures up
Like three fit wines in a cup,
And thou shalt quaff it; — thou shalt hear
Distant harvest-carols clear;
Rustle of the reapèd corn;
Sweet birds antheming the morn;
And in the same moment — hark!
'T is the early April lark,
Or the rooks, with busy caw,
Foraging for sticks and straw.
Thou shalt, at one glance, behold
The daisy and the marigold;
White-plumed lilies, and the first
Hedge-grown primrose that hath burst;
Shaded hyacinth, alway

[191]

Sapphire queen of the mid-May;
And every leaf, and every flower
Pearlèd with the self-same shower.
Thou shalt see the field-mouse peep
Meagre from its cellèd sleep;
And the snake all winter-thin
Cast on sunny bank its skin;
Freckled nest-eggs thou shalt see
Hatching in the hawthorn tree,
When the hen-bird's wing doth rest
Quiet on her mossy nest;
Then the hurry and alarm
When the bee-hive casts its swarm;
Acorns ripe down-pattering
While the autumn breezes sing.

O sweet Fancy! let her loose;
Everything is spoilt by use:
Where's the cheek that doth not fade,
Too much gazed at?   Where's the maid
Whose lip mature is ever new?
Where's the eye, however blue,
Doth not weary?   Where's the face
One would meet in every place?
Where's the voice, however soft,
One would hear so very oft?
At a touch sweet Pleasure melteth
Like to bubbles when rain pelteth.
Let then wingèd Fancy find
Thee a mistress to thy mind:
Dulcet-eyed as Ceres' daughter,

Ere the god of torment taught her
How to frown and how to chide;
With a waist and with a side
White as Hebe's, when her zone
Slipt its golden clasp, and down
Fell her kirtle to her feet
While she held the goblet sweet,
And Jove grew languid. — Break the mesh
Of the Fancy's silken leash;
Quickly break her prison-string,
And such joys as these she'll bring:
— Let the wingèd Fancy roam,
Pleasure never is at home.

ON DEATH

BY JOHN KEATS

Can death be sleep, when life is but a dream,
And scenes of bliss pass as a phantom by?
The transient pleasures as a vision seem,
And yet we think the greatest pain's to die.

How strange it is that man on earth should roam,
And lead a life of woe, but not forsake
His rugged path; nor dare he view alone
His future doom, which is but to awake.

THE STAR-SPANGLED BANNER
BY FRANCIS SCOTT KEY

O say, can you see by the dawn's early light
What so proudly we hailed at the twilight's last gleam-
    ing? —
Whose broad stripes and bright stars, through the
    perilous fight
O'er the ramparts we watched, were so gallantly
    streaming!
And the rocket's red glare, the bombs bursting in air,
Gave proof through the night that our flag was still
    there;
O say, does that star-spangled banner yet wave
O'er the land of the free and the home of the brave?

On that shore, dimly seen through the mists of the
    deep,
Where the foe's haughty host in dread silence reposes,
What is that which the breeze, o'er the towering steep,
As it fitfully blows, now conceals, now discloses?
Now it catches the gleam of the morning's first beam,
In full glory reflected, now shines on the stream;
'T is the star-spangled banner! O, long may it wave
O'er the land of the free and the home of the brave!

And where is that band who so vauntingly swore
That the havoc of war and the battle's confusion
A home and a country should leave us no more?
Their blood has washed out their foul footsteps'
    pollution.

No refuge could save the hireling and slave
From the terror of flight or the gloom of the grave;
And the star-spangled banner in triumph doth wave
O'er the land of the free and the home of the brave!

O, thus be it ever when freemen shall stand
Between their loved homes and the war's desolation!
Blest with vict'ry and peace, may the Heaven-rescued
land
Praise the Power that hath made and preserved us
a nation.
Then conquer we must, when our cause it is just,
And this be our motto, " In God is our trust";
And the star-spangled banner in triumph shall wave
O'er the land of the free and the home of the brave.

RECESSIONAL

BY RUDYARD KIPLING

God of our fathers, known of old,
Lord of our far-flung battle line —
Beneath whose awful hand we hold
Dominion over palm and pine —
Lord God of Hosts, be with us yet,
Lest we forget — lest we forget!

The tumult and the shouting dies —
The Captains and the Kings depart —
Still stands Thine ancient sacrifice,
An humble and a contrite heart.
Lord God of Hosts, be with us yet,
Lest we forget — lest we forget!

[195]

Far-called our navies melt away —
On dune and headland sinks the fire —
Lo, all our pomp of yesterday
Is one with Nineveh and Tyre!
Judge of the Nations, spare us yet,
Lest we forget — lest we forget!

If, drunk with sight of power, we loose
Wild tongues that have not Thee in awe —
Such boasting as the Gentiles use,
Or lesser breeds without the Law —
Lord God of Hosts, be with us yet,
Lest we forget — lest we forget!

For heathen heart that puts her trust
In reeking tube and iron shard —
All valiant dust that builds on dust,
And guarding calls not Thee to guard.
For frantic boast and foolish word,
Thy mercy on Thy People, Lord!

AMEN.

O, WHY SHOULD THE SPIRIT OF MORTAL BE PROUD?

BY WILLIAM KNOX

The following poem was a particular favorite with Abraham Lincoln. It was first shown to him when a young man by a friend, and afterwards he cut it from a newspaper and learned it by heart. He said to a friend, "I would give a great deal to know who wrote it, but have never been able to ascertain." He did afterwards learn the name of the author.

O, why should the spirit of mortal be proud?
Like a swift-fleeting meteor, a fast-flying cloud,
A flash of the lightning, a break of the wave,
He passeth from life to his rest in the grave.

The leaves of the oak and the willow shall fade,
Be scattered around, and together be laid;
As the young and the old, the low and the high,
Shall crumble to dust and together shall lie.

The infant a mother attended and loved,
The mother that infant's affection who proved,
The father that mother and infant who blest, —
Each, all, are away to that dwelling of rest.

The maid on whose brow, on whose cheek, in whose
    eye,
Shone beauty and pleasure, — her triumphs are by;
And alike from the minds of the living erased
Are the memories of mortals who loved her and praised.

The head of the king, that the sceptre hath borne;
The brow of the priest, that the mitre hath worn;

The eye of the sage, and the heart of the brave,—
Are hidden and lost in the depths of the grave.

The peasant, whose lot was to sow and to reap;
The herdsman, who climbed with his goats up the
    steep;
The beggar, who wandered in search of his bread,—
Have faded away like the grass that we tread.

So the multitude goes, like the flower or weed,
That withers away to let others succeed;
So the multitude comes, even those we behold,
To repeat every tale that has often been told.

For we are the same our fathers have been;
We see the same sights our fathers have seen;
We drink the same stream, we see the same sun,
And run the same course our fathers have run.

The thoughts we are thinking our fathers did think;
From the death we are shrinking our fathers did shrink;
To the life we are clinging our fathers did cling,
But it speeds from us all like the bird on the wing.

They loved,—but the story we cannot unfold;
They scorned,—but the heart of the haughty is cold;
They grieved,—but no wail from their slumbers will
    come;
They joyed,—but the tongue of their gladness is
    dumb.

They died, — ah! they died; — we, things that are
    now,
That walk on the turf that lies over their brow,
And make in their dwelling a transient abode,
Meet the things that they met on their pilgrimage
    road.

Yea, hope and despondency, pleasure and pain,
Are mingled together in sunshine and rain:
And the smile and the tear, and the song and the
    dirge,
Still follow each other like surge upon surge.

'T is the wink of an eye; 't is the draught of a breath
From the blossom of health to the paleness of death,
From the gilded saloon to the bier and the shroud;
O, why should the spirit of mortal be proud?

THE OLD FAMILIAR FACES

BY CHARLES LAMB

I have had playmates, I have had companions,
In my days of childhood, in my joyful schooldays;
All, all are gone, the old familiar faces.

I have been laughing, I have been carousing,
Drinking late, sitting late, with my bosom cronies;
All, all are gone, the old familiar faces.

I loved a Love once, fairest among women:
Closed are her doors on me, I must not see her, —
All, all are gone, the old familiar faces.

[199]

I have a friend, a kinder friend has no man
Like an ingrate, I left my friend abruptly;
Left him, to muse on the old familiar faces.

Ghost-like I paced round the haunts of my childhood,
Earth seemed a desert I was bound to traverse,
Seeking to find the old familiar faces.

Friend of my bosom, thou more than a brother,
Why wert not thou born in my father's dwelling?
So might we talk of the old familiar faces.

How some they have died, and some they have left me,
And some are taken from me; all are departed;
All, all are gone, the old familiar faces.

THE ARROW AND THE SONG

BY HENRY WADSWORTH LONGFELLOW

I shot an arrow into the air,
It fell to earth, I knew not where;
For, so swiftly it flew, the sight
Could not follow it in its flight.

I breathed a song into the air,
It fell to earth, I knew not where;
For who has sight so keen and strong,
That it can follow the flight of song?

Long, long afterward, in an oak
I found the arrow, still unbroke;
And the song, from beginning to end,
I found again in the heart of a friend.

[200]

THE CHILDREN'S HOUR

BY HENRY WADSWORTH LONGFELLOW

Between the dark and the daylight,
  When night is beginning to lower,
Comes a pause in the day's occupations,
  That is known as the children's hour.

I hear in the chamber above me
  The patter of little feet,
The sound of a door that is opened,
  And voices soft and sweet.

From my study I see in the lamplight,
  Descending the broad hall stair,
Grave Alice and laughing Allegra,
  And Edith with golden hair.

A whisper and then a silence,
  Yet I know by their merry eyes
They are plotting and planning together
  To take me by surprise.

A sudden rush from the stairway,
  A sudden raid from the hall,
By three doors left unguarded,
  They enter my castle wall.

They climb up into my turret,
  O'er the arms and back of my chair;
If I try to escape, they surround me:
  They seem to be everywhere.

[201]

They almost devour me with kisses,
   Their arms about me intwine,
Till I think of the Bishop of Bingen
   In his Mouse-Tower on the Rhine.

Do you think, O blue-eyed banditti,
   Because you have scaled the wall,
Such an old mustache as I am
   Is not a match for you all?

I have you fast in my fortress,
   And will not let you depart,
But put you into the dungeon
   In the round-tower of my heart.

And there will I keep you forever,
   Yes, forever and a day,
Till the walls shall crumble to ruin,
   And moulder in dust away.

GOD'S-ACRE

BY HENRY WADSWORTH LONGFELLOW

I like that ancient Saxon phrase which calls
   The burial-ground God's-Acre! It is just;
It consecrates each grave within its walls,
   And breathes a benison o'er the sleeping dust.

God's-Acre! Yes, that blessed name imparts
   Comfort to those who in the grave have sown
The seed that they had garnered in their hearts,
   Their bread of life, alas! no more their own.

[202]

Into its furrows shall we all be cast,
　　In the sure faith that we shall rise again
At the great harvest, when the archangel's blast
　　Shall winnow, like a fan, the chaff and grain.

Then shall the good stand in immortal bloom,
　　In the fair gardens of that second birth;
And each bright blossom mingle its perfume
　　With that of flowers which never bloomed on earth.

With thy rude ploughshare, Death, turn up the sod,
　.　And spread the furrow for the seed we sow;
This is the field and Acre of our God,
　　This is the place where human harvests grow!

A PSALM OF LIFE

BY HENRY WADSWORTH LONGFELLOW

Tell me not, in mournful numbers,
　　Life is but an empty dream!
For the soul is dead that slumbers,
　　And things are not what they seem.

Life is real! Life is earnest!
　　And the grave is not its goal;
Dust thou art, to dust returnest,
　　Was not spoken of the soul.

Not enjoyment, and not sorrow,
　　Is our destined end or way;
But to act, that each to-morrow
　　Find us farther than to-day.

[203]

Art is long, and Time is fleeting,
  And our hearts, though stout and brave,
Still, like muffled drums, are beating
  Funeral marches to the grave.

In the world's broad field of battle,
  In the bivouac of Life,
Be not like dumb, driven cattle!
  Be a hero in the strife!

Trust no Future, howe'er pleasant!
  Let the dead Past bury its dead!
Act, — act in the living Present!
  Heart within, and God o'erhead!

Lives of great men all remind us
  We can make our lives sublime,
And, departing, leave behind us
  Footprints on the sands of time; —

Footprints, that perhaps another,
  Sailing o'er life's solemn main,
A forlorn and shipwrecked brother,
  Seeing, shall take heart again.

Let us, then, be up and doing,
  With a heart for any fate;
Still achieving, still pursuing,
  Learn to labor and to wait.

RESIGNATION

BY HENRY WADSWORTH LONGFELLOW

There is no flock, however watched and tended,
　But one dead lamb is there!
There is no fireside, howsoe'er defended,
　But has one vacant chair!

The air is full of farewells to the dying,
　And mournings for the dead;
The heart of Rachel, for her children crying,
　Will not be comforted!

Let us be patient!　These severe afflictions
　Not from the ground arise,
But oftentimes celestial benedictions
　Assume this dark disguise.

We see but dimly through the mists and vapors;
　Amid these earthly damps
What seem to us but sad, funereal tapers
　May be heaven's distant lamps.

There is no Death!　What seems so is transition:
　This life of mortal breath
Is but a suburb of the life elysian,
　Whose portal we call Death.

She is not dead, — the child of our affection, —
　But gone into that school
Where she no longer needs our poor protection,
　And Christ himself doth rule.

[205]

In that great cloister's stillness and seclusion,
  By guardian angels led,
Safe from temptation, safe from sin's pollution,
  She lives whom we call dead.

Day after day we think what she is doing
  In those bright realms of air;
Year after year, her tender steps pursuing,
  Behold her grown more fair.

Thus do we walk with her, and keep unbroken
  The bond which nature gives,
Thinking that our remembrance, though unspoken,
  May reach her where she lives.

Not as a child shall we again behold her;
  For when with raptures wild
In our embraces we again enfold her,
  She will not be a child:

But a fair maiden, in her Father's mansion,
  Clothed with celestial grace;
And beautiful with all the soul's expansion
  Shall we behold her face.

And though, at times, impetuous with emotion
  And anguish long suppressed,
The swelling heart heaves moaning like the ocean,
  That cannot be at rest, —

We will be patient, and assuage the feeling
  We may not wholly stay;
By silence sanctifying, not concealing,
  The grief that must have way.

[206]

THE VILLAGE BLACKSMITH

BY HENRY WADSWORTH LONGFELLOW

Under a spreading chestnut-tree
  The village smithy stands;
The smith, a mighty man is he,
  With large and sinewy hands;
And the muscles of his brawny arms
  Are strong as iron bands.

His hair is crisp and black and long;
  His face is like the tan;
His brow is wet with honest sweat, —
  He earns whate'er he can,
And looks the whole world in the face,
  For he owes not any man.

Week in, week out, from morn till night,
  You can hear his bellows blow;
You can hear him swing his heavy sledge,
  With measured beat and slow,
Like a sexton ringing the village bell,
  When the evening sun is low.

And children coming home from school,
  Look in at the open door;
They love to see the flaming forge,
  And hear the bellows roar,
And catch the burning sparks that fly
  Like chaff from the threshing-floor.

[207]

He goes on Sunday to the church,
   And sits among his boys;
He hears the parson pray and preach;
   He hears his daughter's voice,
Singing in the village choir,
   And it makes his heart rejoice.

It sounds to him like her mother's voice,
   Singing in Paradise!
He needs must think of her once more,
   How in the grave she lies;
And with his hard, rough hand he wipes
   A tear out of his eyes.

Toiling, rejoicing, sorrowing,
   Onward through life he goes;
Each morning sees some task begun,
   Each evening sees it close;
Something attempted, something done,
   Has earned a night's repose.

Thanks, thanks to thee, my worthy friend,
   For the lesson thou hast taught!
Thus at the flaming forge of Life
   Our fortunes must be wrought,
Thus on its sounding anvil shaped
   Each burning deed and thought.

SUSPIRIA

BY HENRY WADSWORTH LONGFELLOW

Take them, O Death! and bear away
    Whatever thou canst call thine own!
Thine image, stamped upon this clay,
    Doth give thee that, but that alone!

Take them, O Grave! and let them lie
    Folded upon thy narrow shelves,
As garments by the soul laid by,
    And precious only to ourselves!

Take them, O great Eternity!
    Our little life is but a gust
That bends the branches of thy tree,
    And trails its blossoms in the dust!

FREEDOM

BY JAMES RUSSELL LOWELL

Are we, then, wholly fallen?   Can it be
That thou, North wind, that from thy mountains
    bringest
Their spirit to our plains, and thou, blue sea,
Who on our rocks thy wreaths of freedom flingest,
As on an altar, — can it be that ye
Have wasted inspiration on dead ears,
Dulled with the too familiar clank of chains?
The people's heart is like a harp for years
Hung where some petrifying torrent rains

[209]

Its slow-incrusting spray: the stiffened chords
Faint and more faint make answer to the tears
That drip upon them: idle are all words;
Only a silver plectrum wakes the tone
Deep buried 'neath that ever-thickening stone.

We are not free: Freedom doth not consist
In musing with our faces toward the Past,
While petty cares and crawling interests twist
Their spider-threads about us, which at last
Grow strong as iron chains to cramp and bind
In formal narrowness heart, soul, and mind.
Freedom is recreated year by year,
In hearts wide open on the Godward side,
In souls calm-cadenced as the whirling sphere,
In minds that sway thy future like a tide.
No broadest creeds can hold her, and no codes;
She chooses men for her august abodes,
Building them fair and fronting to the dawn;
Yet, when we seek her, we but find a few
Light footprints, leading morn-ward through the dew;
Before the day had risen, she was gone.

And we must follow: swiftly runs she on,
And, if our steps should slacken in despair,
Half turns her face, half smiles through golden hair,
Forever yielding, never wholly won:
That is not love which pauses in the race
Two close-linked names on fleeting sand to trace;
Freedom gained yesterday is no more ours;
Men gather but dry seeds of last year's flowers:

Still there's a charm ungranted, still a grace,
Still rosy Hope, the free, the unattained,
Makes us Possession's languid hand let fall;
'T is but a fragment of ourselves is gained,—
The Future brings us more, but never all.

And, as the finder of some unknown realm,
Mounting a summit whence he thinks to see
On either side of him the imprisoning sea,
Beholds, above the clouds that overwhelm
The valley-land, peak after snowy peak
Stretch out of sight, each like a silver helm
Beneath its plume of smoke, sublime and bleak,
And what he thought an island finds to be
A continent to him first oped, — so we
Can from our height of Freedom look along
A boundless future, ours if we be strong;
Or if we shrink, better remount our ships
And, fleeing God's express design, trace back
The hero-freighted Mayflower's prophet-track
To Europe, entering her blood-red eclipse.

THE HERITAGE

BY JAMES RUSSELL LOWELL

The rich man's son inherits lands,
    And piles of brick, and stone, and gold;
And he inherits soft white hands,
    And tender flesh, that fears the cold,
    Nor dares to wear a garment old;
A heritage, it seems to me,
One scarce would wish to hold in fee.

The rich man's son inherits cares:
   The bank may break, the factory burn,
A breath may burst his bubble shares,
   And soft white hands could hardly earn
   A living that would serve his turn;
A heritage, it seems to me,
One scarce would wish to hold in fee.

The rich man's son inherits wants,
   His stomach craves for dainty fare;
With sated heart he hears the pants
   Of toiling hinds with brown arms bare,
   And wearies in his easy-chair;
A heritage, it seems to me,
One scarce would wish to hold in fee.

What doth the poor man's son inherit?
   Stout muscles and a sinewy heart,
A hardy frame, a hardier spirit;
   King of two hands, he does his part
   In every useful toil and art;
A heritage, it seems to me,
A king might wish to hold in fee.

What doth the poor man's son inherit?
   Wishes o'erjoyed with humble things,
A rank adjudged with toil-won merit,
   Content that from employment springs,
   A heart that in his labor sings;
A heritage, it seems to me,
A king might wish to hold in fee.

What doth the poor man's son inherit?
　A patience learn'd of being poor,
Courage, if sorrow come, to bear it,
　A fellow-feeling that is sure
　To make the outcast bless his door;
A heritage, it seems to me,
A king might wish to hold in fee.

O rich man's son! there is a toil
　That with all others level stands:
Large charity doth never soil,
　But only whiten, soft white hands,—
　This is the best crop from thy lands;
A heritage, it seems to me,
Worth being rich to hold in fee.

O poor man's son! scorn not thy staté;
　There is worse weariness than thine —
In merely being rich and great:
　Toil only gives the soul to shine,
　And makes rest fragrant and benign,—
A heritage, it seems to me,
Worth being poor to hold in fee.

Both, heirs to some six feet of sod,
　Are equal in the earth at last:
Both, children of the same dear God,
　Prove title to your heirship vast
　By record of a well-fill'd past;
A heritage, it seems to me,
Well worth a life to hold in fee.

[213]

A PRAYER

BY JAMES RUSSELL LOWELL

God! do not let my loved one die,
  But rather wait until the time
That I am grown in purity
  Enough to enter thy pure clime;
Then take me, I will gladly go,
So that my love remain below!

O, let her stay! She is by birth
  What I through death must learn to be,
We need her more on our poor earth,
  Than thou canst need in heaven with thee:
She hath her wings already, I
Must burst this earth-shell ere I fly.

Then, God, take me! We shall be near,
  More near than ever, each to each:
Her angel ears will find more clear
  My heavenly than my earthly speech;
And still, as I draw nigh to thee,
Her soul and mine shall closer be.

A REQUIEM

BY JAMES RUSSELL LOWELL

Ay, pale and silent maiden,
  Cold as thou liest there,
Thine was the sunniest nature
  That ever drew the air,

The wildest and most wayward,
　And yet so gently kind,
Thou seemedst but to body
　A breath of summer wind.

Into the eternal shadow
　That girds our life around,
Into the infinite silence
　Wherewith Death's shore is bound,
Thou hast gone forth, beloved!
　And I were mean to weep,
That thou hast left Life's shallows,
　And dost possess the Deep.

Thou liest low and silent,
　Thy heart is cold and still,
Thine eyes are shut forever,
　And Death hath had his will;
He loved and would have taken,
　I loved and would have kept,
We strove, — and he was stronger,
　And I have never wept.

Let him possess thy body,
　Thy soul is still with me,
More sunny and more gladsome
　Than it was wont to be:
Thy body was a fetter
　That bound me to the flesh,
Thank God that it is broken,
　And now I live afresh!

Now I can see thee clearly;
  The dusky cloud of clay,
That hid thy starry spirit,
  Is rent and blown away:
To earth I give thy body,
  Thy spirit to the sky,
I saw its bright wings growing,
  And knew that thou must fly.

Now I can love thee truly,
  For nothing comes between
The senses and the spirit,
  The seen and the unseen;
Lifts the eternal shadow,
  The silence bursts apart,
And the soul's boundless future
  Is present in my heart.

THE PRESENT CRISIS

BY JAMES RUSSELL LOWELL

When a deed is done for Freedom, through the broad
    earth's aching breast
Runs a thrill of joy prophetic, trembling on from east
    to west,
And the slave, where'er he cowers, feels the soul within
    him climb
To the awful verge of manhood, as the energy sublime
Of a century bursts full-blossomed on the thorny stem
    of Time.

[216]

Through the walls of hut and palace shoots the instan-
    taneous throe,
When the travail of the Ages wrings earth's systems to
    and fro;
At the birth of each new Era, with a recognizing start,
Nation wildly looks at nation, standing with mute lips
    apart,
And glad Truth's yet mightier man-child leaps beneath
    the Future's heart.

So the Evil's triumph sendeth, with a terror and a
    chill,
Under continent to continent, the sense of coming
    ill,
And the slave, where'er he cowers, feels his sympathies
    with God,
In hot tear-drops ebbing earthward, to be drunk up by
    the sod,
Till a corpse crawls round unburied, delving in the
    nobler clod.

For mankind are one in spirit, and an instinct bears
    along,
Round the earth's electric circle, the swift flush of
    right or wrong;
Whether conscious or unconscious, yet Humanity's
    vast frame
Through its ocean-sundered fibres feels the gush of
    joy or shame; —
In the gain or loss of one race all the rest have equal
    claim,

[217]

Once to every man and nation comes the moment to
    decide,
In the strife of Truth with Falsehood, for the good or
    evil side;
Some great causes, God's new Messiah, offering each
    the bloom or blight,
Parts the goats upon the left hand, and the sheep upon
    the right,
And the choice goes by forever 'twixt that darkness
    and that light.

Hast thou chosen, O my people, on whose party thou
    shalt stand,
Ere the Doom from its worn sandals shakes the dust
    against our land?
Though the cause of Evil prosper, yet 'tis Truth alone
    is strong,
And, albeit she wander outcast now, I see around her
    throng
Troops of beautiful, tall angels, to enshield her from all
    wrong.

Backward look across the ages and the beacon-moments
    see,
That, like peaks of some sunk continent, jut through
    Oblivion's sea;
Not an ear in court or market for the low foreboding
    cry
Of those Crises, God's stern winnowers, from whose
    feet earth's chaff must fly;
Never shows the choice momentous till the judgment
    hath passed by.

[218]

Careless seems the great Avenger; history's pages but
 record
One death-grapple in the darkness 'twixt old system
 and the Word;
Truth forever on the scaffold, Wrong forever on the
 throne—
Yet that scaffold sways the Future, and, behind the
 dim unknown,
Standeth God within the shadow, keeping watch above
 his own.

We see dimly in the Present what is small and what is
 great,
Slow of faith, how weak an arm may turn the iron helm
 of fate,
But the soul is still oracular; amid the market's din,
List the ominous stern whisper from the Delphic cave
 within,—
"They enslave their children's children who make
 compromise with sin."

Slavery, the earthborn Cyclops, fellest of the giant
 brood,
Sons of brutish Force and Darkness, who have drenched
 the earth with blood,
Famished in his self-made desert, blinded by our
 purer day,
Gropes in yet unblasted regions for his miserable
 prey;—
Shall we guide his gory fingers where our helpless children play?

Then to side with Truth is noble when we share her
    wretched crust,
Ere her cause bring fame and profit, and 't is prosper-
    ous to be just;
Then it is the brave man chooses, while the coward
    stands aside,
Doubting in his abject spirit, till his Lord is crucified,
And the multitude make virtue of the faith they had
    denied.

Count me o'er earth's chosen heroes, — they were
    souls that stood alone,
While the men they agonized for hurled the contume-
    lious stone,
Stood serene, and down the future saw the golden
    beam incline
To the side of perfect justice, mastered by their faith
    divine,
By one man's plain truth to manhood and to God's
    supreme design.

By the light of burning heretics Christ's bleeding feet
    I track,
Toiling up new Calvaries ever with the cross that turns
    not back,
And these mounts of anguish number how each genera-
    tion learned
One new word of that grand *Credo* which in prophet-
    hearts hath burned
Since the first man stood God-conquered with his face
    to heaven upturned.

For Humanity sweeps onward: where to-day the
    martyr stands,
On the morrow crouches Judas with the silver in his
    hands;
Far in front the cross stands ready and the crackling
    fagots burn,
While the hooting mob of yesterday in silent awe
    return
To glean up the scattered ashes into History's golden
    urn.

'T is as easy to be heroes as to sit the idle slaves
Of a legendary virtue carved upon our fathers'
    graves,
Worshippers of light ancestral make the present light
    a crime; —
Was the Mayflower launched by cowards, steered by
    men behind their time?
Turn those tracks toward Past or Future, that make
    Plymouth rock sublime?

They were men of present valor, stalwart old icono-
    clasts,
Unconvinced by axe or gibbet that all virtue was the
    Past's;
But we make their truth our falsehood, thinking that
    hath made us free,
Hoarding it in mouldy parchments, while our tender
    spirits flee
The rude grasp of that great Impulse which drove
    them across the sea.

[221]

They have rights who dare maintain them; we are
    traitors to our sires,
Smothering in their holy ashes Freedom's new-lit
    altar-fires;
Shall we make their creed our jailer? Shall we, in
    our haste to slay,
From the tombs of the old prophets steal the funeral
    lamps away
To light up the martyr-fagots round the prophets of
    to-day?

New occasions teach new duties; Time makes ancient
    good uncouth;
They must upward still, and onward, who would keep
    abreast of Truth;
Lo, before us gleam her camp-fires! we ourselves must
    Pilgrims be,
Launch our Mayflower, and steer boldly through the
    desperate winter sea,
Nor attempt the Future's portal with the Past's blood-
    rusted key.

TOO LATE

BY FITZ HUGH LUDLOW

There sat an old man on a rock,
   And unceasing bewailed him of Fate —
That concern where we all must take stock,
   Though our vote has no bearing or weight;
     And the old man sang him an old, old song,
     Never sang voice so clear and strong
     That could drown the old man's song,
      For he sang the song, "Too late! too late."

[222]

When we want, we have for our pains
  The promise that if we but wait
Till the want has burned out of our brains,
    Every means shall be present to sate;
      While we send for the napkin the soup grows cold,
      While the bonnet is trimming the face grows old,
      When we've matched our buttons the pattern is
        sold,
        And everything comes too late — too late.

When strawberries seemed like red heavens,
  Terrapin stew a wild dream,
When my brain was at sixes and sevens,
  If my mother had "folks" and ice cream,
    Then I gazed with a lickerish hunger
    At the restaurant man and fruit monger,
    But, O, how I wished I were younger
      When the goodies all came in a stream — in a
        stream.

I've a splendid blood-horse, and a liver
  That it jars into torture to trot;
My row-boat's the gem of the river —
  Gout made every knuckle a knot!
    I can buy boundless credits in Paris and Rome,
    But no palate for menus, no eyes for a dome —
    Those belong to the youth who must tarry at home,
      When no home but an attic he'd got — he'd got.

How I longed, in that lonest of garrets,
  Where the tiles baked my brain all July,

[223]

For the ground to grow two pecks of carrots,
　　Two pigs of my own in a sty,
　　　A rosebush — a little thatched cottage —
　　　Two spoons — love — a basin of pottage!
　　　Now in freestone I sit — and my dotage —
　　　　With a woman's chair empty close by — close
　　　　　by!

Ah! now, though I sit on a rock,
　　I have shared one seat with the great;
I have sat — knowing naught of the clock —
　　On Love's high throne of state;
　　　But the lips that kissed and the arms that caressed,
　　　To a mouth grown stern with delay were pressed,
　　　And circled a breast that their clasp had blessed
　　　　Had they only not come too late — too late.

ANTONY AND CLEOPATRA
BY WILLIAM HAINES LYTLE

I am dying, Egypt, dying,
　　Ebbs the crimson life-tide fast,
And the dark Plutonian shadows
　　Gather on the evening blast;
Let thine arms, O Queen, enfold me,
　　Hush thy sobs and bow thine ear;
Listen to the great heart-secrets,
　　Thou, and thou alone, must hear.

Though my scarr'd and veteran legions
　　Bear their eagles high no more,
And my wreck'd and scatter'd galleys

[224]

Strew dark Actium's fatal shore,
Though no glittering guards surround me,
  Prompt to do their master's will,
I must perish like a Roman,
  Die the great Triumvir still.

Let not Cæsar's servile minions
  Mock the lion thus laid low;
'Twas no foeman's arm that fell'd him,
  'Twas his own that struck the blow;
His who, pillow'd on thy bosom,
  Turn'd aside from glory's ray,
His who, drunk with thy caresses,
  Madly threw a world away.

Should the base plebeian rabble
  Dare assail my name at Rome,
Where my noble spouse, Octavia,
  Weeps within her widow'd home,
Seek her; say the gods bear witness —
  Altars, augurs, circling wings —
That her blood, with mine commingled,
  Yet shall mount the throne of kings.

As for thee, star-eyed Egyptian,
  Glorious sorceress of the Nile,
Light the path to Stygian horrors
  With the splendors of thy smile.
Give the Cæsar crowns and arches,
  Let his brow the laurel twine;
I can scorn the Senate's triumphs,
  Triumphing in love like thine.

[225]

I am dying, Egypt, dying;
   Hark! the insulting foeman's cry.
They are coming! quick, my falchion,
   Let me front them ere I die.
Ah! no more amid the battle
   Shall my heart exulting swell;
Isis and Osiris guard thee!
   Cleopatra, Rome, farewell!

THE WATER MILL

BY DANIEL CRAIG MCCALLUM

In a copy of this poem presented to the editor, the author inserted the word "again" in the last line of each verse, and in the third verse substituted "thy kindness sow broadcast" for "true love alone will last."

Oh! listen to the Water-Mill, through all the livelong
   day,
As the clicking of the wheel wears hour by hour
   away;
How languidly the Autumn wind doth stir the withered
   leaves,
As on the field the reapers sing, while binding up the
   sheaves.
A solemn proverb strikes my mind, and as a spell is
   cast,
" The mill will never grind again with water that is
   past."

Soft summer winds revive no more, leaves strewn o'er
   earth and main,

[226]

The sickle nevermore will reap the yellow-garnered
    grain;
The rippling stream flows ever on, aye tranquil, deep
    and still,
But never glideth back again, to busy Water-Mill.
The solemn proverb speaks to all, with meaning deep
    and vast.
" The mill will never grind again with water that is
    past."

Oh! clasp the proverb to thy soul, dear loving heart
    and true,
For golden years are fleeting by, and youth is passing
    too.
Ah! learn to make the most of life, nor lose one happy
    day,
For time will ne'er return sweet joys, neglected, thrown
    away,
Nor leave one tender word unsaid, thy kindness sow
    broadcast,
" The mill will never grind again with water that is
    past."

Oh! the wasted hours of life, that have swiftly drifted
    by;
Alas! the good we might have done, all gone without
    a sigh;
Love that we might once have saved, by a single kindly
    word,
Thoughts conceived but ne'er expressed, perishing
    unpenned, unheard.

[227]

Oh! take the lesson to thy soul, forever clasp it fast,
" The mill will never grind again with water that is
    past."

Work on while yet the sun doth shine, thou man of
    strength and will,
The streamlet ne'er doth useless glide by clicking
    water-mill;
Nor wait until to-morrow's light, beams brightly on
    thy way,
For all that thou can'st call thine own, lies in the
    phrase to-day.
Possessions, power, and blooming health must all be
    lost at last,
" The mill will never grind again with water that is
    past."

Oh! love thy God and fellow men, thyself consider last,
For come it will when thou must scan dark errors of
    the past.
Soon will this fight of life be o'er, and earth recede
    from view,
And Heaven in all its glory shine, where all is pure and
    true.
Ah! then thou'lt see more clearly still, the proverb
    deep and vast,
" The mill will never grind again with water that is
    past."

WHOM GOD HATH JOINED
BY T. G. MC CLAUGHRY

We have sipped the cup of sorrow,
    Thou and I;
We have waited a to-morrow,
    Thou and I;
We have watched beside a bed,
Bending o'er a little head,
Crushed beneath a weight of dread,
    Thou and I.

We have owned our helplessness,
    Thou and I;
We have sought God in distress,
    Thou and I;
We have shed a common tear
When no other help was near,
Prayed together in our fear,
    Thou and I.

Shall we break the ties that bind us,
    Thou and I?
Shall we put those days behind us,
    Thou and I?
God has wed with grief and pain,
Shall we prove that union vain,
Shall we go our ways again,
    Thou and I?

OPPORTUNITY

BY WALTER MALONE

They do me wrong who say I come no more
When once I knock and fail to find you in;
For every day I stand outside your door,
And bid you wake and rise to fight and win.
Wail not for precious chances passed away,
Weep not for golden ages on the wane;
Each night I burn the records of the day,
At sunrise every soul is born again.
Laugh like a boy at splendors that have sped,
To vanished joys be blind and deaf and dumb;
My judgments seal the dead past with its dead,
But never bind a moment yet to come.
Though deep in mire, wring not your hands and weep,
I lend my arm to all who say: "I can;"
No shamefaced outcast ever sank so deep
But he might rise and be again a man.

LINCOLN, THE MAN OF THE PEOPLE

BY EDWIN MARKHAM

When the Norn Mother saw the Whirlwind Hour
Greatening and darkening as it hurried on,
She left the Heaven of Heroes and came down
To make a man to meet the mortal need.
She took the tried clay of the common road —
Clay warm yet with the ancient heat of Earth,
Dashed through it all a strain of prophecy;

Tempered the heap with thrill of human tears;
Then mixed a laughter with the serious stuff.
Into the shape she breathed a flame to light
That tender, tragic, ever-changing face.
Here was a man to hold against the world,
A man to match the mountains and the sea.

The color of the ground was in him, the red earth;
The smack and tang of elemental things:
The rectitude and patience of the cliff;
The good-will of the rain that loves all leaves;
The friendly welcome of the wayside well;
The courage of the bird that dares the sea;
The gladness of the wind that shakes the corn;
The mercy of the snow that hides all scars;
The secrecy of streams that make their way
Beneath the mountain to the rifted rock;
The undelaying justice of the light
That gives as freely to the shrinking flower
As to the great oak flaring to the wind —
To the grave's low hill as to the Matterhorn
That shoulders out the sky.

                    Sprung from the West,
The strength of virgin forests braced his mind,
The hush of spacious prairies stilled his soul.
Up from log cabin to the Capitol,
One fire was on his spirit, one resolve —
To send the keen axe to the root of wrong,
Clearing a free way for the feet of God.
And evermore he burned to do his deed

With the fine stroke and gesture of a king:
He built the rail-pile as he built the State,
Pouring his splendid strength through every blow,
The conscience of him testing every stroke,
To make his deed the measure of a man.

So came the Captain with the thinking heart;
And when the judgment thunders split the house,
Wrenching the rafters from their ancient rest,
He held the ridgepole up, and spiked again
The rafters of the Home.   He held his place —
Held the long purpose like a growing tree —
Held on through blame and faltered not at praise.
And when he fell in whirlwind, he went down
As when a lordly cedar, green with boughs,
Goes down with a great shout upon the hills,
And leaves a lonesome place against the sky.

O, LAY THY HAND IN MINE, DEAR

BY GERALD MASSEY

O, lay thy hand in mine, dear!
    We're growing old;
But Time hath brought no sign, dear,
    That hearts grow cold.
'T is long, long since our new love
    Made life divine;
But age enricheth true love,
    Like noble wine.

And lay thy cheek to mine, dear,
  And take thy rest;
Mine arms around thee twine, dear,
  And make thy nest.
A many cares are pressing
  On this dear head;
But Sorrow's hands in blessing
  Are surely laid.

O, lean thy life on mine, dear!
  'T will shelter thee.
Thou wert a winsome vine, dear,
  On my young tree:
And so, till boughs are leafless,
  And songbirds flown,
We'll twine, then lay us, griefless,
  Together down.

ON HIS BLINDNESS

BY JOHN MILTON

When I consider how my light is spent
  Ere half my days, in this dark world and wide,
  And that one talent, which is death to hide,
  Lodged with me useless, though my soul more bent
To serve therewith my Maker, and present
  My true account, lest he returning chide;
  " Doth God exact day-labor, light denied? "
  I fondly ask. But Patience, to prevent
That murmur, soon replies, " God doth not need
  Either man's work or his own gifts; who best

[233]

Bear his mild yoke, they serve him best: his state
Is kingly; thousands at his bidding speed,
    And post o'er land and ocean without rest;
    They also serve who only stand and wait."

A VISIT FROM ST. NICHOLAS

BY CLEMENT C. MOORE

'T was the night before Christmas, when all through
    the house
Not a creature was stirring, not even a mouse;
The stockings were hung by the chimney with care,
In hopes that St. Nicholas soon would be there;
The children were nestled all snug in their beds,
While visions of sugar-plums danced in their heads;
And mamma in her kerchief, and I in my cap,
Had just settled our brains for a long winter's nap, —
When out on the lawn there arose such a clatter,
I sprang from my bed to see what was the matter.
Away to the window I flew like a flash,
Tore open the shutters and threw up the sash.
The moon on the breast of the new-fallen snow
Gave a lustre of midday to objects below;
When what to my wondering eyes should appear,
But a miniature sleigh and eight tiny reindeer,
With a little old driver, so lively and quick
I knew in a moment it must be St. Nick.
More rapid than eagles his coursers they came,
And he whistled and shouted, and called them by name:
" Now, Dasher! now, Dancer! now, Prancer and
    Vixen!

[234]

On, Comet! on, Cupid! on, Donder and Blitzen!
To the top of the porch, to the top of the wall!
Now dash away, dash away, dash away all! "
As dry leaves that before the wild hurricane fly,
When they meet with an obstacle, mount to the sky,
So up to the house-top the coursers they flew,
With the sleigh full of toys, — and St. Nicholas too.
And then in a twinkling I heard on the roof
The prancing and pawing of each little hoof.
As I drew in my head, and was turning around,
Down the chimney St. Nicholas came with a bound.
He was dressed all in fur from his head to his foot,
And his clothes were all tarnished with ashes and soot;
A bundle of toys he had flung on his back,
And he looked like a pedler just opening his pack.
His eyes how they twinkled! his dimples how merry!
His cheeks were like roses, his nose like a cherry;
His droll little mouth was drawn up like a bow,
And the beard on his chin was as white as the snow.
The stump of a pipe he held tight in his teeth,
And the smoke it encircled his head like a wreath.
He had a broad face and a little round belly
That shook, when he laughed, like a bowl full of jelly.
He was chubby and plump, — a right jolly old elf;
And I laughed, when I saw him, in spite of myself.
A wink of his eye and a twist of his head
Soon gave me to know I had nothing to dread.
He spoke not a word, but went straight to his work,
And filled all the stockings; then turned with a jerk,
And laying his finger aside of his nose,
And giving a nod, up the chimney he rose.

[235]

He sprang to his sleigh, to his team gave a whistle,
And away they all flew like the down of a thistle;
But I heard him exclaim, ere he drove out of sight,
"Happy Christmas to all, and to all a good-night!"

COME, REST IN THIS BOSOM
BY THOMAS MOORE

Come, rest in this bosom, my own stricken deer,
Though the herd have fled from thee, thy home is still
    here;
Here still is the smile, that no cloud can o'ercast,
And a heart and a hand all thy own to the last.

Oh! what was love made for, if 't is not the same
Through joy and through torment, through glory and
    shame?
I know not, I ask not, if guilt's in that heart,
I but know that I love thee, whatever thou art.

Thou hast called me thy Angel in moments of bliss,
And thy Angel I'll be, mid the horrors of this,
Through the furnace, unshrinking, thy steps to pur-
    sue,
And shield thee, and save thee, — or perish there too!

FAREWELL! BUT WHENEVER
BY THOMAS MOORE

Farewell! — but whenever you welcome the hour
That awakens the night-song of mirth in your bower,
Then think of the friend who once welcomed it too,
And forgot his own griefs, to be happy with you.

[236]

His griefs may return — not a hope may remain
Of the few that have brightened his pathway of pain —
But he ne'er can forget the short vision that threw
Its enchantment around him while lingering with you!

And still on that evening when Pleasure fills up
To the highest top sparkle each heart and each cup,
Where'er my path lies, be it gloomy or bright,
My soul, happy friends! will be with you that night;
Shall join in your revels, your sports, and your wiles,
And return to me, beaming all o'er with your smiles —
Too blest if it tell me that, mid the gay cheer,
Some kind voice has murmured, " I wish he were here! "

Let Fate do her worst, there are relics of joy,
Bright dreams of the past, which she cannot destroy;
Which come, in the night-time of sorrow and care,
And bring back the features which joy used to wear.
Long, long be my heart with such memories filled!
Like the vase in which roses have once been distilled —
You may break, you may shatter the vase, if you will,
But the scent of the roses will hang round it still.

GO WHERE GLORY WAITS THEE

BY THOMAS MOORE

Go where glory waits thee,
But, while fame elates thee,
   O, still remember me!
When the praise thou meetest
To thine ear is sweetest,

O, then remember me!
Other arms may press thee,
Dearer friends caress thee,
All the joys that bless thee,
   Sweeter far may be;
But when friends are nearest,
And when joys are dearest,
   O, then remember me!

When at eve thou rovest
By the star thou lovest,
   O, then remember me!
Think, when home returning,
Bright we've seen it burning,
   O, thus remember me!
Oft as summer closes,
On its lingering roses,
   Once so loved by thee,
Think of her who wove them,
Her who made thee love them,
   O, then remember me!

When, around thee dying,
Autumn leaves are lying,
   O, then remember me!
And, at night, when gazing
On the gay hearth blazing,
   O, still remember me!
Then should music, stealing
All the soul of feeling,
To thy heart appealing,

[238]

Draw one tear from thee;
Then let memory bring thee
Strains I used to sing thee, —
    O, then remember me!

OFT IN THE STILLY NIGHT

BY THOMAS MOORE

Oft in the stilly night,
    Ere slumber's chain has bound me,
Fond Memory brings the light
    Of other days around me:
        The smiles, the tears,
        Of boyhood's years,
    The words of love then spoken;
        The eyes that shone,
        Now dimmed and gone,
    The cheerful hearts now broken.
Thus in the stilly night,
    Ere slumber's chain has bound me,
Sad Memory brings the light
    Of other days around me.

When I remember all
    The friends so linked together
I've seen around me fall,
    Like leaves in wintry weather,
        I feel like one
        Who treads alone
    Some banquet-hall deserted,
        Whose lights are fled,

[239]

Whose garlands dead,
And all but he departed.
Thus in the stilly night,
Ere slumber's chain has bound me,
Sad Memory brings the light
Of other days around me.

THOSE EVENING BELLS

BY THOMAS MOORE

Those evening bells! those evening bells!
How many a tale their music tells
Of youth, and home, and that sweet time
When last I heard their soothing chime!

Those joyous hours are passed away;
And many a heart that then was gay
Within the tomb now darkly dwells,
And hears no more those evening bells.

And so 't will be when I am gone, —
That tuneful peal will still ring on;
While other bards shall walk these dells,
And sing your praise, sweet evening bells.

MY MOTHER'S BIBLE

BY GEORGE P. MORRIS

This book is all that's left me now!
Tears will unbidden start, —
With faltering lip and throbbing brow
I press it to my heart.

[240]

For many generations past,
 Here is our family tree:
My mother's hand this Bible clasped;
 She, dying, gave it me.

Ah! well do I remember those
 Whose names these records bear,
Who round the hearthstone used to close
 After the evening prayer,
And speak of what these pages said,
 In tones my heart would thrill!
Though they are with the silent dead,
 Here are they living still!

My father read this holy book
 To brothers, sisters, dear;
How calm was my poor mother's look,
 Who leaned God's word to hear.
Her angel-face — I see it yet!
 What thronging memories come!
Again that little group is met
 Within the halls of home!

Thou truest friend man ever knew,
 Thy constancy I've tried;
Where all were false I found thee true,
 My counsellor and guide.
The mines of earth no treasure give
 That could this volume buy:
In teaching me the way to live,
 It taught me how to die.

WOODMAN, SPARE THAT TREE

BY GEORGE P. MORRIS

"One day I was driving in the vicinity of New York with George Morris, the American poet," says Henry Russell, the English musical composer. "We turned into Bloomfield Road, then a woodland lane of great natural beauty, to view a stately old tree which had been planted by the poet's grandfather. As we neared the homely cottage that had once housed the Morris family, we saw an old man, evidently the occupant of the cottage, sharpening an axe. 'What are you going to do?' asked the poet, with a tremor of apprehension; 'you surely do not intend to cut down that tree?' 'Yes, sirree,' was the blunt reply of the old man; 'I need it for firewood!' Morris paid him ten dollars to buy firewood, and the daughter of the woodman pledged her word that the tree should stand as long as she lived. On my suggestion Morris wrote the now well-known poem, 'Oh, Woodman, Spare that Tree,' which I immediately set to music."

Woodman, spare that tree!
    Touch not a single bough!
In youth it sheltered me,
    And I'll protect it now.
'T was my forefather's hand
    That placed it near his cot;
There, woodman, let it stand,
    Thy axe shall harm it not!

That old familiar tree,
    Whose glory and renown
Are spread o'er land and sea,
    And wouldst thou hew it down?
Woodman, forbear thy stroke!
    Cut not its earth-bound ties;
O, spare that aged oak,
    Now towering to the skies!

[242]

When but an idle boy
   I sought its grateful shade;
In all their gushing joy
   Here too my sisters played.
My mother kissed me here;
   My father pressed my hand —
Forgive this foolish tear,
   But let that old oak stand!

My heart-strings round thee cling,
   Close as thy bark, old friend!
Here shall the wild-bird sing,
   And still thy branches bend.
Old tree! the storm still brave!
   And, woodman, leave the spot;
While I've a hand to save,
   Thy axe shall hurt it not.

NEAR THE LAKE

BY GEORGE P. MORRIS

Near the lake where drooped the willow,
   Long time ago! —
Where the rock threw back the billow,
   Brighter than snow —
Dwelt a maid, beloved and cherished
   By high and low;
But with autumn's leaf she perished,
   Long time ago!

[243]

Rock and tree and flowing water,
    Long time ago! —
Bee and bird and blossom taught her
    Love's spell to know!
While to my fond words she listened,
    Murmuring low,
Tenderly her dove-eyes glistened,
    Long time ago!

Mingled were our hearts for ever,
    Long time ago!
Can I now forget her? — Never!
    No — lost one — no!
To her grave these tears are given,
    Ever to flow:
She's the star I missed from heaven,
    Long time ago!

THE LAND O' THE LEAL

BY CAROLINA, BARONESS NAIRNE

I'm wearing awa', Jean,
Like snaw when it's thaw, Jean;
I'm wearing awa'
  To the land o' the leal.
There's nae sorrow there, Jean,
There's neither cauld nor care, Jean,
The day is aye fair
  In the land o' the leal.

[244]

Ye were aye leal and true, Jean;
Your task's ended noo, Jean,
And I'll welcome you
   To the land o' the leal.
Our bonnie bairn's there, Jean,
She was baith guid and fair, Jean:
O, we grudged her right sair
   To the land o' the leal!

Then dry that tearfu' e'e, Jean,
My soul langs to be free, Jean,
And angels wait on me
   To the land o' the leal!
Now fare ye weel, my ain Jean,
This warld's care is vain, Jean;
We'll meet and aye be fain
   In the land o' the leal.

BINGEN ON THE RHINE

BY MRS. CAROLINE E. S. NORTON

A soldier of the Legion lay dying in Algiers,
There was lack of woman's nursing, there was dearth
   of woman's tears;
But a comrade stood beside him, while his lifeblood
   ebbed away,
And bent, with pitying glances, to hear what he might
   say.
The dying soldier faltered, and he took that comrade's
   hand,

And he said, " I nevermore shall see my own, my
    native land;
Take a message and a token to some distant friends
    of mine,
For I was born at Bingen, — at Bingen on the Rhine.

" Tell my brothers and companions, when they meet
    and crowd around,
To hear my mournful story, in the pleasant vineyard
    ground,
That we fought the battle bravely, and when the day
    was done,
Full many a corse lay ghastly pale beneath the setting
    sun;
And, mid the dead and dying, were some grown old
    in wars, —
The death-wound on their gallant breasts, the last
    of many scars;
And some were young, and suddenly beheld life's
    morn decline, —
And one had come from Bingen, — fair Bingen on
    the Rhine.

" Tell my mother that her other son shall comfort
    her old age;
For I was still a truant bird, that thought his home a
    cage.
For my father was a soldier, and even as a child
My heart leaped forth to hear him tell of struggles
    fierce and wild;
And when he died, and left us to divide his scanty
    hoard,

[246]

I let them take whate'er they would, — but kept my
    father's sword;
And with boyish love I hung it where the bright light
    used to shine,
On the cottage wall at Bingen, — calm Bingen on the
    Rhine.

" Tell my sister not to weep for me, and sob with
    drooping head,
When the troops come marching home again with
    glad and gallant tread,
But to look upon them proudly, with a calm and stead-
    fast eye,
For her brother was a soldier too, and not afraid to
    die;
And if a comrade seek her love, I ask her in my name
To listen to him kindly, without regret or shame,
And to hang the old sword in its place (my father's
    sword and mine)
For the honor of old Bingen, — dear Bingen on the
    Rhine.

" There's another, — not a sister; in the happy days
    gone by
You'd have known her by the merriment that sparkled
    in her eye;
Too innocent for coquetry, — too fond for idle scorn-
    ing, —
O friend! I fear the lightest heart makes sometimes
    heaviest mourning!
Tell her the last night of my life (for, ere the moon
    be risen,

[247]

My body will be out of pain, my soul be out of prison),—
I dreamed I stood with *her*, and saw the yellow sun-
  light shine
On the vine-clad hills of Bingen, — fair Bingen on the
  Rhine.

" I saw the blue Rhine sweep along, — I heard, or
  seemed to hear,
The German songs we used to sing in chorus sweet
  and clear;
And down the pleasant river, and up the slanting
  hill,
The echoing chorus sounded, through the evening
  calm and still;
And her glad blue eyes were on me, as we passed, with
  friendly talk,
Down many a path beloved of yore, and well-remem-
  bered walk!
And her little hand lay lightly, confidingly in mine, —
But we'll meet no more at Bingen, — loved Bingen
  on the Rhine."

His trembling voice grew faint and hoarse, — his
  grasp was childish weak, —
His eyes put on a dying look, — he sighed and ceased
  to speak;
His comrade bent to lift him, but the spark of life
  had fled, —
The soldier of the Legion in a foreign land is dead!
And the soft moon rose up slowly, and calmly she
  looked down

[248]

On the red sand of the battle-field, with bloody corses
    strewn;
Yes, calmly on that dreadful scene her pale light
    seemed to shine,
As it shone on distant Bingen, — fair Bingen on the
    Rhine.

THE BIVOUAC OF THE DEAD

BY THEODORE O'HARA

The muffled drum's sad roll has beat
    The soldier's last tattoo;
No more on life's parade shall meet
    That brave and fallen few.
On Fame's eternal camping-ground
    Their silent tents are spread,
And glory guards with solemn sound
    The bivouac of the dead.
No rumor of the foe's advance
    Now swells upon the wind,
No troubled thought at midnight haunts
    Of loved ones left behind;
No vision of the morrow's strife
    The warrior's dream alarms,
No braying horn or screaming fife
    At dawn shall call to arms.
Their shivered swords are red with rust,
    Their plumed heads are bowed,
Their haughty banner trailed in dust
    Is now their martial shroud —
And plenteous funeral tears have washed

The red stains from each brow,
And the proud forms by battle gashed
  Are free from anguish now.
The neighing troop, the flashing blade,
  The bugle's stirring blast,
The charge, the dreadful cannonade,
  The din and shout are passed —
Nor war's wild note, nor glory's peal,
  Shall thrill with fierce delight
Those breasts that never more may feel
  The rapture of the fight.
Like the fierce northern hurricane
  That sweeps his great plateau,
Flushed with the triumph yet to gain
  Came down the serried foe —
Who heard the thunder of the fray
  Break o'er the field beneath,
Knew well the watchword of that day
  Was victory or death.
Full many a mother's breath hath swept
  O'er Angostura's plain,
And long the pitying sky has wept
  Above its moulder'd slain.
The raven's scream or eagle's flight,
  Or shepherd's pensive lay,
Alone now wake each solemn height
  That frowned o'er that dread fray.
Sons of the Dark and Bloody Ground,
  Ye must not slumber there,
Where stranger steps and tongues resound
  Along the heedless air!

Your own proud land's heroic soil
 Shall be your fitter grave;
She claims from war its richest spoil —
 The ashes of her brave.
Thus 'neath their parent turf they rest,
 Far from the gory field,
Borne to a Spartan mother's breast
 On many a bloody shield.
The sunshine of their native sky
 Shines sadly on them here,
And kindred eyes and hearts watch by
 The heroes' sepulchre.
Rest on, embalmed and sainted dead!
 Dead as the blood ye gave;
No impious footsteps here shall tread
 The herbage of your grave!
Nor shall your glory be forgot
 While Fame her record keeps,
Or Honor points the hallowed spot
 Where Valor proudly sleeps.
Yon marble minstrel's voiceless stone
 In deathless song shall tell,
When many a vanished year hath flown,
 The story how ye fell;
Nor wreck, nor change, nor winter's blight,
 Nor time's remorseless doom,
Can dim one ray of holy light
 That gilds your glorious tomb.

HOME, SWEET HOME

FROM THE OPERA OF "CLARI, THE MAID OF MILAN."

BY JOHN HOWARD PAYNE

Mid pleasures and palaces though we may roam,
Be it ever so humble there's no place like home!
A charm from the sky seems to hallow us there,
Which, seek through the world, is ne'er met with else-
      where.
    Home! home! sweet, sweet home!
    There's no place like home!

An exile from home, splendor dazzles in vain:
O, give me my lowly thatched cottage again!
The birds singing gayly that came at my call; —
Give me them, — and the peace of mind dearer than
      all!
    Home! home! sweet, sweet home!
    There's no place like home!

WARREN'S ADDRESS

BY JOHN PIERPONT

Stand! the ground's your own, my braves!
Will ye give it up to slaves?
Will ye look for greener graves?
    Hope ye mercy still?
What's the mercy despots feel?
Hear it in that battle-peal!
Read it on yon bristling steel!
    Ask it, — ye who will.

[252]

Fear ye foes who kill for hire?
Will ye to your *homes* retire?
Look behind you! — they're afire!
    And, before you, see
Who have done it! From the vale
On they come! — and will ye quail?
Leaden rain and iron hail
    Let their welcome be!

In the God of battles trust!
Die we may, — and die we must:
But, O, where can dust to dust
    Be consigned so well,
As where heaven its dews shall shed
On the martyred patriot's bed,
And the rocks shall raise their head,
    Of his deeds to tell?

THE BELLS

BY EDGAR ALLAN POE

Hear the sledges with the bells —
    Silver bells!
What a world of merriment their melody foretells!
    How they tinkle, tinkle, tinkle,
      In the icy air of night!
    While the stars that oversprinkle
    All the heavens seem to twinkle
      With a crystalline delight, —
    Keeping time, time, time,
    In a sort of Runic rhyme,

[253]

To the tintinnabulation that so musically wells
From the bells, bells, bells, bells,
Bells, bells, bells, —
From the jingling and the tinkling of the bells.

Hear the mellow wedding bells —
Golden bells!
What a world of happiness their harmony foretells!
Through the balmy air of night
How they ring out their delight!
From the molten-golden notes,
And all in tune,
What a liquid ditty floats
To the turtle-dove that listens, while she gloats
On the moon!
O, from out the sounding cells,
What a gush of euphony voluminously wells!
How it swells!
How it dwells
On the Future! how it tells
Of the rapture that impels
To the swinging and the ringing
Of the bells, bells, bells,
Of the bells, bells, bells bells,
Bells, bells, bells, —
To the rhyming and the chiming of the bells.

Hear the loud alarum bells —
Brazen bells!
What a tale of terror, now, their turbulency tells!
In the startled ear of night

[254]

How they scream out their affright!
  Too much horrified to speak,
  They can only shriek, shriek,
   Out of tune,
In the clamorous appealing to the mercy of the fire,
In a mad expostulation with the deaf and frantic fire
  Leaping higher, higher, higher,
  With a desperate desire,
 And a resolute endeavor,
 Now — now to sit, or never,
By the side of the pale-faced moon.
  O the bells, bells, bells,
  What a tale their terror tells
Hear the tolling of the bells —
   Iron bells!
What a world of solemn thought their monody compels!
  In the silence of the night,
  How we shiver with affright
At the melancholy menace of their tone!
  For every sound that floats
  From the rust within their throats
   Is a groan.
 And the people — ah, the people —
 They that dwell up in the steeple,
   All alone,
 And who tolling, tolling, tolling,
  In that muffled monotone,
 Feel a glory in so rolling
  On the human heart a stone, —
 They are neither man nor woman, —
 They are neither brute nor human, —

They are ghouls:
And their king it is who tolls;
And he rolls, rolls, rolls,
Rolls,
A pæan from the bells!
And his merry bosom swells
With the pæan of the bells!
And he dances and he yells;
Keeping time, time, time,
In a sort of Runic rhyme,
To the pæan of the bells, —
Of the bells:
Keeping time, time, time,
In a sort of Runic rhyme,
To the throbbing of the bells, —
Of the bells, bells, bells, —
To the sobbing of the bells;
Keeping time, time, time,
As he knells, knells, knells,
In a happy Runic rhyme,
To the rolling of the bells, —
Of the bells, bells, bells, —
To the tolling of the bells,
Of the bells, bells, bells, bells —
Bells, bells, bells, —
To the moaning and the groaning of the bells.

THE RAVEN

BY EDGAR ALLEN POE

In the *Evening Mirror*, January 29, 1845, "The Raven" was published with a highly commendatory card from N. P. Willis, the editor, and a few days later *The American Whig Review* for February, from the advance sheets of which this poem had been copied, was the prey of editorial scissors throughout the country. In the magazine the author was masked under the pseudonym "Quarles," but in this journal he had been named as E. A. Poe. No great poem ever established itself so immediately, so widely, and so imperishably in men's minds. "The Raven" became in some sort a national bird, and its author the most notorious American of the hour. — GEORGE E. WOODBURY.

Once upon a midnight dreary, while I pondered, weak
      and weary,
Over many a quaint and curious volume of forgotten
      lore, —
While I nodded, nearly napping, suddenly there came
      a tapping,
As of some one gently rapping, rapping at my chamber
      door.
" 'T is some visitor," I muttered, " tapping at my
      chamber door;
    Only this, and nothing more."

Ah, distinctly I remember, it was in the bleak December,
And each separate dying ember wrought its ghost
      upon the floor.
Eagerly I wished the morrow; vainly I had sought
      to borrow

From my books surcease of sorrow, — sorrow for the
      lost Lenore, —
For the rare and radiant maiden whom the angels
      named Lenore, —
      Nameless here forevermore.

And the silken, sad, uncertain rustling of each purple
      curtain
Thrilled me, — filled me with fantastic terrors never
      felt before;
So that now, to still the beating of my heart, I stood
      repeating,
" 'T is some visitor entreating entrance at my chamber
      door, —
Some late visitor entreating entrance at my chamber
      door;
      That it is, and nothing more."

Presently my soul grew stronger; hesitating then no
      longer,
" Sir," said I, " or madam, truly your forgiveness I
      implore;
But the fact is, I was napping, and so gently you came
      rapping,
And so faintly you came tapping, tapping at my cham-
      ber door,
That I scarce was sure I heard you "— Here I opened
      wide the door;
      Darkness there, and nothing more.

Deep into that darkness peering, long I stood there,
      wondering, fearing,

Doubting, dreaming dreams no mortal ever dared to
      dream before;
But the silence was unbroken, and the darkness gave
      no token,
And the only word there spoken was the whispered
      word " Lenore! "
This I whispered, and an echo murmured back the
      word " Lenore! "
      Merely this, and nothing more.

Back into the chamber turning, all my soul within me
      burning,
Soon again I heard a tapping, something louder than
      before:
" Surely," said I, " surely that is something at my
      window-lattice;
Let me see then what thereat is, and this mystery
      explore, —
Let my heart be still a moment, and this mystery
      explore; —
      'T is the wind, and nothing more."

Open then I flung the shutter, when, with many a
      flirt and flutter,
In there stepped a stately raven of the saintly days
      of yore.
Not the least obeisance made he; not an instant
      stopped or stayed he;
But, with mien of lord or lady, perched above my
      chamber door, —

Perched upon a bust of Pallas, just above my chamber
    door, —
        Perched, and sat, and nothing more.

Then this ebony bird beguiling my sad fancy into
    smiling,
By the grave and stern decorum of the countenance
    it wore,
" Though thy crest be shorn and shaven, thou," I said,
    " art sure no craven;
Ghastly, grim, and ancient raven, wandering from the
    nightly shore,
Tell me what thy lordly name is on the night's Plu-
    tonian shore? "
        Quoth the raven, " Nevermore! "

Much I marvelled this ungainly fowl to hear discourse
    so plainly,
Though its answer little meaning, little relevancy bore;
For we cannot help agreeing that no living human
    being
Ever yet was blessed with seeing bird above his cham-
    ber door,
Bird or beast upon the sculptured bust above his
    chamber door,
        With such name as " Nevermore! "

But the raven, sitting lonely on the placid bust, spoke
    only
That one word, as if his soul in that one word he did
    outpour.

Nothing further then he uttered, — not a feather
    then he fluttered, —
Till I scarcely more than muttered, " Other friends
    have flown before, —
On the morrow he will leave me, as my hopes have
    flown before."
       Then the bird said, " Nevermore! "

Startled at the stillness, broken by reply so aptly
    spoken,
" Doubtless," said I, " what it utters is its only stock
    and store,
Caught from some unhappy master, whom unmerciful
    disaster
Followed fast and followed faster, till his song one
    burden bore,
Till the dirges of his hope that melancholy burden
    bore, —
       Of ' Nevermore, — nevermore! ' "

But the raven still beguiling all my sad soul into
    smiling,
Straight I wheeled a cushioned seat in front of bird
    and bust and door,
Then, upon the velvet sinking, I betook myself to
    linking
Fancy unto fancy, thinking what this ominous bird
    of yore —
What this grim, ungainly, ghastly, gaunt, and ominous
    bird of yore —
       Meant in croaking " Nevermore! "

[261]

This I sat engaged in guessing, but no syllable ex-
    pressing
To the fowl whose fiery eyes now burned into my
    bosom's core;
This and more I sat divining, with my head at ease
    reclining
On the cushion's velvet lining that the lamplight
    gloated o'er,
But whose velvet violet lining, with the lamplight
    gloating o'er,
       She shall press — ah! nevermore!

Then methought the air grew denser, perfumed from
    an unseen censer,
Swung by seraphim, whose footfalls tinkled on the
    tufted floor.
" Wretch," I cried, " thy God hath lent thee, — by
    these angels he hath sent thee
Respite, — respite and nepenthe from the memories
    of Lenore!
Quaff, O, quaff this kind nepenthe, and forget this
    lost Lenore! "
       Quoth the raven, " Nevermore! "

" Prophet! " said I, " thing of evil! — prophet still,
    if bird or devil!
Whether tempter sent, or whether tempest tossed thee
    here ashore,
Desolate yet all undaunted, on this desert land en-
    chanted, —
On this home by horror haunted, — tell me truly, I
    implore, —

Is there — is there balm in Gilead? — tell me, — tell
    me, I implore! "
    Quoth the raven, " Nevermore! "

" Prophet! " said I, " thing of evil! — prophet still,
    if bird or devil!
By that heaven that bends above us, — by that God
    we both adore,
Tell this soul with sorrow laden, if, within the distant
    Aidenn,
It shall clasp a sainted maiden, whom the angels
    name Lenore,
Clasp a fair and radiant maiden, whom the angels
    name Lenore! "
    Quoth the raven, " Nevermore! "

" Be that word our sign of parting, bird or fiend! "
    I shrieked, upstarting, —
" Get thee back into the tempest and the night's
    Plutonian shore!
Leave no black plume as a token of that lie thy soul
    hath spoken!
Leave my loneliness unbroken! — quit the bust above
    my door!
Take thy beak from out my heart, and take thy form
    from off my door! "
    Quoth the raven, " Nevermore! "

And the raven, never flitting, still is sitting, still is
    sitting
On the pallid bust of Pallas, just above my chamber
    door;

[263]

And his eyes have all the seeming of a demon that is
    dreaming,
And the lamplight o'er him streaming throws his
    shadow on the floor;
And my soul from out that shadow that lies floating
    on the floor
      Shall be lifted — *nevermore!*

OVER THE RIVER

BY NANCY WOODBURY PRIEST

Over the river they beckon to me,
  Loved ones who've crossed to the farther side,
The gleam of their snowy robes I see,
  But their voices are lost in the dashing tide.
There's one with ringlets of sunny gold,
  And eyes the reflection of heaven's own blue;
He crossed in the twilight gray and cold,
  And the pale mist hid him from mortal view.
We saw not the angels who met him there,
  The gates of the city we could not see:
Over the river, over the river,
  My brother stands waiting to welcome me.

Over the river the boatman pale
  Carried another, the household pet;
Her brown curls waved in the gentle gale,
  Darling Minnie! I see her yet.
She crossed on her bosom her dimpled hands,
  And fearlessly entered the phantom bark;
We felt it glide from the silver sands,

And all our sunshine grew strangely dark;
We know she is safe on the farther side,
    Where all the ransomed and angels be:
Over the river, the mystic river,
    My childhood's idol is waiting for me.

For none return from those quiet shores,
    Who cross with the boatman cold and pale;
We hear the dip of the golden oars,
        And catch a gleam of the snowy sail;
And lo! they have passed from our yearning hearts,
    They cross the stream and are gone for aye.
We may not sunder the veil apart
    That hides from our vision the gates of day;
We only know that their barks no more
    May sail with us o'er life's stormy sea;
Yet somewhere, I know, on the unseen shore,
    They watch, and beckon, and wait for me.

And I sit and think, when the sunset's gold
    Is flushing river and hill and shore,
I shall one day stand by the water cold,
    And list for the sound of the boatman's oar;
I shall watch for a gleam of the flapping sail,
    I shall hear the boat as it gains the strand,
I shall pass from sight with the boatman pale,
    To the better shore of the spirit land.

I shall know the loved who have gone before,
    And joyfully sweet will the meeting be,
When over the river, the peaceful river,
    The angel of death shall carry me.

A LOST CHORD

BY ADELAIDE ANNE PROCTER

Seated one day at the organ,
　I was weary and ill at ease,
And my fingers wandered idly
　Over the noisy keys.

I do not know what I was playing,
　Or what I was dreaming then,
But I struck one chord of music,
　Like the sound of a great Amen.

It flooded the crimson twilight,
　Like the close of an angel's psalm,
And it lay on my fevered spirit,
　With a touch of infinite calm.

It quieted pain and sorrow,
　Like love overcoming strife;
It seemed the harmonious echo
　From our discordant life.

It linked all perplexed meanings
　Into one perfect peace,
And trembled away into silence,
　As if it were loath to cease.

I have sought, but I seek it vainly,
　That one lost chord divine,
That came from the soul of the organ,
　And entered into mine.

It may be that Death's bright angel
   Will speak in that chord again;
It may be that only in heaven
   I shall hear that grand Amen.

A WOMAN'S QUESTION

BY ADELAIDE ANNE PROCTER

Before I trust my fate to thee,
   Or place my hand in thine,
Before I let thy future give
   Color and form to mine,
Before I peril all for thee,
Question thy soul to-night for me.

I break all slighter bonds, nor feel
   A shadow of regret:
Is there one link within the past
   That holds thy spirit yet?
Or is thy faith as clear and free
As that which I can pledge to thee?

Does there within thy dimmest dreams
   A possible future shine,
Wherein thy life could henceforth breathe,
   Untouched, unshared by mine?
If so, at any pain or cost,
O, tell me before all is lost!

Look deeper still: if thou canst feel,
   Within thy inmost soul,

That thou hast kept a portion back,
   While I have staked the whole,
Let no false pity spare the blow,
But in true mercy tell me so.

Is there within thy heart a need
   That mine cannot fulfil?
One chord that any other hand
   Could better wake or still?
Speak now, lest at some future day
My whole life wither and decay.

Lives there within thy nature hid
   The demon-spirit, change,
Shedding a passing glory still
   On all things new and strange?
It may not be thy fault alone, —
But shield my heart against thine own.

Couldst thou withdraw thy hand one day
   And answer to my claim,
That fate, and that to-day's mistake, —
   Not thou, — had been to blame?
Some soothe their conscience thus; but thou
Wilt surely warn and save me now.

Ay, answer *not*, — I dare not hear;
   The words would come too late;
Yet I would spare thee all remorse,
   So comfort thee, my fate:
Whatever on my heart may fall,
Remember, I *would* risk it all!

IN THE OLD CHURCH CHOIR

BY LOWELL OTUS REESE

The world was young in those days of ours.
  The world was so young and new,
All builded of birds and of sweet spring flowers,
  And to-morrow fresh wonders grew;
But the world rolled back and love reigned instead
  And smote on a magic lyre —
For Someone sat in the seat ahead
  When we sang in the old church choir.

Someone with eyes of the downcast brown.
  And lips that were wondrous rare;
Dark waves of glory that tumbled down
  From the crimson " tam " set there
At a rakish slant. Oh, that pure delight!
  Life! grant me but one desire —
To see and feel as I felt that night
  When we sang in the old church choir!

The Preacher prayed with a will. And when
  He prayed for " those near and dear,"
The deacons shouted a loud " Amen! "
  And I felt that the Lord was near.
The Preacher preached of the bleeding Lamb,
  And his words were as words of fire;
But I worshipped the girl with the crimson tam
  When we sang in the old church choir.

The church is gone, and the Preacher long
  In the land that he loved so well.

Hark! out of the new church, deep and strong,
   Hear the great pipes joyous swell!
I sit and dream and contented am,
   For Someone is by my fire,
Sweet as in the days of the crimson tam,
   When we sang in the old church choir.

THE OLD SWIMMIN'–HOLE
BY JAMES WHITCOMB RILEY

Oh! the old swimmin'-hole! whare the crick so still
   and deep
Looked like a baby-river that was lying half asleep,
And the gurgle of the worter round the drift jest below
Sounded like the laugh of something we onc't ust to
   know
Before we could remember anything but the eyes
Of the angels lookin' out as we left Paradise;
But the merry days of youth is beyond our controle,
And it's hard to part ferever with the old swimmin'-
   hole.

Oh! the old swimmin'-hole! In the happy days of yore,
When I ust to lean above it on the old sickamore,
Oh! it showed me a face in its warm sunny tide
That gazed back at me so gay and glorified,
It made me love myself, as I leaped to caress
My shadder smilin' up at me with sich tenderness.
But them days is past and gone, and old Time's tuck
   his toll
From the old man come back to the old swimmin'-
   hole.

[270]

Oh! the old swimmin'-hole! In the long, lazy days
When the hum-drum of school made so many run-a·
    ways,
How pleasant was the jurney down the old dusty lane,
Whare the tracks of our bare feet was all printed so
    plane
You could tell by the dent of the heel and the sole
They was lots o' fun on hand at the old swimmin'-
    hole.
But the lost joys is past!　Let your tears in sorrow roll
Like the rain that ust to dapple up the old swimmin'-
    hole.

Thare the bulrushes growed, and the cattails so tall,
And the sunshine and shadder fell over it all;
And it mottled the worter with amber and gold
Tel the glad lilies rocked in the ripples that rolled;
And the snake-feeder's four gauzy wings fluttered by
Like the ghost of a daisy dropped out of the sky,
Or a wownded apple-blossom in the breeze's controle
As it cut acrost some orchurd to'rds the old swimmin'-
    hole.

Oh! the old swimmin'-hole! When I last saw the place,
The scenes was all changed, like the change in my face;
The bridge of the railroad now crosses the spot
Whare the old divin'-log lays sunk and fergot.
And I stray down the banks whare the trees ust to
    be —
But never again will theyr shade shelter me!
And I wish in my sorrow I could strip to the soul,
And dive off in my grave like the old swimmin'-hole.

LITTLE ORPHANT ANNIE

BY JAMES WHITCOMB RILEY

Little Orphant Annie's come to our house to stay,
An' wash the cups an' saucers up, an' brush the crumbs
    away,
An' shoo the chickens off the porch, an' dust the hearth,
    an' sweep,
An' make the fire, an' bake the bread, an' earn her
    board-an'-keep;
An' all us other children, when the supper things is done,
We set around the kitchen fire an' has the mostest fun
A-list'nin' to the witch-tales 'at Annie tells about,
An' the Gobble-uns 'at gits you
        Ef you
          Don't
            Watch
              Out!

Onc't they was a little boy wouldn't say his prayers, —
So when he went to bed at night, away up stairs,
His Mammy heerd him holler, an' his Daddy heerd
    him bawl,
An' when they turn't the kivvers down, he wasn't
    there at all!
An' they seeked him in the rafter-room, an' cubby-
    hole, an' press,
An' seeked him up the chimbly-flue, an' ever'wheres,
    I guess;
But all they ever found was thist his pants an' rounda-
    bout: —

An' the Gobble-uns'll git you
      Ef you
         Don't
            Watch
               Out!

An' one time a little girl 'ud allus laugh an' grin,
An' make fun of ever'one, an' all her blood an' kin;
An' onc't, when they was "company," an' ole folks
    was there,
She mocked 'em an' shocked 'em, an' said she didn't care!
An' thist as she kicked her heels, an' turn't to run an'
    hide,
They was two great big Black Things a-standin' by
    her side,
An' they snatched her through the ceilin' 'fore she
    knowed what she's about!
An' the Gobble-uns'll git you
      Ef you
         Don't
            Watch
               Out!

An' little Orphant Annie says when the blaze is blue,
An' the lamp-wick sputters, an' the wind goes *woo-oo!*
An' you hear the crickets quit, an' the moon is gray,
An' the lightnin'-bugs in dew is all squenched away, —
You better mind yer parents, an' yer teachers fond an'
    dear,
An' churish them 'at loves you, an' dry the orphant's
    tear,

[273]

An' he'p the pore an' needy ones 'at clusters all about,
Er the Gobble-uns'll git you
       Ef you
           Don't
             Watch
               Out!

AN OLD SWEETHEART OF MINE

BY JAMES WHITCOMB RILEY

As one who cons at evening o'er an album all alone,
And muses on the faces of the friends that he has known,
So I turn the leaves of fancy till, in shadowy design,
I find the smiling features of an old sweetheart of mine.

The lamplight seems to glimmer with a flicker of sur-
      prise,
As I turn it low to rest me of the dazzle in my eyes,
And light my pipe in silence, save a sigh that seems to
      yoke
Its fate with my tobacco and to vanish with the smoke.

'Tis a fragrant retrospection — for the loving thoughts
      that start
Into being are like perfume from the blossom of the
      heart;
And to dream the old dreams over is a luxury divine —
When my truant fancy wanders with that old sweet-
      heart of mine.

Though I hear, beneath my study, like a fluttering of
      wings,

[274]

The voices of my children, and the mother as she sings,
I feel no twinge of conscience to deny me any theme
When Care has cast her anchor in the harbor of a
    dream.

In fact, to speak in earnest, I believe it adds a charm
To spice the good a trifle with a little dust of harm —
For I find an extra flavor in Memory's mellow wine
That makes me drink the deeper to that old sweetheart
    of mine.

A face of lily-beauty, with a form of airy grace,
Floats out of my tobacco as the genii from the vase;
And I thrill beneath the glances of a pair of azure eyes
As glowing as the summer and as tender as the skies.

I can see the pink sunbonnet and the little checkered
    dress
She wore when first I kissed her and she answered the
    caress
With the written declaration that "as surely as the
    vine
Grew round the stump" she loved me — that old
    sweetheart of mine.

And again I feel the pressure of her slender little hand
As we used to talk together of the future we had
    planned —
When I should be a poet, and with nothing else to do
But write the tender verses that she set the music to:

[275]

When we should live together in a cozy little cot
Hid in a nest of roses, with a fairy garden-spot,
Where the vines were ever fruited, and the weather
 ever fine,
And the birds were ever singing for that old sweetheart
 of mine:

When I should be her lover forever and a day,
And she my faithful sweetheart till the golden hair was
 gray;
And we should be so happy that when either's lips
 were dumb
They would not smile in Heaven till the other's kiss
 had come.

. . . .

But, ah! my dream is broken by a step upon the
 stair,
And the door is softly opened, and — my wife is standing there;
Yet with eagerness and rapture all my visions I resign
To greet the living presence of that old sweetheart
 of mine.

OLD-FASHIONED ROSES

BY JAMES WHITCOMB RILEY

They ain't no style about 'em,
 And the're sort o' pale and faded;
Yit the doorway here, without 'em,
 Would be lonesomer, and shaded

With a good deal blacker shadder
   Than the mornin'-glories makes,
And the sunshine would look sadder
   For their good old-fashioned sakes.

I like 'em 'cause they kind o'
   Sort o' make a feller like 'em;
And I tell you, when you find a
   Bunch out whur the sun kin strike 'em,
It allus sets me thinkin'
   O' the ones 'at used to grow,
And peek in thro' the chinkin'
   O' the cabin, don't you know.

And then I think o' mother,
   And how she used to love 'em,
When they wuzn't any other,
   'Less she found 'em up above 'em,
And her eyes, afore she shut 'em,
   Whispered with a smile, and said,
We must pluck a bunch and put 'em
   In her hand when she wuz dead.

But, as I wuz a-sayin',
   They ain't no style about 'em
Very gaudy or displayin',
   But I wouldn't be without 'em,
'Cause I'm happier in these posies
   And the hollyhawks and sich
Than the hummin'-bird 'at noses
   In the roses of the rich.

THE LITTLE WHITE HEARSE
BY JAMES WHITCOMB RILEY

As the little white hearse went glimmering by —
  The man on the coal cart jerked his lines,
And smutted the lid of either eye,
  And turned and stared at the business signs;
And the street-car driver stopped and beat
His hands on his shoulders and gazed up street
Till his eye on the long track reached the sky —
As the little white hearse went glimmering by.

As the little white hearse went glimmering by —
  A stranger petted a ragged child
In the crowded walk, and she knew not why,
  But he gave her a coin for the way she smiled;
And a bootblack thrilled with a pleasure strange
As a customer put back his change
With a kindly hand and a grateful sigh —
As the little white hearse went glimmering by.

As the little white hearse went glimmering by —
  A man looked out of a window dim,
And his cheeks were wet and his heart was dry —
  For a dead child even were dear to him!
And he thought of his empty life and said:
" Loveless alive and loveless dead,
Nor wife nor child in earth or sky! " —
As the little white hearse went glimmering by.

GINEVRA

BY SAMUEL ROGERS

If thou shouldst ever come by choice or chance
To Modena, where still religiously
Among her ancient trophies is preserved
Bologna's bucket (in its chain it hangs
Within that reverend tower, the Guirlandina),
Stop at a palace near the Reggio gate,
Dwelt in of old by one of the Orsini.
Its noble gardens, terrace above terrace,
And rich in fountains, statues, cypresses,
Will long detain thee; through their archèd walks,
Dim at noonday, discovering many a glimpse
Of knights and dames, such as in old romance,
And lovers, such as in heroic song,
Perhaps the two, for groves were their delight,
That in the spring-time, as alone they sat,
Venturing together on a tale of love,
Read only part that day. — A summer sun
Sets ere one half is seen; but ere thou go,
Enter the house — prythee, forget it not —
And look awhile upon a picture there. ̄

'T is of a Lady in her earliest youth,
The last of that illustrious race;
Done by Zampieri — but I care not whom.
He who observes it, ere he passes on,
Gazes his fill, and comes and comes again,
That he may call it up when far away.

[279]

She sits inclining forward as to speak,
Her lips half open, and her finger up,
As though she said " Beware! " her vest of gold
Broidered with flowers, and clasped from head to foot,
An emerald stone in every golden clasp;
And on her brow, fairer than alabaster,
A coronet of pearls. But then her face,
So lovely, yet so arch, so full of mirth,
The overflowings of an innocent heart, —
It haunts me still, though many a year has fled,
Like some wild melody!
      Alone it hangs
Over a mouldering heirloom, its companion,
An oaken chest, half eaten by the worm,
But richly carved by Antony of Trent
With Scripture stories from the life of Christ;
A chest that came from Venice, and had held
The ducal robes of some old Ancestor,
That, by the way — it may be true or false —
But don't forget the picture; and thou wilt not
When thou hast heard the tale they told me there.

She was an only child; from infancy
The joy, the pride, of an indulgent Sire;
Her Mother dying of the gift she gave,
That precious gift, what else remained to him?
The young Ginevra was his all in life,
Still as she grew, for ever in his sight;
And in her fifteenth year became a bride,
Marrying an only son, Francesco Doria,
Her playmate from her birth, and her first love.

Just as she looks there in her bridal dress,
She was all gentleness, all gayety,
Her pranks the favorite theme of every tongue.
But now the day was come, the day, the hour;
Now, frowning, smiling, for the hundredth time,
The nurse, that ancient lady, preached decorum;
And, in the lustre of her youth, she gave
Her hand, with her heart in it, to Francesco.

Great was the joy; but at the Bridal-feast,
When all sate down, the bride was wanting there,
Nor was she to be found! Her Father cried,
" 'T is but to make a trial of our love! "
And filled his glass to all; but his hand shook,
And soon from guest to guest the panic spread.
'T was but that instant she had left Francesco,
Laughing and looking back, and flying still,
Her ivory tooth imprinted on his finger.
But now, alas, she was not to be found;
Nor from that hour could anything be guessed,
But that she was not!
                              Weary of his life,
Francesco flew to Venice, and, forthwith,
Flung it away in battle with the Turk.
Orsini lived, — and long mightst thou have seen
An old man wandering as in quest of something,
Something he could not find, he knew not what.
When he was gone, the house remained awhile
Silent and tenantless, — then went to strangers.

Full fifty years were past, and all forgot,
When, on an idle day, a day of search

Mid the old lumber in the Gallery,
That mouldering chest was noticed; and 't was said
By one as young, as thoughtless as Ginevra,
"Why not remove it from its lurking-place?"
'T was done as soon as said; but on the way
It burst, it fell; and lo, a skeleton,
With here and there a pearl, an emerald stone,
A golden clasp, clasping a shred of gold!
All else had perished, — save a nuptial-ring,
And a small seal, her mother's legacy,
Engraven with a name, the name of both,
"GINEVRA."
                    There then had she found a grave!
Within that chest had she concealed herself,
Fluttering with joy, the happiest of the happy;
When a spring-lock, that lay in ambush there,
Fastened her down for ever!

SONG OF THE MYSTIC

BY FATHER ABRAM JOSEPH RYAN

I walk down the Valley of Silence —
    Down the dim, voiceless valley — alone!
And I hear not the fall of a footstep
    Around me, save God's and my own;
And the hush of my heart is as holy
    As hovers where angels have flown!

Long ago was I weary of voices
    Whose music my heart could not win;
Long ago was I weary of noises

[282]

That fretted my soul with their din;
Long ago was I weary of places
　Where I met but the human — and sin.

I walked in the world with the worldly;
　I craved what the world never gave;
And I said: " In the world each Ideal,
　That shines like a star on life's wave,
Is wrecked on the shores of the Real,
　And sleeps like a dream in a grave."

And still did I pine for the Perfect,
　And still found the False with the True;
I sought 'mid the Human for Heaven,
　But caught a mere glimpse of its Blue.
And I wept when the clouds of the Mortal
　Veiled even that glimpse from my view.

And I toiled on, heart-tired of the Human;
　And I moaned 'mid the mazes of men;
Till I knelt, long ago, at an altar
　And I heard a voice call me: — since then
I walk down the Valley of Silence
　That lies far beyond mortal ken.

Do you ask what I found in the Valley?
　'T is my Trysting Place with the Divine.
And I fell at the feet of the Holy,
　And above me a voice said: " Be mine."
And there arose from the depths of my spirit
　An echo — " My heart shall be thine."

[283]

Do you ask how I live in the Valley?
　I weep — and I dream — and I pray.
But my tears are as sweet as the dewdrops
　That fall on the roses in May;
And my prayer, like a perfume from Censers,
　Ascendeth to God night and day.

In the hush of the Valley of Silence
　I dream all the songs that I sing;
And the music floats down the dim Valley,
　Till each finds a word for a wing,
That to hearts, like the Dove of the Deluge,
　A message of Peace they may bring.

But far on the deep there are billows
　That never shall break on the beach;
And I have heard songs in the Silence,
　That never shall float into speech;
And I have had dreams in the Valley,
　Too lofty for language to reach.

And I have seen Thoughts in the Valley —
　Ah! me, how my spirit was stirred!
And they wear holy veils on their faces,
　Their footsteps can scarcely be heard:
They pass through the Valley like Virgins,
　Too pure for the touch of a word!

Do you ask me the place of the Valley?
　Ye hearts that are harrowed by Care?
It lieth afar between mountains,

[284]

And God and His angels are there:
And one is the dark mount of Sorrow,
    And one the bright mountain of Prayer!

ARE THE CHILDREN AT HOME?

BY MARGARET E. SANGSTER

Each day, when the glow of sunset
    Fades in the western sky,
And the wee ones, tired of playing,
    Go tripping lightly by,
I steal away from my husband,
    Asleep in his easy-chair,
And watch from the open doorway
    Their faces fresh and fair.

Alone in the dear old homestead
    That once was full of life,
Ringing with girlish laughter,
    Echoing boyish strife,
We two are waiting together;
    And oft, as the shadows come,
With tremulous voice he calls me,
    " It is night! are the children home? "

" Yes, love! " I answer him gently,
    " They're all home long ago ";
And I sing, in my quivering treble,
    A song so soft and low,
Till the old man drops to slumber,
    With his head upon his hand,

[285]

And I tell to myself the number
  At home in the better land.

At home, where never a sorrow
  Shall dim their eyes with tears!
Where the smile of God is on them
  Through all the summer years!
I know, — yet my arms are empty,
  That fondly folded seven,
And the mother heart within me
  Is almost starved for heaven.

Sometimes, in the dusk of evening,
  I only shut my eyes,
And the children are all about me,
  A vision from the skies:
The babes whose dimpled fingers
  Lost the way to my breast,
And the beautiful ones, the angels,
  Passed to the world of the blest.

With never a cloud upon them,
  I see their radiant brows;
My boys that I gave to freedom, —
  The red sword sealed their vows!
In a tangled Southern forest,
  Twin brothers bold and brave,
They fell; and the flag they died for,
  Thank God! floats over their grave.

A breath, and the vision is lifted
  Away on wings of light,

And again we two are together,
  All alone in the night.
They tell me his mind is failing,
  But I smile at idle fears;
He is only back with the children,
  In the dear and peaceful years.

And still, as the summer sunset
  Fades away in the west,
And the wee ones, tired of playing,
  Go trooping home to rest,
My husband calls from his corner,
  " Say, love, have the children come? "
And I answer, with eyes uplifted,
  " Yes, dear, they are all at home."

IRENE

BY MARGARET E. SANGSTER

[Written on the death of a young friend.]

In sweetest blush of maiden bloom,
A flower so rare in tint and line,
The Gardener lifts thee to illume
Some chosen place in realms divine.

And deep must be the shadow here,
Where thy fair presence ever made
(So gentle wert thou, and so dear)
A sunshine in the darkest shade.

No memory of thy life is sad,
We think of thee, with pure delight,

[287]

As alway making others glad,
And ever speaking for the right.

Like music set to tender words,
Thy duties moved through quiet days,
And still thy voice, like morning birds,
Was only heard in tones of praise.

While yet the dew was on the leaf,
Thy heart was given to Christ the King;
We dreamed not then that all too brief
Would seem thy life, who saw thee bring

Sweet gifts, the gold of sacrifice,
The myrrh of never doubting love,
And all thou hadst of worth or price
To offer to the Lord above.

Our fair Irene! Our child of peace,
Our hearts are rent with grief and pain,
But thou of pain hast now surcease,
Thou shalt not taste its draught again.

Thy bitterness is over now,
The Cross no more on thee shall press,
No fear shall ever veil thy brow,
Or sorrow give thy soul distress.

Thou art with Him who loved thee more
Than earthly friends, than nearest kin;
We wait like watchers on the shore,
But thou, to port, hath entered in.

And there, beyond the storm and strife,
Beyond these tides with ebb and flow,
Serene, in heaven's immortal life,
Thy place is safe till we shall go.

As *one by one*, we all must cross
The stream so deep and dark and cold,
Which leads us, far from mortal loss,
To dwell within the gates of gold.

O! mourning ones! through tears and dread
Of lonely days, this comfort glean,
Your darling sleeps. She is not dead,
With Christ she lives! your blessed Irene.

OUR OWN

BY MARGARET E. SANGSTER

If I had known, in the morning,
  How wearily all the day
The words unkind would trouble my mind
  That I said when you went away,
I had been more careful, darling,
  Nor given you needless pain;
But — we vex our own with look and tone
  We might never take back again.

For though in the quiet evening
  You may give me the kiss of peace,
Yet it well might be that never for me
  The pain of the heart should cease;

[289]

How many go forth at morning
　Who never come home at night,
And hearts have broken for harsh words spoken
　That sorrow can ne'er set right.

We have careful thought for the stranger,
　And smiles for the sometime guest,
But oft for our own the bitter tone,
　Though we love our own the best.
Ah, lip with the curve impatient,
　Ah, brow with the shade of scorn,
'T were a cruel fate were the night too late
　To undo the work of morn.

A LIFE ON THE OCEAN WAVE

BY EPES SARGENT

A life on the ocean wave,
　A home on the rolling deep;
Where the scatter'd waters rave,
　And the winds their revels keep!
Like an eagle caged I pine
　On this dull, unchanging shore:
Oh, give me the flashing brine,
　The spray and the tempest's roar!

Once more on the deck I stand,
　Of my own swift-gliding craft:
Set sail! farewell to the land;
　The gale follows fair abaft.

We shoot through the sparkling foam,
   Like an ocean-bird set free, —
Like the ocean-bird, our home
   We'll find far out on the sea.

The land is no longer in view,
   The clouds have begun to frown;
But with a stout vessel and crew,
   We'll say, Let the storm come down!
And the song of our hearts shall be,
   While the winds and the waters rave,
A home on the rolling sea!
   A life on the ocean wave!

TREASURE IN HEAVEN

BY JOHN GODFREY SAXE

RESPECTFULLY DEDICATED TO GEORGE PEABODY, ESQ.

> *"What I spent, I had; what I left,*
> *I lost; what I gave, I have!"*
> OLD EPITAPH

Every coin of earthly treasure
   We have lavished, upon earth,
For our simple worldly pleasure,
   May be reckoned something worth;
For the spending was not losing,
   Though the purchase were but small;
It has perished with the using:
   We have had it, — that is all!

All the gold we leave behind us
   When we turn to dust again
(Though our avarice may blind us),
   We have gathered quite in vain;
Since we neither can direct it,
   By the winds of fortune tossed,
Nor in other worlds expect it:
   What we hoarded, we have lost.

But each merciful oblation —
   (Seed of pity wisely sown),
What we gave in self-negation,
   We may safely call our own;
For the treasure freely given
   Is the treasure that we hoard,
Since the angels keep in Heaven
   What is lent unto the Lord!

THE OLD MAN'S MOTTO

BY JOHN GODFREY SAXE

"Give me a motto!" said a youth
   To one whom years had rendered wise;
"Some pleasant thought, or weighty truth,
   That briefest syllables comprise;
Some word of warning or of cheer
To grave upon my signet here.

"And, reverend father," said the boy,
   "Since life, they say, is ever made
A mingled web of grief and joy;

[292]

Since cares may come and pleasures fade,—
Pray, let the motto have a range
Of meaning matching every change."

"Sooth!" said the sire, "methinks you ask
    A labor something over-nice,
That well a finer brain might task.
    What think you, lad, of this device
(Older than I, though I am gray),
'T is simple,—'This will pass away'?

"When wafted on by Fortune's breeze,
    In endless peace thou seem'st to glide,
Prepare betimes for rougher seas,
    And check the boast of foolish pride;
Though smiling joy is thine to-day,
Remember, 'This will pass away!'

"When all the sky is draped in black,
    And, beaten by tempestuous gales,
Thy shuddering ship seems all a-wrack,
    Then trim again thy tattered sails;
To grim Despair be not a prey;
Bethink thee, 'This will pass away!'

"Thus, O my son, be not o'er-proud,
    Nor yet cast down; judge thou aright;
When skies are clear, expect the cloud;
    In darkness, wait the coming light;
Whatever be thy fate to-day,
Remember, 'This will pass away!'"

[293]

THE SUPERFLUOUS MAN

BY JOHN GODFREY SAXE

"It is ascertained by inspection of the registers of many countries, that the uniform proportion of male to female births is as 21 to 20: accordingly, in respect to marriage, every 21st man is naturally superfluous."—TREATISE ON POPULATION.

I long have been puzzled to guess,
　　And so I have frequently said,
What the reason could really be
　　That I never have happened to wed;
But now it is perfectly clear,
　　I am under a natural ban;
The girls are already assigned,—
　　And I'm a superfluous man!

Those clever statistical chaps
　　Declare the numerical run
Of women and men in the world,
　　Is Twenty to Twenty-and-one;
And hence in the pairing, you see,
　　Since wooing and wedding began,
For every connubial score,
　　They've got a superfluous man!

By twenties and twenties they go,
　　And giddily rush to their fate,
For none of the number, of course,
　　Can fail of a conjugal mate;
But while they are yielding in scores
　　To Nature's inflexible plan,
There's never a woman for me,—
　　For I'm a superfluous man!

[294]

It is n't that I am a churl,
  To solitude over-inclined;
It isn't that I am at fault
  In morals or manner or mind;
Then what is the reason, you ask,
  I'm still with the bachelor-clan?
I merely was numbered amiss,—
  And I'm a superfluous man!

It isn't that I am in want
  Of personal beauty or grace,
For many a man with a wife
  Is uglier far in the face;
Indeed, among elegant men
  I fancy myself in the van;
But what is the value of that,
  When I'm a superfluous man?

Although I am fond of the girls,
  For aught I could ever discern
The tender emotion I feel
  Is one that they never return;
'T is idle to quarrel with fate,
  For, struggle as hard as I can,
They're mated already, you know,—
  And I'm a superfluous man!

No wonder I grumble at times,
  With women so pretty and plenty,
To know that I never was born
  To figure as one of the Twenty;

But yet, when the average lot
With critical vision I scan,
I think it may be for the best
That I'm a superfluous man!

BREATHES THERE THE MAN

BY SIR WALTER SCOTT

[From "The Lay of the Last Minstrel," Canto VI.]

Breathes there the man with soul so dead
Who never to himself hath said,
  This is my own, my native land!
Whose heart hath ne'er within him burned,
As home his footsteps he hath turned
  From wandering on a foreign strand?
If such there breathe, go, mark him well;
For him no minstrel raptures swell;
High though his titles, proud his name,
Boundless his wealth as wish can claim,
Despite those titles, power, and pelf,
The wretch, concentred all in self,
Living, shall forfeit fair renown,
And, doubly dying, shall go down
To the vile dust from whence he sprung,
Unwept, unhonored, and unsung.

THE FOOL'S PRAYER

BY EDWARD ROWLAND SILL

The royal feast was done; the king
  Sought some new sport to banish care,
And to his jester cried: "Sir Fool,
  Kneel now, and make for us a prayer!"

The jester doffed his cap and bells,
  And stood the mocking court before:
They could not see the bitter smile
  Behind the painted grin he wore.

He bowed his head, and bent his knee
  Upon the monarch's silken stool;
His pleading voice arose, "O Lord,
  Be merciful to me, a fool!

"No pity, Lord, could change the heart
  From red with wrong to white as wool;
The rod must heal the sin; but, Lord,
  Be merciful to me, a fool!

"'Tis not by guilt the onward sweep
  Of truth and right, O Lord, we stay;
'Tis by our follies that so long
  We hold the earth from heaven away.

"These clumsy feet still in the mire,
  Go crushing blossoms without end;
These hard, well-meaning hands we thrust
  Among the heartstrings of a friend.

[297]

"The ill-timed truth we might have kept, —
    Who knows how sharp it pierced and stung?
The word we had not sense to say, —
    Who knows how grandly it had rung?

"Our faults no tenderness should ask,
    The chastening stripes must cleanse them all;
But for our blunders, — oh, in shame
    Before the eyes of heaven we fall.

"Earth bears no balsam for mistakes;
    Men crown the knave, and scourge the tool
That did his will; but Thou, O Lord,
    Be merciful to me, a fool!"

The room was hushed; in silence rose
    The king, and sought his gardens cool,
And walked apart, and murmured low:
    "Be merciful to me, a fool!"

IF I SHOULD DIE TO-NIGHT

BY ARABELLE E. SMITH

If I should die to-night,
My friends would look upon my quiet face
Before they laid it in its resting-place,
And deem that death had left it almost fair;
And, laying snow-white flowers against my hair,
Would smooth it down with tearful tenderness,
And fold my hands with lingering caress, —
Poor hands, so empty and so cold to-night!

If I should die to-night,
My friends would call to mind, with loving thought,
Some kindly deed the icy hands had wrought;
Some gentle word the frozen lips had said;
Errands on which the willing feet had sped;
The memory of my selfishness and pride,
My hasty words, would all be put aside,
And so I should be loved and mourned to-night.

If I should die to-night,
Even hearts estranged would turn once more to me,
Recalling other days remorsefully;
The eyes that chill me with averted glance
Would look upon me as of yore, perchance,
And soften, in the old familiar way;
For who could war with dumb, unconscious clay!
So I might rest, forgiven of all, to-night.

Oh, friends, I pray to-night,
Keep not your kisses for my dead, cold brow —
The way is lonely, let me feel them now.
Think gently of me; I am travel-worn;
My faltering feet are pierced with many a thorn.
Forgive, oh, hearts estranged, forgive, I plead!
When dreamless rest is mine I shall not need
The tenderness for which I long to-night.

AMERICA

BY SAMUEL F. SMITH

My country, 't is of thee,
Sweet land of liberty,
   Of thee I sing;
Land where my fathers died,
Land of the pilgrims' pride,
From every mountain-side
   Let freedom ring.

My native country, thee —
Land of the noble, free —
   Thy name I love;
I love thy rocks and rills,
Thy woods and templed hills;
My heart with rapture thrills
   Like that above.

Let music swell the breeze,
And ring from all the trees
   Sweet freedom's song:
Let mortal tongues awake;
Let all that breathe partake;
Let rocks their silence break, —
   The sound prolong.

Our fathers' God, to Thee,
Author of liberty,
   To Thee we sing;
Long may our land be bright
With freedom's holy light;
Protect us by Thy might,
   Great God, our King.

[300]

THE PAUPER'S DEATH–BED

BY CAROLINE ANNE BOWLES SOUTHEY

Tread softly, — bow the head, —
  In reverent silence bow, —
No passing-bell doth toll,
Yet an immortal soul
  Is passing now.

Stranger! however great,
  With lowly reverence bow;
There's one in that poor shed —
One by that paltry bed —
  Greater than thou.

Beneath that beggar's roof,
  Lo! Death doth keep his state.
Enter, no crowds attend;
Enter, no guards defend
  This palace gate.

That pavement, damp and cold,
  No smiling courtiers tread;
One silent woman stands,
Lifting with meagre hands
  A dying head.

No mingling voices sound, —
  An infant wail alone;
A sob suppressed, — again
That short deep gasp, and then —
  The parting groan.

[301]

O change! O wondrous change!
  Burst are the prison bars, —
This moment, *there*, so low,
So agonized, and now, —
  Beyond the stars.

O change! stupendous change!
  There lies the soulless clod;
The sun eternal breaks,
The new immortal wakes, —
  Wakes with his God!

THE BOYS THAT RUN THE FURROW
BY FRANK L. STANTON

You can write it down as gospel,
  With the flags of peace unfurled,
The boys that run the furrow
  Are the boys that rule the world!

It is written on the hilltops,
  In the fields where blossoms blend:
Prosperity is ending
  Where the furrow has an end!

The glory of the battle,
  Of clashing swords blood-red,
Is nothing to the warfare
  Of the battle-hosts of bread!

The waving banners of the fields
  O'er the broad land unfurled —
The boys that run the furrow
  Are the boys that rule the world!

[302]

A LITTLE HAND

BY FRANK L. STANTON

Perhaps there are tenderer, sweeter things
   Somewhere in this sun-bright land;
But I thank the Lord for His blessing,
   And the clasp of a little hand.

A little hand that softly stole
   Into my own that day,
When I needed the touch that I loved so much,
   To strengthen me on the way.

Softer it seemed than the softest down
   On the breast of the gentlest dove;
But its timid press and its faint caress
   Were strong in the strength of love!

It seemed to say in a strange, sweet way,
   " I love you and understand,"
And calmed my fears as my hot heart tears
   Fell over that little hand.

. . . .

Perhaps there are tenderer, sweeter things
   Somewhere in this sun-bright land;
But I thank the Lord for His blessing,
   And the clasp of a little hand.

[303]

THE DOORSTEP

BY EDMUND CLARENCE STEDMAN

The conference-meeting through at last,
  We boys around the vestry waited
To see the girls come tripping past
  Like snowbirds willing to be mated.

Not braver he that leaps the wall
  By level musket-flashes litten,
Than I, who stepped before them all,
  Who longed to see me get the mitten.

But no; she blushed and took my arm!
  We let the old folks have the highway,
And started towards the Maple Farm
  Along a kind of lovers' by-way.

I can't remember what we said,
  'Twas nothing worth a song or story;
Yet that rude path by which we sped
  Seemed all transformed and in a glory.

The snow was crisp beneath our feet,
  The moon was full, the fields were gleaming;
By hood and tippet sheltered sweet,
  Her face with youth and health was beaming.

The little hand outside her muff —
  O sculptor, if you could but mould it!
So lightly touched my jacket-cuff,
  To keep it warm I had to hold it.

To have her with me there alone, —
   'T was love and fear and triumph blended.
At last we reached the foot-worn stone
   Where that delicious journey ended.

The old folks, too, were almost home;
   Her dimpled hand the latches fingered,
We heard the voices nearer come,
   Yet on the doorstep still we lingered.

She took her ringlets from her hood,
   And with a " Thank you, Ned," dissembled;
But yet I knew she understood
   With what a daring wish I trembled.

A cloud past kindly overhead,
   The moon was slyly peeping through it,
Yet hid its face, as if it said,
   " Come, now or never! do it! *do it!* "

My lips till then had only known
   The kiss of mother and of sister,
But somehow full upon her own
   Sweet, rosy, darling mouth — I kissed her!

Perhaps 'twas boyish love, yet still,
   O, listless woman! weary lover!
To feel once more that fresh, wild thrill
   I'd give — but who can live youth over?

[305]

CHRISTMAS AT SEA

BY ROBERT LOUIS STEVENSON

The sheets were frozen hard, and they cut the naked
    hand;
The decks were like a slide, where a seaman scarce
    could stand;
The wind was a nor'wester, blowing squally off the
    sea;
And cliffs and spouting breakers were the only things
    a-lee.

They heard the surf a-roaring before the break of
    day;
But 'twas only with the peep of light we saw how ill
    we lay.
We tumbled every hand on deck instanter, with a
    shout,
And we gave her the maintops'l, and stood by to go
    about.

All day we tacked and tacked between the South Head
    and the North;
All day we hauled the frozen sheets, and got no further
    forth;
All day as cold as charity, in bitter pain and dread,
For very life and nature we tacked from head to head.

We gave the South a wider berth, for there the tide-
    race roared;
But every tack we made we brought the North Head
    close aboard:

[306]

So's we saw the cliffs and houses, and the breakers
running high,
And the coastguard in his garden, with his glass against
his eye.

The frost was on the village roofs as white as ocean
foam;
The good red fires were burning bright in every 'long-
shore home;
The windows sparkled clear, and the chimneys volleyed
out;
And I vow we sniffed the victuals as the vessel went
about.

The bells upon the church were rung with a mighty
jovial cheer;
For it's just that I should tell you how (of all days
in the year)
This day of our adversity was blessed Christmas
morn,
And the house above the coastguard's was the house
where I was born.

O well I saw the pleasant room, the pleasant faces there,
My mother's silver spectacles, my father's silver hair;
And well I saw the firelight, like a flight of homely
elves,
Go dancing round the china-plates that stand upon the
shelves.

And well I knew the talk they had, the talk that was
of me,

[307]

Of the shadow on the household and the son that went
　　to sea;
And O the wicked fool I seemed, in every kind of way,
To be here and hauling frozen ropes on blessed Christ-
　　mas Day.

They lit the high sea-light, and the dark began to fall.
"All hands to loose topgallant sails," I heard the cap-
　　tain call.
"By the Lord, she'll never stand it," our first mate,
　　Jackson, cried.
"It's the one way or the other, Mr. Jackson," he replied.

She staggered to her bearings, but the sails were new
　　and good,
And the ship smelt up to windward just as though she
　　understood.
As the winter's day was ending, in the entry of the
　　night,
We cleared the weary headland, and passed below the
　　light.

And they heaved a mighty breath, every soul on board
　　but me,
As they saw her nose again pointing handsome out to
　　sea;
But all that I could think of, in the darkness and the
　　cold,
Was just that I was leaving home and my folks were
　　growing old.

[308]

THE DEPARTED FRIEND
BY ROBERT LOUIS STEVENSON

Though he that ever kind and true
Kept stoutly step by step with you,
Your whole long, gusty lifetime through,
    Be gone a while before —
Be now a moment gone before,
Yet doubt not; anon the seasons shall restore
    Your friend to you.

He has but turned a corner — still
He pushes on with right good will
Through mire and marsh, by heugh and hill,
    That self-same arduous way —
That self-same upland hopeful way
That you and he through many a doubtful day
    Attempted still.

He is not dead, this friend — not dead,
But in the path we mortals tread
Got some few, trifling steps ahead
    And nearer to the end,
So that you, too, once past the bend,
Shall meet again, as face to face, this friend
    You fancy dead.

Push gayly on, strong heart; the while
You travel forward mile by mile,
He loiters with a backward smile
    Till you can overtake,
And strains his eyes to search his wake,
Or, whistling, as he sees you through the brake,
    Waits on a stile.

[309]

BEFORE THE BEGINNING OF YEARS
BY ALGERNON CHARLES SWINBURNE

Before the beginning of years
  There came to the making of man
Time, with a gift of tears;
  Grief, with a glass that ran;
Pleasure, with pain for leaven;
  Summer, with flowers that fell;
Remembrance, fallen from heaven;
  And madness risen from hell;
Strength, without hands to smite;
  Love, that endures for a breath;
Night, the shadow of light,
  And life, the shadow of death.

And the high gods took in hand
  Fire, and the falling of tears,
And a measure of sliding sand
  From under the feet of the years;
And froth and drift of the sea;
  And dust of the laboring earth;
And bodies of things to be
  In the houses of death and of birth;
And wrought with weeping and laughter,
  And fashion'd with loathing and love,
With life before and after,
  And death beneath and above,
For a day and a night and a morrow,
  That his strength might endure for a span
With travail and heavy sorrow,
  The holy spirit of man.

From the winds of the north and the south
 They gather'd as unto strife;
They breathed upon his mouth,
 They fill'd his body with life;
Eyesight and speech they wrought
 For the veils of the soul therein,
A time for labor and thought,
 A time to serve and to sin;
They gave him light in his ways,
 And love, and a space for delight,
And beauty and length of days,
 And night, and sleep in the night.
His speech is a burning fire;
 With his lips he travaileth;
In his heart is a blind desire,
 In his eyes foreknowledge of death;
He weaves, and is clothed with derision;
 Sows, and he shall not reap;
His life is a watch or a vision
 Between a sleep and a sleep.

THE SONG OF THE CAMP

BY BAYARD TAYLOR

" Give us a song! " the soldiers cried,
 The outer trenches guarding,
When the heated guns of the camps allied
 Grew weary of bombarding.

The dark Redan, in silent scoff,
 Lay grim and threatening under;

[311]

And the tawny mound of the Malakoff
  No longer belch'd its thunder.

There was a pause. A guardsman said:
  " We storm the forts to-morrow;
Sing while we may, another day
  Will bring enough of sorrow."

They lay along the battery's side,
  Below the smoking cannon:
Brave hearts from Severn and from Clyde,
  And from the banks of Shannon.

They sang of love, and not of fame;
  Forgot was Britain's glory:
Each heart recall'd a different name,
  But all sang " Annie Laurie."

Voice after voice caught up the song,
  Until its tender passion
Rose like an anthem, rich and strong, —
  Their battle-eve confession.

Dear girl, her name he dared not speak,
  But as the song grew louder,
Something upon the soldier's cheek
  Wash'd off the stains of powder.

Beyond the darkening ocean burn'd
  The bloody sunset's embers,
While the Crimean valleys learn'd
  How English love remembers.

[312]

And once again a fire of hell
   Rain'd on the Russian quarters,
With scream of shot, and burst of shell,
   And bellowing of the mortars!

And Irish Nora's eyes are dim;
   For a singer dumb and gory;
And English Mary mourns for him
   Who sang of " Annie Laurie."

Sleep, soldiers! still in honor'd rest
   Your truth and valor wearing:
The bravest are the tenderest, —
   The loving are the daring.

BREAK, BREAK, BREAK

BY ALFRED TENNYSON

Break, break, break,
   On thy cold gray stones, O sea!
And I would that my tongue could utter
   The thoughts that arise in me.

O well for the fisherman's boy
   That he shouts with his sister at play!
O well for the sailor lad
   That he sings in his boat on the bay!

And the stately ships go on,
   To the haven under the hill;

But O for the touch of a vanished hand,
    And the sound of a voice that is still!

Break, break, break,
    At the foot of thy crags, O sea!
But the tender grace of a day that is dead
    Will never come back to me.

THE BUGLE

BY ALFRED TENNYSON

[From " The Princess."]

The splendor falls on castle walls
    And snowy summits old in story:
The long light shakes across the lakes,
    And the wild cataract leaps in glory.
Blow, bugle, blow, set the wild echoes flying,
Blow, bugle; answer, echoes, dying, dying, dying.

O hark! O hear! how thin and clear,
    And thinner, clearer, farther going!
O sweet and far, from cliff and scar,
    The horns of Elfland faintly blowing!
Blow, let us hear the purple glens replying:
Blow, bugle; answer, echoes, dying, dying, dying.

O love, they die in yon rich sky,
    They faint on hill or field or river;
Our echoes roll from soul to soul,
    And grow forever and forever.
Blow, bugle, blow, set the wild echoes flying,
And answer, echoes, answer, dying, dying, dying.

[314]

CHARGE OF THE LIGHT BRIGADE

BY ALFRED TENNYSON

Half a league, half a league,
　Half a league onward,
All in the valley of Death
　Rode the six hundred.
" Forward, the Light Brigade!
Charge for the guns! " he said;
Into the valley of Death
　Rode the six hundred.

" Forward, the Light Brigade! "
Was there a man dismayed?
Not though the soldier knew
　Some one had blundered:
Theirs not to make reply,
Theirs not to reason why,
Theirs but to do and die:
Into the valley of Death
　Rode the six hundred.

Cannon to right of them,
Cannon to left of them,
Cannon in front of them
　Volleyed and thundered;
Stormed at with shot and shell,
Boldly they rode and well;
Into the jaws of Death,
Into the mouth of Hell,
　Rode the six hundred.

[315]

Flashed all their sabres bare,
Flashed as they turned in air,
Sabring the gunners there,
Charging an army, while
   All the world wondered:
Plunged in the battery-smoke,
Right through the line they broke:
Cossack and Russian
Reeled from the sabre-stroke,
   Shattered and sundered.
Then they rode back, but not —
   Not the six hundred.

Cannon to right of them,
Cannon to left of them,
Cannon behind them
   Volleyed and thundered:
Stormed at with shot and shell,
While horse and hero fell,
They that had fought so well
Came through the jaws of Death
Back from the mouth of Hell, —
All that was left of them,
   Left of six hundred.

When can their glory fade?
O the wild charge they made!
   All the world wondered.
Honor the charge they made!
Honor the Light Brigade,
   Noble six hundred!

[316]

CROSSING THE BAR

BY ALFRED TENNYSON

Sunset and evening star,
  And one clear call for me!
And may there be no moaning of the bar
  When I put out to sea,

But such a tide as moving seems asleep,
  Too full for sound and foam,
When that which drew from out the boundless deep
  Turns again home.

Twilight and evening bell,
  And after that the dark!
And may there be no sadness of farewell
  When I embark;

For tho' from out our bourne of Time and Place
  The flood may bear me far,
I hope to see my Pilot face to face
  When I have crost the bar.

LADY CLARA VERE DE VERE

BY ALFRED TENNYSON

Lady Clara Vere de Vere,
  Of me you shall not win renown;
You thought to break a country heart
  For pastime, ere you went to town.

[317]

At me you smiled, but unbeguiled
   I saw the snare, and I retired:
The daughter of a hundred Earls,
   You are not one to be desired.

Lady Clara Vere de Vere,
   I know you proud to bear your name;
Your pride is yet no mate for mine,
   Too proud to care from whence I came.
Nor would I break for your sweet sake
   A heart that dotes on truer charms.
A simple maiden in her flower
   Is worth a hundred coats-of-arms.

Lady Clara Vere de Vere,
   Some meeker pupil you must find,
For were you queen of all that is,
   I could not stoop to such a mind.
You sought to prove how I could love,
   And my disdain is my reply.
The lion on your old stone gates
   Is not more cold to you than I.

Lady Clara Vere de Vere,
   You put strange memories in my head.
Not thrice your branching limes have blown
   Since I beheld young Laurence dead.
O your sweet eyes, your low replies:
   A great enchantress you may be;
But there was that across his throat
   Which you had hardly cared to see.

[318]

Lady Clara Vere de Vere,
  When thus he met his mother's view,
She had the passions of her kind,
  She spake some certain truths of you.
Indeed I heard one bitter word
  That scarce is fit for you to hear;
Her manners had not that repose
  Which stamps the caste of Vere de Vere.

Lady Clara Vere de Vere,
  There stands a spectre in your hall:
The guilt of blood is at your door:
  You changed a wholesome heart to gall.
You held your course without remorse,
  To make him trust his modest worth,
And, last, you fixed a vacant stare,
  And slew him with your noble birth.

Trust me, Clara Vere de Vere,
  From yon blue heavens above us bent
The grand old gardener and his wife
  Smile at the claims of long descent.
Howe'er it be, it seems to me,
  'T is only noble to be good.
Kind hearts are more than coronets,
  And simple faith than Norman blood.

I know you, Clara Vere de Vere:
  You pine among your halls and towers:
The languid light of your proud eyes
  Is wearied of the rolling hours.

[319]

In glowing health, with boundless wealth,
　　But sickening of a vague disease,
You know so ill to deal with time,
　　You needs must play such pranks as these.

Clara, Clara Vere de Vere,
　　If Time be heavy on your hands,
Are there no beggars at your gate,
　　Nor any poor about your lands?
Oh! teach the orphan-boy to read,
　　Or teach the orphan-girl to sew,
Pray Heaven for a human heart,
　　And let the foolish yeoman go.

LADY CLARE

BY ALFRED TENNYSON

It was the time when lilies blow,
　　And clouds are highest up in air,
Lord Ronald brought a lily-white doe
　　To give his cousin, Lady Clare.

I trow they did not part in scorn:
　　Lovers long betroth'd were they:
They two will wed the morrow morn:
　　God's blessing on the day!

" He does not love me for my birth,
　　Nor for my lands so broad and fair;
He loves me for my own true worth,
　　And that is well," said Lady Clare.

[320]

In there came old Alice the nurse,
   Said, " Who was this that went from thee ? "
" It was my cousin," said Lady Clare,
   " To-morrow he weds with me."

" Oh, God be thank'd! " said Alice the nurse,
   " That all comes round so just and fair:
Lord Ronald is heir of all your lands,
   And you are not the Lady Clare."

" Are ye out of your mind, my nurse, my nurse ? "
   Said Lady Clare, " that ye speak so wild ? "
" As God's above," said Alice the nurse,
   " I speak the truth: you are my child.

The old earl's daughter died at my breast;
   I speak the truth, as I live by bread!
I buried her like my own sweet child,
   And put my child in her stead."

" Falsely, falsely have ye done,
   O mother," she said, " if this be true,
To keep the best man under the sun
   So many years from his due."

" Nay now, my child," said Alice the nurse,
   " But keep the secret for your life,
And all you have will be Lord Ronald's,
   When you are man and wife."

" If I'm a beggar born," she said,
   " I will speak out, for I dare not lie.

[321]

Pull off, pull off the brooch of gold,
   And fling the diamond necklace by."

" Nay now, my child," said Alice the nurse,
   " But keep the secret all ye can."
She said, " Not so: but I will know
   If there be any faith in man."

" Nay now, what faith? " said Alice the nurse,
   " The man will cleave unto his right."
" And he shall have it," the lady replied,
   " Though I should die to-night."

" Yet give one kiss to your mother, dear!
   Alas, my child, I sinn'd for thee."
" O mother, mother, mother," she said,
   " So strange it seems to me!

" Yet here's a kiss for my mother dear,
   My mother dear, if this be so,
And lay your hand upon my head,
   And bless me, mother, ere I go."

She clad herself in a russet gown,
   She was no longer Lady Clare:
She went by dale, and she went by down,
   With a single rose in her hair.

The lily-white doe Lord Ronald had brought
   Leapt up from where she lay,
Dropp'd her head in the maiden's hand,
   And follow'd her all the way.

Down stepp'd Lord Ronald from his tower:
　" O Lady Clare, you shame your worth!
Why come you dress'd like a village maid,
　That are the flower of the earth? "

" If I come dress'd like a village maid,
　I am but as my fortunes are:
I am a beggar born," she said,
　" And not the Lady Clare."

" Play me no tricks," said Lord Ronald,
　" For I am yours in word and in deed.
Play me no tricks," said Lord Ronald,
　" Your riddle is hard to read."

Oh, and proudly stood she up!
　Her heart within her did not fail:
She look'd into Lord Ronald's eyes,
　And told him all her nurse's tale.

He laugh'd a laugh of merry scorn:
　He turn'd and kiss'd her where she stood:
" If you are not the heiress born,
　And I," said he, " the next in blood —

" If you are not the heiress born,
　And I," said he, " the lawful heir,
We two will wed to-morrow morn,
　And you shall still be Lady Clare."

THE MAY QUEEN

BY ALFRED TENNYSON

You must wake and call me early, call me early,
    mother dear;
To-morrow 'll be the happiest time of all the glad
    new-year, —
Of all the glad new-year, mother, the maddest, merri-
    est day;
For I'm to be Queen o' the May, mother, I'm to be
    Queen o' the May.

There's many a black, black eye, they say, but none
    so bright as mine;
There's Margaret and Mary, there's Kate and Caro-
    line;
But none so fair as little Alice in all the land, they say:
So I'm to be Queen o' the May, mother, I'm to be
    Queen o' the May.

I sleep so sound all night, mother, that I shall never
    wake,
If you do not call me loud when the day begins to
    break;
But I must gather knots of flowers and buds, and
    garlands gay;
For I'm to be Queen o' the May, mother, I'm to be
    Queen o' the May.

As I came up the valley, whom think ye should I see
But Robin leaning on the bridge beneath the hazel-
    tree?

He thought of that sharp look, mother, I gave him
    yesterday, —
But I'm to be Queen o' the May, mother, I'm to be
    Queen o' the May.

He thought I was a ghost, mother, for I was all in
    white;
And I ran by him without speaking, like a flash of
    light.
They call me cruel-hearted, but I care not what they
    say,
For I'm to be Queen o' the May, mother, I'm to be
    Queen o' the May.

They say he's dying all for love, — but that can never
    be;
They say his heart is breaking, mother, — what is
    that to me?
There's many a bolder lad 'll woo me any summer
    day;
And I'm to be Queen o' the May, mother, I'm to be
    Queen o' the May.

Little Effie shall go with me to-morrow to the green,
And you'll be there, too, mother, to see me made the
    Queen;
For the shepherd lads on every side 'll come from far
    away;
And I'm to be Queen o' the May, mother, I'm to be
    Queen o' the May.

The honeysuckle round the porch has woven its wavy
    bowers,
And by the meadow-trenches blow the faint sweet
    cuckoo-flowers;
And the wild marsh-marigold shines like fire in swamps
    and hollows gray;
And I'm to be Queen o' the May, mother, I'm to be
    Queen o' the May.

The night-winds come and go, mother, upon the
    meadow-grass,
And the happy stars above them seem to brighten as
    they pass;
There will not be a drop of rain the whole of the live-
    long day;
And I'm to be Queen o' the May, mother, I'm to be
    Queen o' the May.

All the valley, mother, 'll be fresh and green and
    still,
And the cowslip and the crowfoot are over all the
    hill,
And the rivulet in the flowery dale 'll merrily glance
    and play,
For I'm to be Queen o' the May, mother, I'm to be
    Queen o' the May.

So you must wake and call me early, call me early,
    mother dear;
To-morrow'll be the happiest time of all the glad
    new-year;

To-morrow'll be of all the year the maddest, merriest
    day,
For I'm to be Queen o' the May, mother, I'm to be
    Queen o' the May.

NEW-YEAR'S EVE

If you're waking, call me early, call me early, mother
    dear,
For I would see the sun rise upon the glad new-year.
It is the last new-year that I shall ever see, —
Then you may lay me low i' the mould, and think no
    more of me.

To-night I saw the sun set, — he set and left behind
The good old year, the dear old time, and all my peace
    of mind;
And the new-year's coming up, mother; but I shall
    never see
The blossom on the blackthorn, the leaf upon the tree.

Last May we made a crown of flowers; we had a merry
    day, —
Beneath the hawthorn on the green they made me
    Queen of May;
And we danced about the May-pole and in the hazel
    copse,
Till Charles's Wain came out above the tall white
    chimney-tops.

There's not a flower on all the hills, — the frost is on
    the pane;
I only wish to live till the snowdrops come again.

I wish the snow would melt and the sun come out on
    high, —
I long to see a flower so before the day I die.

The building rook'll caw from the windy tall elm-tree,
And the tufted plover pipe along the fallow lea,
And the swallow'll come back again with summer
    o'er the wave,
But I shall lie alone, mother, within the mouldering
    grave.

Upon the chancel-casement, and upon that grave of
    mine,
In the early, early morning the summer sun'll shine
Before the red cock crows from the farm upon the
    hill, —
When you are warm-asleep mother, and all the world
    is still.

When the flowers come again, mother, beneath the
    waning light
You'll never see me more in the long gray fields at
    night;
When from the dry dark wold the summer airs blow
    cool
On the oat-grass and the sword-grass, and the bulrush
    in the pool.

You'll bury me, my mother, just beneath the hawthorn
    shade,
And you'll come sometimes and see me where I am
    lowly laid.

I shall not forget you, mother; I shall hear you when
    you pass,
With your feet above my head in the long and pleasant
    grass.

I have been wild and wayward, but you'll forgive me
    now;
You'll kiss me, my own mother, upon my cheek and
    brow;
Nay, nay, you must not weep, nor let your grief be
    wild;
You should not fret for me, mother — you have
    another child.

If I can, I'll come again, mother, from out my resting-
    place;
Though you'll not see me, mother, I shall look upon
    your face;
Though I cannot speak a word, I shall hearken what
    you say,
And be often, often with you when you think I'm far
    away.

Good night! good night! when I have said good
    night forevermore,
And you see me carried out from the threshold of the
    door,
Don't let Effie come to see me till my grave be growing
    green, —
She'll be a better child to you then ever I have
    been.

She'll find my garden tools upon the granary floor.
Let her take 'em — they are hers; I shall never garden
    more.
But tell her, when I'm gone, to train the rosebush that
    I set
About the parlor window and the box of mignonette.

Good night, sweet mother! Call me before the day
    is born.
All night I lie awake, but I fall asleep at morn;
But I would see the sun rise upon the glad new-
    year,—
So, if you're waking, call me, call me early, mother
    dear.

CONCLUSION

I thought to pass away before, and yet alive I am;
And in the fields all round I hear the bleating of the
    lamb.
How sadly, I remember, rose the morning of the year!
To die before the snowdrop came, and now the violet's
    here.

O, sweet is the new violet, that comes beneath the
    skies;
And sweeter is the young lamb's voice to me that
    cannot rise;
And sweet is all the land about, and all the flowers
    that blow;
And sweeter far is death than life, to me that long to
    go.

[330]

It seemed so hard at first, mother, to leave the blessed
    sun,
And now it seems as hard to stay; and yet, His will
    be done!
But still I think it can't be long before I find release;
And that good man, the clergyman, has told me words
    of peace.

O, blessings on his kindly voice, and on his silver hair!
And blessings on his whole life long, until he meet
    me there!
O, blessings on his kindly heart and on his silver
    head!
A thousand times I blest him, as he knelt beside my
    bed.

He taught me all the mercy, for he showed me all the
    sin;
Now, though my lamp was lighted late, there's One
    will let me in.
Nor would I now be well, mother, again, if that could
    be;
For my desire is but to pass to Him that died for me.

I did not hear the dog howl, mother, or the death-
    watch beat, —
There came a sweeter token when the night and morn-
    ing meet;
But sit beside my bed, mother, and put your hand in
    mine,
And Effie on the other side, and I will tell the sign.

[331]

All in the wild March-morning I heard the angels
 call, —
It was when the moon was setting, and the dark was
 over all;
The trees began to whisper, and the wind began to
 roll,
And in the wild March-morning I heard them call my
 soul.

For, lying broad awake, I thought of you and Effie
 dear;
I saw you sitting in the house, and I no longer here;
With all my strength I prayed for both, — and so I
 felt resigned,
And up the valley came a swell of music on the wind.

I thought that it was fancy, and I listened in my bed;
And then did something speak to me, — I know not
 what was said;
For great delight and shuddering took hold of all my
 mind,
And up the valley came again the music on the wind.

But you were sleeping; and I said, "It's not for them,
 — it's mine";
And if it comes three times, I thought, I take it for
 a sign.
And once again it came, and close beside the window-
 bars;
Then seemed to go right up to heaven and die among
 the stars.

[332]

So now I think my time is near; I trust it is. I know
The blessed music went that way my soul will have to
    go.
And for myself, indeed, I care not if I go to-day;
But Effie, you must comfort her when I am past away.

And say to Robin a kind word, and tell him not to
    fret;
There's many a worthier than I, would make him
    happy yet.
If I had lived — I cannot tell — I might have been
    his wife;
But all these things have ceased to be, with my desire
    of life.

O, look ! the sun begins to rise! the heavens are in a
    glow;
He shines upon a hundred fields, and all of them I
    know.
And there I move no longer now, and there his light
    may shine, —
Wild flowers in the valley for other hands than mine.

O, sweet and strange it seems to me, that ere this
    day is done
The voice that now is speaking may be beyond the
    sun, —

Forever and forever with those just souls and true, —
And what is life, that we should moan? why make
    we such ado?

[333]

Forever and forever, all in a blessed home,
And there to wait a little while till you and Effie come, —
To lie within the light of God, as I lie upon your
    breast, —
And the wicked cease from troubling, and the weary
    are at rest.

TO–MORROW

BY ALFRED TENNYSON

Her that yer Honor was spakin' to ? Whin, yer Honor ?
    last year —
Standin' here be the bridge, whin last yer Honor was
    here;
An', yer Honor, ye gev her the top o' the mornin';
    " To-morra," says she.
What did they call her, yer Honor ? They call'd her
    Molly Magee.
An' yer Honor's the thrue ould blood that always
    manes to be kind,
But there's rason in all things, yer Honor, for Molly
    was out o' her mind.

Shure, an' meself remimbers wan night comin' down be
    the sthrame,
An' it seems to me now like a bit o' yisterday in a
    dhrame —
Here where yer Honor seen her — there was but a
    slip of a moon,
But I hard thim — Molly Magee wid her batchelor,
    Danny O'Roon —

[334]

" You've been takin' a dhrop o' the crathur," and
    Danny says, " Troth, an' I been
Dhrinkin' yer health wid Shamus O'Shea at Katty's
    shebeen; *

But I must be lavin' ye soon." " Ochone, are ye goin'
    away ? "
" Goin' to cut the Sassenach whate," he says, " over
    the say "—
" An' whin will ye meet me agin? " An' I hard him,
    " Molly asthore,
" I'll meet ye agin to-morra," says he, " be the chapel-
    door."
" And whin' are ye goin' to lave me?" " Oh, Mon-
    day mornin'," says he;
" An' shure, thin, ye'll meet me to-morra?" " To-
    morra, to-morra, machree! "

Thin Molly's ould mother, yer Honor, that had no
    likin' for Dan,
Call'd from her cabin an' tould her to come away from
    the man;
An' Molly Magee kem flyin' acrass me, as light as a
    lark,
An' Dan stood there for a minute, an' thin wint into
    the dark.
But wirrah! the storm that night — the tundher, and
    rain that fell,
An' the sthrames runnin' down at the back o' the glin
    'ud 'a' dhrownded hell.

* Grog-shop.

[335]

But airth was at pace nixt mornin', an' hivin in its
    glory smiled,
As the Holy Mother o' Glory that smiles at her sleepin'
    child —
Ethen — she stept an the chapel-green, an' she turn'd
    herself roun',
Wid a diamond dhrop in her eye, for Danny was not
    to be foun';
An' many's the time that I watch'd her at mass,
    lettin' down the tear,
For the divil a Danny was there, yer Honor, for forty
    year.

Och, Molly Magee, wid the red o' the rose an' the
    white o' the May,
An' yer hair as black as the night, an' yer eyes as bright
    as the day!
Achora, yer laste little whishper was sweet as the lilt
    of a bird!
Acushla, ye set me heart batin' to music wid ivery
    word!
An' sorra the queen wid her sceptre in sich an illigant
    han',
An' the fall o' yer foot in the dance was as light as
    snow an the lan'.

An' the sun kem out of a cloud whiniver ye walkt in
    the shtreet,
An' Shamus O'Shea was yer shadda, an' laid himself
    undher yer feet;

[336]

An' I loved ye meself wid a heart an' a half, me darlin',
    an' he
'Ud 'a' shot his own soul for a kiss o' ye, Molly Magee.

But shure we wor betther frinds whin I cracked his
    skull for her sake,
An' he ped me back wid the best he could give at ould
    Donovan's wake —
For the boys wor about her agin, whin Dan didn't
    come to the fore,
An' Shamus along wid the rest, but she put thim all
    to the door.
An', afther, I thried her meself, av the bird 'ud come
    to me call,
But Molly, begorrah, 'ud listen to naither at all, at all.

An' her nabours an' frinds 'ud consowl an' condowl
    wid her, airly an' late.
" Your Danny," they says, " niver crasst over say to
    the Sassenach whate;
He's gone to the States, aroon, an' he's married another
    wife,
An' ye'll niver set eyes on the face of the thraithur agin
    in life!
An' to dhrame of a married man, death alive, is a
    mortial sin."
But Molly says, " I'd his hand-promise, an' shure
    he'll meet me agin."

An' afther her parints had inter'd glory, an' both in
    wan day,

She began to spake to herself, the crathur, an' whish-
    per, an' say,
"To-morra, to-morra!" An' Father Molowny he
    tuk her in han',
"Molly, ye're manin'," he says, "me dear, av I und-
    herstan',
Then ye'll meet yer parints agin an' yer Danny O'Roon
    afore God,
Wid His blessed marthyrs an' saints"; an' she gev him
    a frindly nod,
"To-morra, to-morra," she says, an' she didn't intind
    to desave,
But her wits wor dead, an' her hair was as white as
    the snow an a grave.

Arrah, now, here last month they wor diggin' the bog,
    an' they foun',
Dhrownded in black bog-wather, a corp' lyin' un-
    dher groun'.
Arrah, thin, they laid this body they foun' an the grass
Be the chapel-door, an' the people 'ud see it that wint
    into mass —
But a frish gineration had riz, an' most o' the ould
    was few,
An' I didn't know him meself, an' none o' the parish
    knew.

But Molly kem limpin' up wid her stick — she was
    lamed iv a knee.
Thin a slip of a gossoon call'd, "Div ye know him,
    Molly Magee?"

An' she stood up straight as the queen o' the world, —
    she lifted her head —
" He said he would meet me to-morra! " an' dhropt
    down dead an the dead.

Och, Molly, we thought, machree, ye would start
    back agin into life,
Whin we laid yez aich be aich, at yer wake, like hus-
    ban' an' wife.
Sorra the dhry eye thin but was wet for the frinds that
    was gone!
Sorra the silent throat but we hard it cryin' " Ochone! "
An' Shamus O'Shea, that has now ten childer, han'-
    some an' tall,
Him an' his childer wor keenin' as if he had lost thim
    all.

Thin his Riverence buried thim both in wan grave be
    the elder-tree,
The young man, Danny O'Roon, wid his ould woman,
    Molly Magee.

May all the flowers o' Jeroosilim blossom an' spring
    from the grass,
Imbrashin' an' kissin' aich other — as ye did — over
    yer Crass!
An' the lark fly out o' the flowers wid his song to the
    sun an' the moon,
An' tell thim in hivin about Molly Magee an' her
    Danny O'Roon,
Till holy St. Pether gets up wid his kays an' opens the
    gate!

An' shure, be the Crass, that's betther nor cuttin' the
    Sassenach whate,
To be there wid the Blessed Mother, an' saints an'
    marthyrs galore,
An' singin' yer " aves " an' " pathers " foriver an'
    ivermore.

LITTLE BILLEE

BY WILLIAM MAKEPEACE THACKERAY

There were three sailors of Bristol City
    Who took a boat and went to sea,
But first with beef and captain's biscuits
    And pickled pork they loaded she.

There was gorging Jack, and guzzling Jimmy,
    And the youngest he was little Billee;
Now when they'd got as far as the Equator,
    They'd nothing left but one split pea.

Says gorging Jack to guzzling Jimmy,
    " I am extremely hungaree."
To gorging Jack says guzzling Jimmy,
    " We've nothing left, us must eat we."

Says gorging Jack to guzzling Jimmy,
    " With one another we shouldn't agree!
Ther's little Bill, he's young and tender,
    We're old and tough, so let's eat he."

" O Billy! we're going to kill and eat you,
    So undo the button of your chemie."

[340]

When Bill received this information,
  He used his pocket-handkerchie.

" First let me say my catechism
  Which my poor mother taught to me."
" Make haste! make haste! " says guzzling Jimmy,
  While Jack pulled out his snickersnee.

Billy went up to the main-top-gallant mast,
  And down he fell on his bended knee,
He scarce had come to the Twelfth Commandment
  When up he jumps — " There's land I see!

" Jerusalem and Madagascar
  And North and South Amerikee,
There's the British flag a riding at anchor,
  With Admiral Napier, K. C. B."

So when they got aboard of the Admiral's,
  He hanged fat Jack and flogged Jimmee,
But as for little Bill he made him
  The Captain of a Seventy-three.

THE MAHOGANY-TREE

BY WILLIAM MAKEPEACE THACKERAY

Christmas is here;
Winds whistle shrill,
Icy and chill,
Little care we;

Little we fear
Weather without,
Sheltered about
The mahogany-tree.

Once on the boughs
Birds of rare plume
Sang, in its bloom;
Night-birds are we;
Here we carouse,
Singing, like them,
Perched round the stem
Of the jolly old tree.

Here let us sport,
Boys, as we sit, —
Laughter and wit
Flashing so free.
Life is but short,—
When we are gone,
Let them sing on,
Round the old tree.

Evenings we knew,
Happy as this;
Faces we miss,
Pleasant to see.
Kind hearts and true,
Gentle and just,
Peace to your dust!
We sing round the tree.

Care, like a dun,
Lurks at the gate:
Let the dog wait;
Happy we'll be!
Drink, every one;
Pile up the coals;
Fill the red bowls,
Round the old tree!

Drain we the cup. —
Friend, art afraid?
Spirits are laid
In the Red Sea.
Mantle it up;
Empty it yet;
Let us forget,
Round the old tree!

Sorrows, begone!
Life and its ills,
Duns and their bills,
Bid we to flee.
Come with the dawn,
Blue-devil sprite;
Leave us to-night,
Round the old tree!

THE VANISHING ARMY — G. A. R.

BY ARTHUR LEWIS TUBBS

From the wave-washed strand of the Golden Land
　　To the shores of the Eastern sea;
From the mountains that fringe the frozen North
　　To the Southland's flowery lea,
Comes the tramp of feet to the drummer's beat,
　　And the fife with its martial lay,
For the soldier boys are marching again,
　　To keep Memorial Day.

They were heroes all when the trumpet's call
　　Was heard in the days gone by;
For their hearts were brave and their hearts were true,
　　When they heard their country's cry.
But now, as they come to the fife and drum,
　　'Tis a loving tribute to pay,
And a path of flowers for these heroes of ours
　　Is spread on Memorial Day.

For the Stripes and Stars and the gleaming bars
　　To a nation of peace belong,
And a friendly cheer is all they hear,
　　Or the children's voices in song.
The weapons are rusted and silent now
　　That once they used in the fray;
They have only to bear the flowers fair,
　　As they march on Memorial Day.

The ranks grow thinner, the marchers few,
　　And to-day the grasses grow

On many a mound that was not found
    But one short year ago.
Whether they sleep the dreamless sleep,
    Or a little longer stay,
We'll never forget the boundless debt
    The nation can never pay.

Let Northern blossoms and Southern blooms
    Their tendrils intertwine:
A token of peace that years increase
    And love hath made divine.
And whether the heroes wore the blue,
    Or whether they wore the gray,
We own them ours and scatter the flowers
    For all, on Memorial Day.

WHEN BABY LAUGHS

BY A. J. WATERHOUSE

I wonder what she's dreaming 'bout,
    'Long some time in the night,
When of a sudden she laughs out
    In infantile delight.
I guess some angel from above,
    Swift winging to and fro,
Doth pause to whisper to my love
    Such words as babies know.

And when she laughs I guess he flies
    Straight where God's hosts rejoice,
And bears beyond the bending skies
    The music of her voice.

[345]

Then, through the mighty anthem's swell
    Her laughter striketh clear,
Sweeter than tone of any bell,
    And angels pause to hear.

For what hath Heaven compared with this:
    The laughter of a child,
Who still the note of pain doth miss,
    By dreams of night beguiled?
There beat so many voices here
    Of anguish and despair,
What wonder if they hold it dear,
    The laugh that hides no care?

So when my baby's laugh rings out,
    I watch her fleeting smile,
And say, " Some angel is about,"
    And listen for a while
To try to catch the whisper, too,
    In vain, in vain I try;
For angels heed what babies do,
    But pass their elders by.

THE HOLY CITY

BY F. E. WEATHERLY

Last night I lay a sleeping,
There came a dream so fair,
I stood in old Jerusalem
Beside the temple there.
I heard the children singing,

[346]

And ever as they sang,
Methought the voice of Angels
From Heav'n in answer rang;
Methought the voice of Angels
From Heav'n in answer rang.
Jerusalem! Jerusalem!
Lift up your gates and sing,
Hosanna in the highest!
Hosanna to your King!

And then methought my dream was chang'd,
The streets no longer rang,
Hush'd were the glad Hosannas
The little children sang.
The sun grew dark with mystery,
The morn was cold and chill
As the shadow of a cross arose upon a lonely hill.
As the shadow of a cross arose upon a lonely hill.
Jerusalem! Jerusalem!
Hark! how the Angels sing,
Hosanna in the highest,
Hosanna to your King.

And once again the scene was chang'd,
New earth there seem'd to be,
I saw the Holy City
Beside the tideless sea;
The light of God was on its streets,
The gates were open wide,
And all who would might enter,
And no one was denied.

[347]

No need of moon or stars by night,
Or sun to shine by day,
It was the new Jerusalem
That would not pass away,
It was the new Jerusalem
That would not pass away.
Jerusalem! Jerusalem!
Sing for the night is o'er!
Hosanna in the highest,
Hosanna for evermore!
Hosanna in the highest,
Hosanna for evermore!

THE QUESTIONER

BY CARL WERNER

I called the boy to my knee one day,
    And I said: "You're just past four;
Will you laugh in that same light-hearted way
    When you're turned, say, thirty more?"
Then I thought of a past I'd fain erase —
    More clouded skies than blue —
And I anxiously peered in his upturned face
    For it seemed to say:
    "Did you?"

I touched my lips to his tiny own
    And I said to the boy: "Heigh, ho!
Those lips are as sweet as the hay, new-mown;
    Will you keep them always so?"
Then back from those years came a rakish song —

With a ribald jest or two —
And I gazed at the child who knew no wrong,
  And I thought he asked:
  "Did you?"

I looked in his eyes, big, brown and clear,
  And I cried: "Oh, boy of mine!
Will you keep them true in the after-year?
  Will you leave no heart to pine?"
Then out of the past came another's eyes—
  Sad eyes of tear-dimmed blue —
Did he know they were not his mother's eyes?
  For he answered me:
  "Did you?"

LINES ON THE DEATH OF HIS SON CHARLES

BY DANIEL WEBSTER

My son, thou wast my heart's delight,
Thy morn of life was gay and cheery;
That morn has rushed to sudden night,
Thy father's house is sad and dreary.

I held thee on my knee, my son!
And kissed thee laughing, kissed thee weeping.
But ah! thy little day is done,
Thou'rt with thy angel sister sleeping.

The staff, on which my years should lean,
Is broken, ere those years come o'er me;
My funeral rites thou shouldst have seen,
But thou art in the tomb before me.

[349]

Thou rear'st to me no filial stone,
No parent's grave with tears beholdest;
Thou art my ancestor, my son!
And stand in Heaven's account the oldest.

On earth my lot was soonest cast,
Thy generation after mine,
Thou hast thy predecessors past;
Earlier eternity is thine.

I should have set before thine eyes
The road to Heaven, and showed it clear;
But thou untaught spring'st to the skies,
And leav'st thy teacher lingering here.

Sweet Seraph, I would learn of thee,
And hasten to partake thy bliss!
And oh! to thy world welcome me,
As first I welcomed thee to this.

Dear Angel, thou art safe in Heaven;
No prayers for thee need more be made;
Oh! let thy prayers for those be given
Who oft have blessed thy infant head.

My Father! I beheld thee born
And led thy tottering steps with care;
Before me risen to Heaven's bright morn,
My son! My Father! guide me there.

THE ANGELS OF BUENA VISTA

JOHN GREENLEAF WHITTIER

Speak and tell us, our Ximena, looking northward far
    away,
O'er the camp of the invaders, o'er the Mexican
    array,
Who is losing? who is winning? are they far or come
    they near?
Look abroad, and tell us, sister, whither rolls the
    storm we hear.

"Down the hills of Angostura still the storm of battle
    rolls;
Blood is flowing, men are dying; God have mercy
    on their souls!"
Who is losing? who is winning? — "Over hill and
    over plain,
I see but smoke of cannon clouding through the moun-
    tain rain."

Holy Mother! keep our brothers! Look, Ximena,
    look once more.
"Still I see the fearful whirlwind rolling darkly as
    before,
Bearing on, in strange confusion, friend and foeman,
    foot and horse,
Like some wild and troubled torrent sweeping down
    its mountain-course."

Look forth once more, Ximena! "Ah! the smoke
  has roll'd away;
And I see the Northern rifles gleaming down the
  ranks of gray.
Hark! that sudden blast of bugles! there the troop
  of Minon wheels;
There the Northern horses thunder, with the cannon
  at their heels.

"Jesu, pity! how it thickens! now retreat and now
  advance!
Right against the blazing cannon shivers Puebla's
  charging lance!
Down they go, the brave young riders; horse and foot
  together fall:
Like a ploughshare in the fallow, through them ploughs
  the Northern ball." ·

Nearer came the storm, and nearer, rolling fast and
  frightful on:
Speak, Ximena, speak and tell us, who has lost, and
  who has won?
"Alas! alas! I know not; friend and foe together
  fall,
O'er the dying rush the living; pray, my sisters, for
  them all!

"Lo! the wind the smoke is lifting: Blessed Mother,
  save my brain!
I can see the wounded crawling slowly out from heaps
  of slain.

Now they stagger, blind and bleeding; now they fall,
    and strive to rise;
Hasten, sisters, haste and save them, lest they die
    before our eyes!

"O my heart's love! O my dear one! lay thy poor
    head on my knee:
Dost thou know the lips that kiss thee? Canst thou
    hear me? canst thou see?
O my husband, brave and gentle! O my Bernal,
    look once more
On the blessed cross before thee! Mercy! mercy!
    all is o'er!"

Dry thy tears, my poor Ximena; lay thy dear one
    down to rest;
Let his hands be meekly folded, lay the cross upon
    his breast;
Let his dirge be sung hereafter, and his funeral masses
    said;
To-day, thou poor bereaved one, the living ask thy
    aid.

Close beside her, faintly moaning, fair and young, a
    soldier lay,
Torn with shot and pierced with lances, bleeding slow
    his life away;
But, as tenderly before him the lorn Ximena knelt,
She saw the Northern eagle shining on his pistol-
    belt.

[353]

With a stifled cry of horror straight she turn'd away
    her head;
With a sad and bitter feeling look'd she back upon
    her dead;
But she heard the youth's low moaning, and his
    struggling breath of pain,
And she raised the cooling water to his parching lips
    again.

Whispered low the dying soldier, press'd her hand and
    faintly smiled:
Was that pitying face his mother's? did she watch
    beside her child?
All his stranger words with meaning her woman's
    heart supplied;
With her kiss upon his forehead, "Mother!" mur-
    mured he and died!

"A bitter curse upon them, poor boy, who led thee
    forth,
From some gentle sad-eyed mother, weeping, lonely,
    in the North!"
Spake the mournful Mexic woman, as she laid him
    with her dead,
And turn'd to soothe the living, and bind the wounds
    which bled.

Look forth once more, Ximena! "Like a cloud before
    the wind
Rolls the battle down the mountain, leaving blood
    and death behind;

[354]

Ah! they plead in vain for mercy; in the dust the
    wounded strive;
Hide your faces, holy angels! O thou Christ of God,
    forgive!''

Sink, O night, among thy mountains! let the cool
    gray shadows fall;
Dying brothers, fighting demons, drop thy curtain
    over all!
Through the thickening winter twilight, wide apart
    the battle roll'd,
In its sheath the sabre rested, and the cannon's lips
    grew cold.

But the noble Mexic women still their holy task pur-
    sued,
Through that long, dark night of sorrow, worn and
    faint and lacking food;
Over weak and suffering brothers, with a tender care
    they hung,
And the dying foeman bless'd them in a strange and
    Northern tongue.

Not wholly lost, O Father! is this evil world of ours;
Upward, through its blood and ashes, spring afresh
    the Eden flowers;
From its smoking hell of battle, Love and Pity send
    their prayer,
And still thy white-wing'd angels hover dimly in our
    air.

[355]

THE BAREFOOT BOY

BY JOHN GREENLEAF WHITTIER

Blessings on thee, little man,
Barefoot boy, with cheek of tan!
With thy turned-up pantaloons,
And thy merry whistled tunes;
With thy red lip, redder still
Kissed by strawberries on the hill;
With the sunshine on thy face,
Through thy torn brim's jaunty grace;
From my heart I give thee joy, —
I was once a barefoot boy!
Prince thou art, — the grown-up man
Only is republican.
Let the million-dollared ride!
Barefoot, trudging at his side,
Thou hast more than he can buy
In the reach of ear and eye, —
Outward sunshine, inward joy:
Blessings on thee, barefoot boy!

O for boyhood's painless play,
Sleep that wakes in laughing day,
Health that mocks the doctor's rules,
Knowledge never learned of schools,
Of the wild bee's morning chase,
Of the wild-flower's time and place,
Flight of fowl and habitude
Of the tenants of the wood;
How the tortoise bears his shell,

How the woodchuck digs his cell,
And the ground-mole sinks his well;
How the robin feeds her young,
How the oriole's nest is hung;
Where the whitest lilies blow,
Where the freshest berries grow,
Where the ground-nut trails its vine,
Where the wood-grape's clusters shine;
Of the black wasp's cunning way,
Mason of his walls of clay,
And the architectural plans
Of gray hornet artisans!—
For, eschewing books and tasks,
Nature answers all he asks;
Hand in hand with her he walks,
Face to face with her he talks,
Part and parcel of her joy,—
Blessings on the barefoot boy!

O for boyhood's time of June,
Crowding years in one brief moon,
When all things I heard or saw,
Me, their master, waited for.
I was rich in flowers and trees,
Humming-birds and honey-bees;
For my sport the squirrel played,
Plied the snouted mole his spade;
For my taste the blackberry cone
Purpled over hedge and stone;
Laughed the brook for my delight
Through the day and through the night

[357]

Whispering at the garden wall,
Talked with me from fall to fall;
Mine the sand-rimmed pickerel pond,
Mine the walnut slopes beyond,
Mine, on bending orchard trees,
Apples of Hesperides!
Still as my horizon grew,
Larger grew my riches too;
All the world I saw or knew
Seemed a complex Chinese toy,
Fashioned for a barefoot boy!

O for festal dainties spread,
Like my bowl of milk and bread, —
Pewter spoon and bowl of wood,
On the door-stone, gray and rude!
O'er me, like a regal tent,
Cloudy-ribbed, the sunset bent,
Purple-curtained, fringed with gold,
Looped in many a wind-swung fold;
While for music came the play
Of the pied frogs' orchestra;
And, to light the noisy choir,
Lit the fly his lamp of fire.
I was monarch: pomp and joy
Waited on the barefoot boy!

Cheerly, then, my little man,
Live and laugh, as boyhood can!
Though the flinty slopes be hard,
Stubble-speared the new-mown sward,

Every morn shall lead thee through
Fresh baptisms of the dew;
Every evening from thy feet
Shall the cool wind kiss the heat.
All too soon these feet must hide
In the prison cells of pride,
Lose the freedom of the sod,
Like a colt's for work be shod,
Made to tread the mills of toil,
Up and down in ceaseless moil:
Happy if their track be found
Never on forbidden ground;
Happy if they sink not in
Quick and treacherous sands of sin.
Ah! that thou couldst know thy joy,
Ere it passes, barefoot boy!

IN SCHOOL–DAYS

BY JOHN GREENLEAF WHITTIER

Still sits the school-house by the road,
  A ragged beggar sunning;
Around it still the sumachs grow,
  And blackberry-vines are running.

Within, the master's desk is seen,
  Deep scarred by raps official;
The warping floor, the battered seats,
  The jack-knife's carved initial;

The charcoal frescos on its wall;
  Its door's worn sill, betraying

[359]

The feet that, creeping slow to school,
  Went storming out to playing!

Long years ago a winter sun
  Shone over it at setting;
Lit up its western window-panes,
  And low eaves' icy fretting.

It touched the tangled golden curls,
  And brown eyes full of grieving,
Of one who still her steps delayed
  When all the school were leaving.

For near her stood the little boy
  Her childish favor singled;
His cap pulled low upon a face
  Where pride and shame were mingled.

Pushing with restless feet the snow
  To right and left, he lingered; —
As restlessly her tiny hands
  The blue-checked apron fingered.

He saw her lift her eyes; he felt
  The soft hand's light caressing,
And heard the tremble of her voice,
  As if a fault confessing.

" I'm sorry that I spelt the word:
    I hate to go above you,
Because," — the brown eyes lower fell, —
    " Because, you see, I love you! "

[360]

Still memory to a gray-haired man
    That sweet child-face is showing.
Dear girl! the grasses on her grave
    Have forty years been growing!

He lives to learn, in life's hard school,
    How few who pass above him
Lament their triumph and his loss,
    Like her, — because they love him.

MAUD MULLER

BY JOHN GREENLEAF WHITTIER

Maud Muller, on a summer's day,
Raked the meadow sweet with hay.

Beneath her torn hat glowed the wealth
Of simple beauty and rustic health.

Singing, she wrought, and her merry glee
The mock-bird echoed from his tree.

But, when she glanced to the far-off town,
White from its hill-slope looking down,

The sweet song died, and a vague unrest
And a nameless longing filled her breast, —

A wish, that she hardly dared to own,
For something better than she had known.

[361]

The Judge rode slowly down the lane,
Smoothing his horse's chestnut mane.

He drew his bridle in the shade
Of the apple-trees, to greet the maid,

And ask a draught from the spring that flowed
Through the meadow, across the road.

She stooped where the cool spring bubbled up,
And filled for him her small tin cup,

And blushed as she gave it, looking down
On her feet so bare, and her tattered gown.

" Thanks! " said the Judge, " a sweeter draught
From a fairer hand was never quaffed."

He spoke of the grass and flowers and trees,
Of the singing birds and the humming bees;

Then talked of the haying, and wondered whether
The cloud in the west would bring foul weather.

And Maud forgot her brier-torn gown,
And her graceful ankles, bare and brown,

And listened, while a pleased surprise
Looked from her long-lashed hazel eyes.

At last, like one who for delay
Seeks a vain excuse, he rode away.

Maud Muller looked and sighed: " Ah me!
That I the Judge's bride might be!

" He would dress me up in silks so fine,
  And praise and toast me at his wine.

" My father should wear a broadcloth coat,
  My brother should sail a painted boat.

" I'd dress my mother so grand and gay,
  And the baby should have a new toy each day.

" And I'd feed the hungry and clothe the poor,
  And all should bless me who left our door."

The Judge looked back as he climbed the hill,
And saw Maud Muller standing still:

" A form more fair, a face more sweet,
  Ne'er hath it been my lot to meet.

" And her modest answer and graceful air
  Show her wise and good as she is fair.

" Would she were mine, and I to-day,
  Like her, a harvester of hay.

" No doubtful balance of rights and wrongs,
  Nor weary lawyers with endless tongues,

" But low of cattle, and song of birds,
  And health, and quiet, and loving words."

[363]

But he thought of his sister, proud and cold,
And his mother, vain of her rank and gold.

So, closing his heart, the Judge rode on,
And Maud was left in the field alone.

But the lawyers smiled that afternoon,
When he hummed in court an old love tune;

And the young girl mused beside the well,
Till the rain on the unraked clover fell.

He wedded a wife of richest dower,
Who lived for fashion, as he for power.

Yet oft, in his marble hearth's bright glow,
He watched a picture come and go:

And sweet Maud Muller's hazel eyes
Looked out in their innocent surprise.

Oft, when the wine in his glass was red,
He longed for the wayside well instead,

And closed his eyes on his garnished rooms,
To dream of meadows and clover blooms;

And the proud man sighed with a secret pain
" Ah, that I were free again!

" Free as when I rode that day
Where the barefoot maiden raked the hay."

[364]

She wedded a man unlearned and poor,
And many children played round her door.

But care and sorrow, and child-birth pain,
Left their traces on heart and brain.

And oft, when the summer sun shone hot
On the new-mown hay in the meadow lot,

And she heard the little spring brook fall
Over the roadside, through the wall,

In the shade of the apple-tree again
She saw a rider draw his rein,

And, gazing down with a timid grace,
She felt his pleased eyes read her face.

Sometimes her narrow kitchen walls
Stretched away into stately halls;

The weary wheel to a spinnet turned,
The tallow candle an astral burned;

And for him who sat by the chimney lug,
Dozing and grumbling o'er pipe and mug,

A manly form at her side she saw,
And joy was duty and love was law.

Then she took up her burden of life again,
Saying only, " It might have been."

[365]

Alas for maiden, alas for judge,
For rich repiner and household drudge!

God pity them both! and pity us all,
Who vainly the dreams of youth recall;

For of all sad words of tongue or pen,
The saddest are these: " It might have been! "

Ah, well! for us all some sweet hope lies
Deeply buried from human eyes;

And, in the hereafter, angels may
Roll the stone from its grave away!

THE SHEPHERD'S RESOLUTION

BY GEORGE WITHER

Shall I, wasting in despair,
Die because a woman's fair?
Or make pale my cheeks with care
'Cause another's rosy are?
Be she fairer than the day,
Or the flowery meads in May, —
  If she be not so to me,
  What care I how fair she be?

Shall my foolish heart be pined
'Cause I see a woman kind?
Or a well-disposèd nature
Joinèd with a lovely feature?

Be she meeker, kinder than
The turtle-dove or pelican, —
    If she be not so to me,
      What care I how kind she be?

Shall a woman's virtues move
Me to perish for her love?
Or, her well deservings known,
Make me quite forget mine own?
Be she with that goodness blest
Which may merit name of best, —
    If she be not such to me,
      What care I how good she be?

'Cause her fortune seems too high,
Shall I play the fool and die?
Those that bear a noble mind
Where they want of riches find,
Think what with them they would do
That without them dare to woo:
    And unless that mind I see,
      What care I how great she be?

Great, or good, or kind, or fair,
I will ne'er the more despair:
If she love me, this believe, —
I will die ere she shall grieve.
If she slight me when I woo,
I can scorn and let her go; —
    For if she be not for me,
      What care I for whom she be?

[367]

BURIAL OF SIR JOHN MOORE

BY CHARLES WOLFE

Not a drum was heard, not a funeral note,
　As his corse to the rampart we hurried;
Not a soldier discharged his farewell shot
　O'er the grave where our hero we buried.

We buried him darkly, at dead of night,
　The sods with our bayonets turning;
By the struggling moonbeams' misty light,
　And the lantern dimly burning.

No useless coffin enclosed his breast,
　Not in sheet or in shroud we wound him;
But he lay, like a warrior taking his rest,
　With his martial cloak around him,

Few and short were the prayers we said,
　And we spoke not a word of sorrow;
But we steadfastly gazed on the face of the dead,
　And we bitterly thought of the morrow.

We thought, as we hollowed his narrow bed,
　And smoothed down his lonely pillow,
That the foe and the stranger would tread o'er his head,
　And we far away on the billow!

Lightly they'll talk of the spirit that's gone,
　And o'er his cold ashes upbraid him;
But little he'll reck, if they let him sleep on
　In the grave where a Briton has laid him!

[368]

But half of our heavy task was done,
    When the clock struck the hour for retiring;
And we heard the distant and random gun
    That the foe was suddenly firing.

Slowly and sadly we laid him down,
    From the field of his fame fresh and gory!
We carved not a line, and we raised not a stone,
    But we left him alone with his glory.

IF I HAD THOUGHT THOU COULDST HAVE DIED

BY CHARLES WOLFE

If I had thought thou couldst have died,
    I might not weep for thee;
But I forgot, when by thy side,
    That thou couldst mortal be!
It never through my mind had passed,
    The time would e'er be o'er, —
And I on thee should look my last,
    And thou shouldst smile no more!

And still upon that face I look,
    And think 'twill smile again;
And still the thought I will not brook
    That I must look in vain!
But when I speak, thou dost not say
    What thou ne'er left'st unsaid;
And now I feel, as well I may,
    Sweet Mary! thou art dead!

[369]

If thou wouldst stay, e'en as thou art,
   All cold and all serene, —
I still might press thy silent heart,
   And where thy smiles have been!
While e'en thy chill, bleak corse I have,
   Thou seemest still mine own;
But then I lay thee in thy grave, —
   And I am now alone!

I do not think, where'er thou art,
   Thou hast forgotten me;
And I, perhaps, may soothe this heart,
   In thinking too of thee:
Yet there was round thee such a dawn
   Of light ne'er seen before, —
As fancy never could have drawn,
   And never can restore!

THE OLD OAKEN BUCKET
BY SAMUEL WOODWORTH

How dear to this heart are the scenes of my childhood,
   When fond recollection presents them to view!
The orchard, the meadow, the deep-tangled wildwood,
   And every loved spot which my infancy knew;
The wide-spreading pond, and the mill which stood
      by it,
   The bridge, and the rock where the cataract fell;
The cot of my father, the dairy-house nigh it,
   And e'en the rude bucket which hung in the well, —
The old oaken bucket, the iron-bound bucket,
The moss-covered bucket which hung in the well.

That moss-covered vessel I hail as a treasure;
 For often, at noon, when returned from the field,
I found it the source of an exquisite pleasure,
 The purest and sweetest that nature can yield.
How ardent I seized it, with hands that were glowing!
 And quick to the white-pebbled bottom it fell;
Then soon, with the emblem of truth overflowing,
 And dripping with coolness, it rose from the well,—
The old oaken bucket, the iron-bound bucket,
The moss-covered bucket, arose from the well.

How sweet from the green mossy brim to receive it,
 As, poised on the curb, it inclined to my lips!
Not a full blushing goblet could tempt me to leave it,
 Though filled with the nectar that Jupiter sips.
And now, far removed from the loved situation,
 The tear of regret will intrusively swell,
As fancy reverts to my father's plantation,
 And sighs for the bucket which hangs in the well,—
The old oaken bucket, the iron-bound bucket,
The moss-covered bucket which hangs in the well.

WE ARE SEVEN

BY WILLIAM WORDSWORTH

  A simple child,
 That lightly draws its breath,
And feels its life in every limb,
 What should it know of death?

I met a little cottage girl:
 She was eight years old, she said;

[371]

Her hair was thick with many a curl
  That clustered round her head.

She had a rustic, woodland air,
  And she was wildly clad;
Her eyes were fair, and very fair;—
  Her beauty made me glad.

"Sisters and brothers, little maid,
  How many may you be?"
"How many? Seven in all," she said,
  And wondering looked at me.

"And where are they? I pray you tell."
  She answered, "Seven are we;
And two of us at Conway dwell,
  And two are gone to sea;

"Two of us in the churchyard lie,
  My sister and my brother;
And, in the churchyard cottage, I
  Dwell near them with my mother."

"You say that two at Conway dwell,
  And two are gone to sea,
Yet ye are seven! I pray you tell,
  Sweet maid, how this may be."

Then did the little maid reply,
  "Seven boys and girls are we;
Two of us in the churchyard lie
  Beneath the churchyard tree."

[372]

" You run about, my little maid;
   Your limbs they are alive;
If two are in the churchyard laid,
   Then ye are only five."

" Their graves are green, they may be seen,"
   The little maid replied:
" Twelve steps or more from my mother's door,
   And they are side by side.

" My stockings there I often knit,
   My kerchief there I hem;
And there upon the ground I sit,
   And sing a song to them.

" And often after sunset, sir,
   When it is light and fair,
I take my little porringer
   And eat my supper there.

" The first that died was Sister Jane;
   In bed she moaning lay,
Till God released her of her pain;
   And then she went away.

" So in the churchyard she was laid;
   And, when the grass was dry,
Together round her grave we played,
   My brother John and I.

" And when the ground was white with snow.
   And I could run and slide,

[373]

My brother John was forced to go,
  And he lies by her side."

" How many are you, then," said I,
  " If they two are in heaven? "
Quick was the little maid's reply!
  " O Master! we are seven."

" But they are dead; those two are dead!
  Their spirits are in heaven! "
'T was throwing words away; for still
The little maid would have her will,
  And said, " Nay, we are seven."

THE BEAUTIFUL GATE

AUTHOR UNKNOWN

When mysterious whispers are floating about,
  And voices that will not be still
Shall summon me hence from the slippery shore
  To the waves that are silent and still;
When I look with changed eyes at the home of the
    blest,
  Far out of the reach of the sea,
Will any one stand at that beautiful gate
  Waiting and watching for me?

There are friendless and suffering strangers around,
  There are tempted and poor I must meet;
There are dear ones at home I may bless with my love,
  There are wretched ones pacing the street;

[374]

There are many unthought of, whom, happy and blest,
  In the land of the good I shall see:
Will any of these at the beautiful gate
  Be waiting and watching for me?

There are old and forsaken, who linger awhile
  In the homes which their dearest have left,
And an action of love and a few gentle words
  Might cheer the sad spirit bereft;
But the reaper is near to the long-standing corn,
  The weary shall soon be set free;
Will any of these at the beautiful gate
  Be waiting and watching for me?

There are little ones glancing about on my path
  In need of a friend or a guide;
There are dim little eyes looking up into mine,
  Whose tears could be easily dried;
But Jesus may beckon the children away
  In the midst of their grief or their glee:
Will any of them at the beautiful gate
  Be waiting and watching for me?

I may be brought there by the manifold grace
  Of the Saviour who loved to forgive,
Though I bless not the hungry ones near to my side,
  Only pray for myself while I live;
But I think I should mourn o'er my selfish neglect,
  If sorrow in heaven can be,
If no one should stand at that beautiful gate
  Waiting and watching for me!

[375]

BLUE AND GRAY

AUTHOR UNKNOWN

" O mother! what do they mean by blue?
   And what do they mean by gray?"
Was heard from the lips of a little child,
   As she bounded in from play.
The mother's eyes filled up with tears:
   She turned to her darling fair,
And smoothed away from the sunny brow
   Its treasures of golden hair.

" Why, mother's eyes are blue, my sweet,
   And grandpa's hair is gray;
And the love we bear our darling child,
   Grows stronger every day."
" But what did they mean?" persisted the child:
   " For I saw two cripples to-day;
And one of them said he fought for the blue;
   The other, he fought for the gray.

" Now, he of the blue had lost a leg;
   The other had but one arm:
And both seemed worn and weary and sad;
   Yet their greeting was kind and warm.
They told of battles in days gone by,
   Till it made my young blood thrill:
The leg was lost in the Wilderness fight;
   And the arm, on Malvern Hill.

" They sat on the stones by the farm-yard gate,
   And talked for an hour or more,

[376]

Till their eyes grew bright, and their hearts seemed
    warm,
  With fighting their battles o'er.
And parting at last with a friendly grasp,
  In a kindly, brotherly way,
Each called on God to speed the time
  Uniting the blue and the gray."

Then the mother thought of other days,—
  Two stalwart boys from her riven;
How they knelt at her side, and, lisping, prayed,—
  "Our Father which art in heaven";
How one wore the gray, and the other the blue;
  How they passed away from sight,
And had gone to the land where gray and blue
  Are merged in colors of light.

And she answered her darling with golden hair,—
  While her heart was sadly wrung
With the thoughts awakened in that sad hour
  By her innocent, prattling tongue,—
"The blue and the gray are the colors of God:
  They are seen in the sky at even;
And many a noble, gallant soul
  Has found them passports to heaven."

CONGRESSMAN JONES

BY AN UNKNOWN AUTHOR IN THE
CHICAGO RECORD-HERALD

When Jones left Badger's Corners he was racked by
doubt and fear,
And a weight was on his shoulders as he heard his
neighbors cheer;
He was going where great statesmen with majestic
brows would stand,
In the halls of marble, wisely making statutes for the
land.

In his heart Jones knew how little he excelled the
common ones,
Who were sending him to mingle with and challenge
the "big guns";
In his fancy he could plainly see himself unnoticed
there,
Where the splendid statesmen towered and with
wisdom filled the air.

Jones was awed when he beheld them and first heard
them called by name;
Still the glamour was upon them, he was dazzled by
their fame,
And he watched them, full of wonder, yet a little sadly,
too,
For in searching out the giants he found very, very few.

Day by day he saw and heard them, day by day his
awe decreased;

He had feared and he had doubted, but at length his
    trembling ceased;
He had learned at last that greatness is but being
    stationed where
Almost any one might dazzle if the fates had set him
    there.

DO YE THINK OF THE DAYS THAT ARE GONE?

AUTHOR UNKNOWN

" Do ye think of the days that are gone, Jeanie,
    As ye sit by your fire at night?
Do ye wish that the morn would bring back the time
    When your heart and your step were so light? "
" I think of the days that are gone, Robin,
    And of all that I joyed in then;
But the brightest that ever rose on me
    I have never wished back again! "

" Do ye think of the hopes that are gone, Jeanie,
    As ye sit by your fire at night?
Do ye gather them up as they faded fast,
    Like buds with an early blight? "
" I think of the hopes that are gone, Robin,
    And I mourn not their stay was fleet;
For they fell as the leaves of the red rose fall,
    And were even in falling sweet! "

" Do ye think of the friends that are gone, Jeanie,
    As ye sit by your fire at night?
Do ye wish they were round you again once more,

[379]

By the hearth that they made so bright?"
"I think of the friends that are gone, Robin,
  They are dear to my heart as then;
But the best and the dearest among them all
  I have never wished back again!"

THE GOOD OLD WAY

AUTHOR UNKNOWN

John Mann had a wife who was kind and true, —
  A wife who loved him well;
She cared for the house and their only child;
  But if I the truth must tell,
She fretted and pined because John was poor
  And his business was slow to pay;
But he only said, when she talked of change,
  "We'll stick to the good old way!"

She saw her neighbors were growing rich
  And dwelling in houses grand;
That she was living in poverty,
  With wealth upon every hand;
And she urged her husband to speculate,
  To risk his earnings at play;
But he only said, "My dearest wife,
  We'll stick to the good old way."

For he knew that the money that's quickly got
  Is the money that's quickly lost;
And the money that stays is the money earned
  At honest endeavor's cost.

[380]

So he plodded along in his honest style,
    And he bettered himself each day,
And he only said to his fretful wife,
    " We'll stick to the good old way."

And at last there came a terrible crash,
    When beggary, want, and shame
Came down on the homes of their wealthy friends,
    While John's remained the same;
For he had no debts and he gave no trust,
    " My motto is this," he'd say, —
" It's a charm against panics of every kind, —
    'Tis stick to the good old way!"

And his wife looked round on the little house
    That was every nail their own,
And she asked forgiveness of honest John
    For the peevish mistrust she had shown;
But he only said, as her tearful face
    Upon his shoulder lay,
" The good old way is the best way, wife;
    We'll stick to the good old way."

THE INDIAN'S PRAYER

AUTHOR UNKNOWN

" Let me go to my home in the far distant west,
To the scenes of my childhood in innocence blest;
Where the tall cedars wave and the bright waters flow,
Where my fathers repose — let me go!   Let me go!

[381]

" Let me go to the spot where the cataract plays,
Where oft I have sported in boyhood's bright days;
And greet my poor mother, whose heart will o'erflow
At the sight of her child — let me go! Let me go!

" Let me go to my sire, by whose battle-scarred side
I have sported so oft in the morn of my pride;
And exulted to conquer the insolent foe —
To my father, the chief, let me go! Let me go!

" And, oh! let me go to my flashing-eyed maid,
Who taught me to love 'neath the green willow's shade,
Whose heart, like the fawn's, leaps as pure as the snow
To the bosom it loves — let me go! Let me go!

" And oh! let me go to my wild forest home —
No more from its life-cheering pleasures to roam:
'Neath the groves of the glen let my ashes lie low —
To my home in the woods let me go! Let me go! "

JOHN HOWARD PAYNE

AUTHOR UNKNOWN

This poem was published in a Washington, D.C., paper in an
article on " The Nation's Song," without the name of the author and
without a title.

'T was Christmas night in Paris,
  Rainy and dark and drear;
But within one gilded mansion
  Was happy Christmas cheer.

Merrily in the perfumed air
  The Christmas carols rung;
Then softly, slowly, sweetly,
  Dear "Home, Sweet Home" was sung.

Without, against the window sill,
  To shield him from the rain,
With streaming eyes and breaking heart,
  Crouched lonely Howard Payne.

" My song," he cried in anguish deep,
  " Is sung in every home,
While I, without a single friend,
  A homeless wand'rer roam.

" Yes, it was on this self-same spot,
  Without a crust of bread,
With not one place to call my own,
  Nowhere to rest my head,

" I sat me down and wrote that song,
  That o'er the world doth ring;
They little think who's listening now —
  Those happy ones that sing."

'Twas true; before that window once,
  Friendless amid the throng,
And yearning for the joys of home,
  He wrote his world-famed song.

LAMENT FOR LAFAYETTE

AUTHOR UNKNOWN

All lonely and cold, in the sepulchre slumbers
  The giant of freedom, the chosen of fame!
Too high in the theme for my harp's lowly numbers;
  Yet fain would I twine me a wreath for that name
Which proudly shines forth in the tablet of glory,
  Unsullied by faction, untarnished by guile;
The loftiest theme for the bard's raptured story;
  The name by which freemen met death with a smile.

Then arise, ye proud bards! give our hearts' mighty
    sadness
  A voice not unworthy a theme so sublime,
For him, the bright day-star of freedom and gladness,
  Whose memory will glow through the far flight of
    time!
He is gone, and forever! the pride of our nation,
  That bright sun of freedom in glory hath set;
The heroes who bled for our country's salvation
  Now joy in thy presence, O brave Lafayette!

Thou camest to our shore when the day-star of freedom
  Was proudly dispelling dark tyranny's night,
When millions awoke to the rank she decreed them,
  And the millions of despots were scattered in flight;
When the star-spangled banner waves sheen in the
    morning
  The heart of the freeman will bound at thy name;
Thou champion of freedom! fell tyranny scorning,
  One world was too small for the blaze of thy fame!

[384]

Bright, bright is the path thou hast left of thy glory,
 Amid the world's darkness, which ne'er shall decline,
For the light of thy fame on the ages before thee,
 With splendor unsullied, forever will shine;
When freedom's bright fabric lay blackened in ruin,
 While bloodthirsty tyrants usurped the dread sway
At the roots of the proud tree of liberty hewing,
 All hopes for the land of thy love died away.

Thou art gone! thy pure soul on its voyage hath
  started;
 From its ashes the phœnix of freedom hath flown,
To join the bright phalanx of heroes departed,
 Who dwell in the light of a fame like thine own.
Farewell, thou last star of that bright constellation
 Of heroes whose glory can never depart;
Thy fame hath no limit of kindred or nation;
 Thy name is enshrined in each patriot's heart.

With Washington's blended, for ever the glory
 Shall form the proud theme of our bard's burning
  lays,
While the banner of freedom shall proudly wave o'er
  thee,
 Thou mighty departed! thou light of our days;
But still! my wild harp, all in vain we lament him;
 His praise must be sung by some loftier lyre;
Let the soul-raptured bard use the gift heaven hath
  lent him,
 And weave for our hero a requiem of fire!

[385]

LINES ON THE DEATH OF BABY

B. H.

One little bud the less,
In nature's garden grows.
One tiny voice more, hush'd
In death's deep calm repose.

Th' prattling birdie sleeps,
Sleeps quietly alone,
While o'er his form th' wind
A requiem low doth moan.

In Paradise will bloom
And beauteously grow
Th' bud cut short and chill'd
By piercing winds below.

Close in his Maker's arms
The little one is press'd,
His playmates seraphim,
A cherub 'mong the bless'd.

LOOK AHEAD

AUTHOR UNKNOWN

Whatever you do in this wonderful world,
In business, in church, or at play;
Whatever of gain or of loss you have met
With the others who go your way,
Keep out of the past
From the first to the last,

[386]

And away from its worries stay;
The present has wealth you would never suspect,
If prudent you are, and wisely elect
To live in the light of to-day.

The things that are past did very well once;
To-day they are rusty and stale.
That trouble you had with your fellow man —
Did you struggle in vain and fail?
What of it, indeed?
There is all the more need
That you start on a different trail.
Don't take to the woods whatever you do,
Just look right ahead; there's a fortune for you
In keeping a well-trimmed sail.

So cramped can we be in our mental states,
So burdened with might-have-beens,
That life will become a woful waste
For its many outs and ins.
But stop and reflect
You will never be wrecked
By your own or another's sins,
If the past you will keep in its proper place
And meet what is yours with a candid face —
'Tis the man of to-day who wins.

MOTHER'S FOOL

AUTHOR UNKNOWN

" 'Tis plain to see," said a farmer's wife,
" These boys will make their mark in life;
They were never made to handle a hoe,
And at once to a college ought to go;
There's Fred, he's little better than a fool,
But John and Henry must go to school."

" Well, really, wife," quoth Farmer Brown,
As he sat his mug of cider down,
" Fred does more work in a day for me
Than both his brothers do in three.
Book larnin' will never plant one's corn,
Nor hoe potatoes, sure's you're born,
Nor mend a rod of broken fence —
For my part give me common sense."

But his wife was bound the roost to rule,
And John and Henry were sent to school,
While Fred, of course, was left behind
Because his mother said he had no mind.

Five years at school the students spent;
Then into business each one went.
John learned to play the flute and fiddle,
And parted his hair, of course, in the middle;
While his brother looked rather higher than he,
And hung out a sign, " H. Brown, M. D."

[388]

Meanwhile, at home, their brother Fred
Had taken a notion into his head;
But he quietly trimmed his apple trees,
And weeded onions and planted peas,
While somehow or other, by hook or crook,
He managed to read full many a book.
Until at last his father said
He was getting " book larnin' " into his head;
" But for all that," added Farmer Brown,
" He's the smartest boy there is in town."

The war broke out and Captain Fred
A hundred men to battle led,
And when the rebel flag came down,
Went marching home as General Brown.
But he went to work on the farm again,
And planted corn and sowed his grain;
He shingled the barn and mended the fence,
Till people declared he had common sense.

Now, common sense was very rare,
And the State House needed a portion there;
And his brothers, who went to the city school,
Came home to live with " mother's fool."

NOW I LAY ME DOWN TO SLEEP

AUTHOR UNKNOWN

[Found in the knapsack of a soldier of the Civil War after he had been slain in battle.]

Near the camp-fire's flickering light,
　　In my blanket bed I lie,
Gazing through the shades of night
　　And the twinkling stars on high;
O'er me spirits in the air
　　Silent vigils seem to keep,
As I breathe my childhood's prayer,
　　" Now I lay me down to sleep."

Sadly sings the whip-poor-will
　　In the boughs of yonder tree;
Laughingly the dancing rill
　　Swells the midnight melody.
Foemen may be lurking near,
　　In the cañon dark and deep;
Low I breathe in Jesus' ear:
　　" I pray Thee, Lord, my soul to keep."

'Mid those stars one face I see —
　　One the Saviour turned away —
Mother, who in infancy
　　Taught my baby lips to pray;
Her sweet spirit hovers near
　　In this lonely mountain-brake.
Take me to her Saviour dear
　　" If I should die before I wake."

Fainter grows the flickering light,
  As each ember slowly dies;
Plaintively the birds of night
  Fill the air with sad'ning cries;
Over me they seem to cry:
  " You may never more awake."
Low I lisp: " If I should die,
  I pray Thee, Lord, my soul to take."

Now I lay me down to sleep;
I pray Thee, Lord, my soul to keep.
If I should die before I wake,
I pray Thee, Lord, my soul to take.

THE OLD SONGS

AUTHOR UNKNOWN

These ragtime songs they're singin' now may be the
    proper thing,
But they don't hit me like the songs us youngsters
    used to sing.
I never hear no ragtime songs, no matter where I roam,
Kin makes the heartstrings quiver like "My Old
    Kentucky Home."
"Lorena" was another song that all our heartstrings
    wrung
Around at social gatherin's when us old folks was
    young.

We'd "Wait Fer the Wagon," an' we'd tell of "Nellie
    Gray,"

An' "Oh, Susannah" 'd get her turn, an' likewise
"Old Dog Tray";
An' "Massa's in the Cold, Cold Ground," we'd sing
that by the hour,
Then, feelin' sad, we'd finish with "A Little Faded
Flower."
Them were the songs that 'round our hearts the spell
o' music flung,
Them were the songs that people sang when us old
folks was young.

We knowed some operatic songs as well as these, b'gee!
"The Heart Bowed Down," likewise its mate, "Then
You'll Remember Me."
An' when we tired of opery and simpler things we'd try
An' make the rafters fairly ring with "Comin' Thro'
the Rye."
Oh, you kin have your ragtime songs; gimme the songs
they sung
Around at social gatherin's when us old folks was
young.

ROCK OF AGES

AUTHOR UNKNOWN

" Rock of ages, cleft for me,"
  Thoughtlessly the maiden sung,
Fell the words unconsciously
  From her girlish, gleeful tongue;
Sang as little children sing;
  Sang as sing the birds of June:

Fell the words like light leaves down,
  On the current of the tune —
" Rock of ages, cleft for me,
  Let me hide myself in thee."

" Rock of ages, cleft for me,"
  'Twas a woman sung them now,
Pleadingly and prayerfully,
  Every word her heart did know;
Rose the song as storm-tossed bird
  Beats with weary wing the air,
Every note with sorrow stirred,
  Every syllable a prayer —
" Rock of ages, cleft for me,
  Let me hide myself in thee."

" Rock of ages, cleft for me,"
  Lips grown aged sung the hymn
Trustingly and tenderly,
  Voice grown weak and eyes grown dim,
" Let me hide myself in thee."
  Trembling though the voice, and low,
Rose the sweet strain peacefully,
  Like a river in its flow;
Sung as only they can sing
  Who life's thorny path have passed;
Sung as only they can sing
  Who behold the promised rest —
" Rock of ages, cleft for me,
  Let me hide myself in thee."

" Rock of ages, cleft for me,"
    Sung above a coffin lid;
Underneath, all restfully,
    All life's joys and sorrows hid.
Nevermore, oh storm-tossed soul,
    Nevermore from wind or tide,
Never more from billow's roll
    Wilt thou need thyself to hide.
Could the sightless, sunken eyes,
    Closed beneath the soft gray hair,
Could the mute and stiffened lips
    Move again in pleading prayer,
Still, aye still, the words would be —
" Let me hide myself in thee."

"SING US A SONG"

AUTHOR UNKNOWN

" Come, sing us a song — a hot one, too!
    (And fill each glass again,)
And, merry and bright, we'll pass the night
    In the joys of manly men.

" What care we for a woman's tears,
    Or childhood's frightened cry?
Come, tickle the harp! Let critics carp,
    And long-haired cynics sigh."

The harper swept, with an airy touch,
    Each true and trusted string,
And the bitter tears of other years
    To his notes seemed answering:

[394]

" I romped in the meadows,
Made love in the shadows;
   I waded the eddying streams,
I basked in the glory
Of youth's bright story
   And sweet was the joy of my dreams —
         Oh,
   Sweet was the joy of my dreams.

"Song birds were singing,
Young hope was springing —
   But, sweetest of music to me,
Was that voice in the gloaming,
When, weary with roaming,
   I knelt at my mother's knee —
         Oh,
   I knelt at my mother's knee —— "

" Ah, bosh on your sentimental drone!
   (Fill the glasses up again!)
Away with the grave, but sing us a stave
   For the laughter of merry men! "

But the harper tenderly swept the strings
   And his soft voice fell once more
Like an elfin strain, borne o'er the plain,
   Or a sigh from a distant shore:

" Though loyalty fadeth,
   Though envy upbraideth,
      The years bring the solace to me —

There's a friendship unshaken,
A friend ne'er forsaken
   I met at my mother's knee —
        Oh,
   I met at my mother's knee —— "

" Come, cheer our hearts with a livelier song
   (No, boys, that wasn't a tear;
It was only the fleck of a tiny speck
   From the top of the foaming beer).

" But the air seems close, and foul, and hot,
   And the drinks have bitter grown —
And I feel the thought in my brain inwrought
   Of a mother, at home — alone.

"So, harper, give us the song once more —
   Those same sweet words again —
For it fills the air with a mother's pray'r,
   And makes us holier men."

THE TEACHER'S DIADEM

AUTHOR UNKNOWN

Sitting 'mid the gathering shadows, weary with the
   Sabbath's care;
Weary with the Sabbath's burdens, that she dearly
   loves to bear;
For she sees a shining pathway, and she gladly presses
   on;

'Tis the first Great Teacher's footprints — it will lead
      where He has gone;
With a hand that's never faltered, with a love that's
      ne'er grown dim,
Long and faithfully she's labored, to His fold the lambs
      to bring.

But to-night her soul grows heavy; through the closed
      lids fall the tears,
As the children pass before her, that she's taught these
      many years;
And she cries in bitter anguish: " Shall not one to me
      be given,
To shine upon my coronet amid the hosts of heaven!
Hear my prayer to-night, my Saviour, in Thy glorious
      home above;
Give to me some little token — some approval of Thy
      love."

Ere the words were scarcely uttered, banishing the
      evening gloom,
Came a soft and shining radiance, brightening all
      within the room;
And an angel in white raiment, brighter than the morn-
      ing sun,
Stood before her, pointing upward, while he softly
      whispered, " Come."
As he paused, she heard the rustle of his starry pinions
      bright,
And she quickly rose and followed, out into the stilly
      night;

Up above the dim blue ether; up above the silver
      stars;
On, beyond the golden portals; through the open
      pearly doors;
Far across the sea of crystal, to the shining sapphire
      Throne,
Where she heard amid the chorus, " Welcome, child;
      thy work's well done."
Surely 'tis her Saviour speaking; 'tis His hands, aye,
      'tis His feet;
And she cries: " Enough! I've seen Him; all my joys
      are now complete."

All forgot earth's care and sorrow; all forgot the
      starry crown;
'Twas enough e'en to be near Him; to behold Him on
      His Throne.
" Not enough," the Saviour answered; " thou wouldst
      know through all these years,
If in vain has been thy teaching, all thy labor and thy
      prayers;
That from thee the end was hidden, did thy faith in
      me grow less?
Thou hast asked some little token, I will grant thee
      thy request."

From out a golden casket, inlaid with many a gem,
He took — glist'ning with countless jewels — a regal
      diadem;
Bright a name shone in each jewel, names of many
      scholars dear,

Who she thought had passed unheeded all her earnest
    thought and care.
" But," she asked, " how came these names here —
    names I never saw before ? "
And the Saviour smiling answered, " 'Tis the fruit
    thy teachings bore;

" 'Tis the seed thy love hath planted, tended by my
    faithful hand;
Though unseen by thee, it's budded, blossoming in
    many lands.
Here are names from darkened Egypt, names from
    Afric's desert sands;
Names from isles amid the ocean, names from India's
    sunny strands;
Some from Greenland's frozen mountains, some from
    burning tropic plains;
From where'er man's found a dwelling, here you'll
    find some chosen name.
When thine earthly mission's ended, that in love to
    thee was given,
This is the crown of thy rejoicing, that awaits thee
    here in heaven."

Suddenly the bright light faded; all was dark within
    the room;
And she sat amid the shadows of the Sabbath evening
    gloom;
But a peaceful, holy incense rested on her soul like
    dew;
Though the end from her was hidden, to her Master
    she'd be true;

Sowing seed at morn and even, pausing not to count
the gain;
If her bread was on the waters, God would give it
back again;
If the harvest she had toiled for other hands than hers
should reap,
He'd repay her for her labor, who had bade her,
" Feed my sheep."

ALTRUISM

AUTHOR UNKNOWN

This poem was discovered by Mr. George Morgan, of the bank-
ing firm of Morgan, Drexel & Co., in a country newspaper. He
carried it in his pocket for five years, occasionally reading it to his
friends. Inquiries for copies of it were so frequent that he finally
had it printed for distribution.

If you have a friend worth loving,
    Love him. Yes, and let him know
That you love him, ere life's evening
    Tinge his brow with sunset glow.
Why should good words ne'er be said
Of a friend till he is dead?

If you hear a song that thrills you,
    Sung by any child of song,
Praise it. Do not let the singer
    Wait deserved praises long.
Why should one who thrills your heart
Lack the joy you may impart?

If you hear a prayer that moves you
    By its humble, pleading tone,

[400]

Join it. Do not let the seeker
   Bow before its God alone.
Why should not your brother share
The strength of " two or three " in prayer?

If you see the hot tears falling
   From a brother's weeping eyes,
Share them. And by kindly sharing
   Own our kinship in the skies.
Why should any one be glad
When a brother's heart is sad?

If a silvery laugh goes rippling
   Through the sunshine on his face,
Share it. 'Tis the wise man's saying —
   For both grief and joy a place.
There's health and goodness in the mirth
In which an honest laugh has birth.

If your work is made more easy
   By a friendly, helping hand,
Say so. Speak out brave and truly
   Ere the darkness veil the land.
Should a brother workman dear
Falter for a word of cheer?

Scatter thus your seeds of kindness
   All enriching as you go —
Leave them. Trust the Harvest Giver;
   He will make each seed to grow.
So, until the happy end,
Your life shall never lack a friend.

AN ANGRY ANARCHIST

BY AN UNKNOWN AUTHOR IN LONDON TIT-BITS

Oh, he preached it from the housetops and he whispered
    it by stealth;
He wrote whole miles of stuff against the awful curse
    of wealth.
He shouted for the poor man, and he called the rich
    man down;
He roasted every king and queen who dared to wear
    a crown.
He clamored for rebellion, and he said he'd lead a band
To exterminate the millionaires and sweep them from
    the land.
He yelled against monopolists, their power he'd defy,
And swore he'd be an anarchist and blow them to the
    sky.
He stormed, he fumed, and ranted, till he made the
    rich men wince,
But an uncle left him money, and he hasn't shouted
    since.

A CONDENSED BIOGRAPHICAL
DICTIONARY OF AUTHORS
REPRESENTED

A CONDENSED BIOGRAPHICAL DICTIONARY OF AUTHORS REPRESENTED

ADAMS, CHARLES FOLLEN (1842). Born at Dorchester, Massachusetts. He was graduated from the common schools into the stern curriculum of war, serving as a soldier in the 13th Massachusetts Infantry. In 1872 he began contributing to various periodicals humorous poems in the German dialect. These poems he afterward collected and published in various books, the first of which was *Leedle Yawcob Strauss, and Other Poems.*

ADAMS, JOHN QUINCY (1767–1848). Born at Braintree, Massachusetts, the son of John Adams, second President of the United States. He was graduated from Harvard in 1787 and, after admission to the bar, entered into Government service and after three years' incumbency of a professorship at Harvard in rhetoric and belles-lettres was appointed Minister to Russia, and then Minister to Great Britain. Returning to America he became Secretary of State under President Monroe, and succeeded him in the Presidency.

AKERS, ELIZABETH ANN (1832). Born in Strong, Maine. At the age of fifteen she began to contribute articles to the press under the name of Florence Percy. Later, her work appeared in the *Atlantic Monthly;* in 1874 she became literary editor of the *Daily Advertiser* of Portland, Maine. Her fame rests on the poem "Rock Me to Sleep, Mother," which was first published in the

[405]

Saturday Evening Post of Philadelphia. It immediately became popular, and there were many claimants to its authorship.

ARNOLD, (SIR) EDWIN (1832–1904). Born at Gravesend, Sussex, England. He received a most thorough education at King's College, London, and at Oxford University, where he won the Newdigate Prize for poetry. In 1856 he was appointed Principal of the Government Deccan College, Poona, India, where he came to know the East, which was to form the subject of his later work. In 1861 he returned to England and turned his attention to journalism, in which he was very successful, becoming the editor of the *London Telegraph*. His best known works are *The Light of Asia* (1879), *Pearls of the Faith* (1883), *The Light of the World* (1891), and *The Tenth Muse* (1895). His work achieved immediate and widespread popularity, securing him a permanent place among English poets.

AYTON, SIR ROBERT (1570–1638). A Scottish poet and courtier, knighted by James I. Dryden pronounced his verses "some of the best of his age."

BABCOCK, MALTBIE DAVENPORT (1858–1901). Born at Syracuse, New York. He was graduated from Syracuse University with the highest honors. Entering the Presbyterian ministry he quickly achieved a reputation for oratory. He wrote a number of fugitive poems, of Emersonian quality, and several hymns of unusual spiritual beauty.

BARBAULD, ANNA LETITIA AIKEN (1743–1825). Born in Leicestershire, England. She wrote a number of books in verse and prose, of which *Poems*, published in 1773, was the first, and her *Hymns in Rhyme*, published long after her death, was the best.

BARR, AMELIA EDITH (HUDDLESTON) (1831). Born at Ulverston, Lancashire, England, and educated at Glasgow·High School. Upon her marriage in 1850 to Robert Barr, she moved to Texas, where her husband and three sons died of yellow fever in 1867. In 1869 she gave her attention to fiction. She has written more than thirty novels, the first being *Jan Vedder's Wife*. She has also written a number of poems which have achieved a popularity scarcely less than that of her fiction.

BOKER, GEORGE HENRY (1823–1890). American diplomat. Wrote several dramas and several volumes of poems. His dramas combine poetic merit with adaptability for acting.

BROOKS, PHILLIPS (1835–1893). Born in Boston, Massachusetts. After graduating from Harvard he entered the Episcopalian ministry. He was rector successively of two churches in Philadelphia, and of Trinity Church, Boston, where, until his death, he enjoyed the reputation of being the most eloquent and influential divine in his denomination. He wrote a number of books fitted with the inspirational quality which distinguished his sermons, and one poem, that which appears in this volume, which is beloved by Christians of all denominations.

BROWNING, ELIZABETH BARRETT (1806–1861). Born at Coxhoe Hall, Durham. She received a very thorough education at home, especially in the

[407]

classics, a deep love for which is very evident in her poems. While still very young she received an injury to her spine from which she never fully recovered. As early as 1826 she began to publish poems, at first anonymously, but later under her own name. In 1845 she met Robert Browning, whom she later married, living in Italy for the remaining years of her life. Her best poems are "The Sonnets from the Portuguese," which are for the most part a revelation of her own love story, and "Aurora Leigh," a love romance in verse. Mrs. Browning is generally considered the greatest of English poetesses, her works being tender and delicate, yet strong and deep in thought.

BROWNING, ROBERT (1812–1889). Born at Camberwell, England. Both of his parents, being people of education, encouraged their son from his earliest years in intellectual pursuits. At the age of twelve he had already written some poems, though these were not published. His first real work was "Pauline," which appeared anonymously in 1833. Recognition came but slowly despite his many works, his subjects being too recondite and his manner of treatment too intricate to interest the great number of readers. He wrote several dramas, none of which, excepting "A Blot on the 'Scutcheon" (1843), ever enjoyed any success on the stage. Browning is most generally known for a few of his shorter poems, as "Evelyn Hope," "A Death in the Desert," and "The Pied Piper of Hamelin." He received many distinctions during his lifetime, and on his death was buried in Westminster Abbey.

BRYANT, WILLIAM CULLEN (1794–1878). Born at Cummington, Massachusetts, of old Puritan stock. He spent one year at Williams College. In 1817 his poem

"Thanatopsis," written at the age of nineteen, appeared in the *North American Review*, and was greeted as the first truly great American poem. He led a very active life, being a successful lawyer, and later gained fame as a journalist in New York, becoming the editor of the *Evening Post*. Bryant's best known poems are "To a Water Fowl," "The Rivulet," "The West Wind," and "The Forest Hymn." His translations of the "Iliad" and "Odyssey" into blank verse are considered among the best renditions of Homer.

BURNS, ROBERT (1759–1796). Born of Scotch peasant stock near Ayr. His father was unfortunate in all his business enterprises, and upon his death, the poet experienced similar difficulties. When in desperation he was on the point of leaving Scotland for the West Indies, some friends dissuaded him, and suggested he publish his poems. These appeared in 1786, but, although very successful, the poet gained little from them financially. On several occasions he was offered remunerative positions, but refused as he did not wish to leave his native countryside. Burns is to-day the most widely read of all British and American poets. He excelled in short lyrical flights of song, which ring so sincere as to touch every heart. "Other poets," says Alfred Austin, "may be the favorites of a class or clique; Burns is the favorite of the whole world." The secret of this universal favor is to be found in the fact that he was born in a lowly condition of life, close to our mother earth, and gave utterance to the rudimentary sentiments, the abiding sorrows, and the constant yearnings of human nature.

BYRON, GEORGE GORDON, 6TH LORD (1788–1824). Born in London. He received a thorough education, culminating with the Master of Arts degree received after three years' study at Cambridge. He travelled extensively for two years in the Mediterranean countries, and, returning to London, wove the impressions of his tour into an heroic poem called "Childe Harold." He married in 1815, and, a year later, after the birth of a daughter, was separated from his wife. He lived much abroad, writing voluminously: dramatic, narrative, descriptive, and lyrical poems; notably, "Don Juan," "The Corsair," and "Manfred." He espoused the cause of Greek liberty, raising troops and leading them against the Turks. He died of fever at Missolonghi, Greece.

CAMPBELL, THOMAS (1777–1844). Born at Glasgow, Scotland, and educated at Glasgow University. While still a student he published his first poem, "The Pleasures of Hope," which achieved a great success. Although he wrote several other longer poems his fame does not rest on these, but on his patriotic and war lyrics, such as "Ye Mariners of England," "Hohenlinden," and "The Battle of the Baltic." Campbell also gained fame as a distinguished literary critic.

CAREY, HENRY (1685 or 1692–1743). Birthplace unknown. He died in London. He is said to have been the natural son of George Savile, Marquis of Halifax. He wrote many musical dramas and over one hundred musical ballads which were popular in their time. Of the ballads "Sally in our Alley" is the most famous. His son George Savile Carey claimed that Henry Carey composed "God Save the King," the national air of the British Empire, but the melody is probably older than his time. He probably arranged and altered it, singing it for the first time in public.

[410]

CARSON, NORMA BRIGHT (1883). Born at Philadelphia, Pennsylvania, and educated in the public schools of that city. Married Robert Carson in 1906. Published *The Dream Child and Other Poems* and *From Irish Castles to French Chateaux*.

CARY, ALICE (1820–1871). Born near Cincinnati, Ohio. When quite young she began writing poems and sketches for the press. In 1850 she and her sister Phœbe published a volume of their poems. In 1852 the sisters removed to New York City, where they lived the rest of their lives. Alice also published a number of novels.

CARY, PHŒBE (1824–1871). Born in Cincinnati, Ohio, and died in Newport, Rhode Island (see biography of Alice Cary, her sister).

COOPER, GEORGE (1840). Born in New York City and educated in its public schools. After practising law a brief time, he abandoned it for the pursuit of literature, contributing to the leading magazines. His poems, especially those for children, were widely admired for their pure sentiment and felicitous expression. He has written much verse for music.

COWPER, WILLIAM (1731–1800). Born at Great Berkhampstead Rectory, England, the son of a clergyman. Educated at Westminster School. He studied law and was appointed Commissioner of Bankrupts. Weakly from a child, he had in manhood periodical attacks of insanity. He died and was buried in Dereham, Norfolk. He wrote much verse, "The Task" being his longest poem. He also translated the "Iliad" and "Odyssey" of Homer.

COZZENS, FREDERICK SWARTWOUT (1818–1869). Born in New York City, the son of a prosperous merchant, who gave him an excellent education. He adopted literature as a pastime and soon became noted as a humorist, both in prose and verse. His sketches, published in book form under the title of *The Sparrowgrass Papers*, had an enormous circulation. He died suddenly in Brooklyn.

DALY, THOMAS AUGUSTINE (1871). Born at Philadelphia, educated at Villanova College and Fordham University. Since 1908 General Manager *Catholic Standard and Times*. Has published two books of verse, *Canzoni* and *Carmina*.

DICKENS, CHARLES (1812–1870). Born at Landport, Portsea, England. His father was unsuccessful in business, being arrested for debt when Charles was ten years of age, and the boy's education was sadly neglected. He worked at small jobs, teaching himself shorthand at night, and at the age of nineteen became Parliamentary reporter for a newspaper. Two years later he began contributing papers to various periodicals; these attracted considerable attention and were collected and published under the title of *Sketches of Boz*. *Boz* being a family soubriquet derived from the pet name of Mose or Moses. *Pickwick Papers*, his first extended work, was published in 1837 and established his reputation as a writer of a new order of fiction, whose distinguishing characteristic was delineation of unique characters. In almost yearly succession until his death he produced the novels which remain to-day the most popular works of English fiction. He twice visited America, in 1842 and in 1867, giving readings from his works, which were even more popular here than at home. He also wrote a number of successful plays, and founded two magazines of great popularity — *Household Words* and *All the Year Round.* He was buried in Westminster Abbey.

DORR, JULIA CAROLINE (RIPLEY) (1825). Born at Charleston, South Carolina. Becoming motherless in infancy, her father took her to Vermont, where she was educated. She married Seneca M. Dorr of New York. Subsequent to his death in 1884 she removed to Vermont, where she now resides. She is the author of a number of novels and books of verse.

DOWNING, FANNIE (MURDAUGH) (1835–1894). In 1851 she married Charles W. Downing, secretary of the State of Florida. She wrote several volumes of verse under her own name and the pseudonyms of "Viola" and Frank Dashmore. Her poems show power, combined with scholarship.

DRAKE, JOSEPH RODMAN (1795–1820). Born at New York. He received a purely scientific education and became a physician. He published one volume of poems which was very popular, especially the poems "The Culprit Fay" and "The American Flag." His early death was caused by consumption. He was buried at Hunt's Point, now in the Borough of the Bronx, New York City.

DUFFERIN, HELEN SELENA (SHERIDAN), COUNTESS OF (1807–1867). Granddaughter of Richard Brinsley Sheridan. She shared the family talent and wrote a good deal of verse, her best known piece being perhaps "The Lament of the Irish Emigrant," which is included in this volume.

DWIGHT, JOHN SULLIVAN (1813–1893). Born in Boston, Massachusetts. He was educated at Harvard University and prepared for the ministry at the Harvard

[413]

Divinity School. Leaving the ministry, he joined the Brook Farm community. Here he edited the musical department of the *Harbinger*, the organ of the community. Upon the failure of the experiment, he continued his work as musical critic in Boston. He wrote verse, as well as composed music, with facility and grace.

ELIOT, GEORGE, pseudonym of Mrs. Mary Ann (Evans) Cross (1819–1880). Born near Nuneaton, Warwickshire, England, and lived quietly at home until her father's death in 1849. She began her literary career with translations and various short articles in the *Westminster Review*. She later became an assistant editor of this paper, in which capacity she was thrown into the society of George Henry Lewes, a prominent journalist and philosopher, with whom she entered into an irregular connection because by a legal technicality he was prohibited from divorcing his wife, though she had eloped with another man. Encouraged by Lewes she began to write fiction, and her first novel, *The Sad Fortunes of the Rev. Amos Barton*, appeared in 1857. Many others followed, of which the best known are *Adam Bede*, *Silas Marner*, *Middlemarch*, and *Daniel Deronda*. Her poetical works are "The Spanish Gipsy," "Agatha," "The Legend of Jubal," and "Armgart." Mr. Lewes died in 1878, and in 1880 George Eliot married John Walter Cross. She died eight months afterward, in the same year. George Eliot was more successful in fiction than in verse. Edmund Clarence Stedman said: "A little poem in blank verse, entitled 'O May I Join the Choir Invisible!' and setting forth her conception of the religion of humanity, is worth all the rest of her poetry, for it is the outburst of an exalted soul foregoing personal immortality and compensated by a vision of the growth and happiness of the human race."

[414]

EMERSON, RALPH WALDO (1803–1882). Born at Boston, Massachusetts. He entered Harvard University in 1817 and, after passing through the usual course there, studied for the ministry, to which he was ordained in 1827. He resigned from the ministry in 1832 and visited Europe, where he met many eminent men and formed a life-long friendship with Carlyle. On his return in 1834 he settled at Concord and took up lecturing. He was regarded as the leader of the transcendentalists and was one of the chief contributors to their organ *The Dial*. In 1847 he paid a second visit to England and delivered a course of lectures in England and Scotland on "Representative Men" which he subsequently published. His works were collected in eleven volumes and include *Essays* (two series), *Conduct of Life*, *Society and Solitude*, *Natural History of Intellect*, and *Poems*. He was a man of singular elevation and purity of character.

FIELD, EUGENE (1850–1895). Born at St. Louis, Missouri. After a varied experience as a journalist in the Far West, he settled down to newspaper work in Chicago. By his poems and tales in the press of that city, especially those relating to children, he achieved national fame. He was also very happy in his translations and travesties of Horace.

Of him William Cranston Lawton says, in his *Introduction to the Study of American Literature*: "Field utters the very heart secrets of boyhood as not even Riley or Stevenson can do. *Wynken, Blynken and Nod* became long ago a kindergarten classic. His echoes of Horace are not mere irreverent travesties, but seize the very essence of the thought, and render it in the most startlingly up-to-date English, spiced both with current slang and with Field's own invented idioms."

[415]

FIELDS, JAMES THOMAS (1816–1881). Born in Portsmouth, New Hampshire. He became a publisher and editor, being one of the founders of the firm of Osgood, Ticknor, Fields and Company, and the editor of the *Atlantic Monthly*. He published a number of volumes of biography and criticism, and of original verse, and edited, with Edwin P. Whipple, the critic *The Family Library of British Poetry*.

FINCH, FRANCIS MILES (1827–1907). Born at Ithaca, New York. He was graduated with honors from Yale, where he had achieved a reputation as a writer of college songs. He promoted the establishment of Cornell University at Ithaca. His most noted poem is "The Blue and the Gray," published in 1867 in the *Atlantic Monthly*.

FOSS, SAM WALTER (1858). Born at Candia, New Hampshire. After his graduation from Brown University he became an editor and a contributor to magazines, chiefly of humorous verse, tinged with philosophy.

FOSTER, STEPHEN COLLINS (1826–1864). Born in Pittsburgh, Pennsylvania. Educated at Cannonsburg College, Pennsylvania. He taught himself music and, at the age of seventeen, while in employment at Louisville, Kentucky, began publishing songs, which speedily became popular all over the country. In 1854 he married, and removed to New York City, where, in rapid succession, he published the songs which made him world famous; such as, "Old Kentucky Home," "Massa's in the Cold, Cold Ground," and "Way Down upon the Swanee River." Altogether he wrote about one hundred and fifty songs, one-fourth of which were negro melodies. In 1861 he wrote his last song, "Old Black Joe."

[416]

FRENCH, L. VIRGINIA (SMITH) (1830–1881). Born in Frederick County, Virginia. She received an excellent education, and established a school in Memphis, Tennessee. Under the name of "L'Inconnue" [the unknown] she contributed articles to various magazines, which won for her a literary reputation. In 1852 she became associate editor of the *Southern Ladies' Book* of New Orleans. In 1856 Mrs. French published her poems under the title of *Wind Whispers*. She also wrote a series of metrical *Legends of the South*, and a tragedy. Later she became editor of *The Crusader* of Atlanta, Georgia.

GOLDSMITH, OLIVER (1728–1774). Born at Pallasmore, Longford, Ireland. He received an excellent education, and he studied for several professions, but never followed any, being rejected as a clergyman, and failing as a physician. He led a rather wild and vagrant life, travelling extensively. In 1757, after a long trip abroad on the continent, he went to London, where he remained during the rest of his life. While here he became associated with the famous circle of which Samuel Johnson was the dictator. Goldsmith has treated every field of literature, history, drama, fiction, essays, and verse. The four great works for which he is famous are *She Stoops to Conquer*, a comedy; *The Vicar of Wakefield*, a novel; and *The Traveller* and *The Deserted Village*, poems.

GRAY, THOMAS (1716–1771). Born in London. Educated at Eton and Cambridge, in which university he spent his life as a Fellow-Commoner and Professor, teaching history and the modern languages. He died at Cambridge, and was buried at Stoke-Pogis in the graveyard which has therefore been identified with the "Country Churchyard" of his famous elegy. General Wolfe,

[417]

on the evening before the battle of Quebec, repeated the poem to his officers, and, as he concluded, said: "I would prefer being the author of that poem to the glory of beating the French to-morrow."

GREENE, ALBERT GORTON (1802–1868). Born in Providence, Rhode Island. Upon graduation from Brown University, he studied law. He took a great interest in literature, in particular making a collection of American poetry, which formed the nucleus of the great collection on that subject now in Brown University. His own poems, of which he wrote a number and which became popular selections for recitation, were never published in collected form.

GUINEY, LOUISE IMOGEN (1861). Born at Boston, Massachusetts. After receiving an excellent education, she began contributing to various magazines. She is the author of a number of volumes of verse and prose and the editor of several critical works. She resides in Oxford, England.

HALLECK, FITZ-GREENE (1790–1867). Born at Guilford, Connecticut. In collaboration with Joseph Rodman Drake he wrote *The Crocker Papers* (1819). A few years later he visited Europe, and the traces of this visit are discernible in his subsequent poems. Halleck's works were very popular during his lifetime, but with a few exceptions are now little read.

HARTE, FRANCIS BRET (1839–1902). Born at Albany, New York. While still a boy he went to California, where he had a rather checkered career as a teacher, miner, and journalist. Later he became a United States consul, first at Crefeld, Germany, and then at Glasgow,

Scotland. In 1885 he went to London, and supported himself by his pen until his death. Harte is best known for his realistic and striking stories of Western life. His poems have enjoyed great popularity because of their rich vein of humor. Edmund Clarence Stedman, in his *Poets of America*, said of Harte's verse: "Like the rhyming of his master, Thackeray, it is the overflow of a rare genius, whose work must be counted among the treasures of the language. Mr. Harte may be termed the founder, and thus far has been the most brilliant exemplar, of our transcontinental school."

HAY, JOHN (1838–1905). Born at Salem, Indiana. Graduated from Brown University. Shortly after his admission to the bar he became private secretary to President Lincoln, whose life he later wrote in conjunction with John G. Nicolay, another secretary of the President. He entered into the diplomatic service, becoming in time Ambassador to England. He was Secretary of State under President McKinley and President Roosevelt. His most notable literary work is *Pike County Ballads*, a little book of Western dialect verse, all of which was written within a week.

HEMANS, FELICIA DOROTHEA (BROWNE) (1793–1835). Born at Liverpool, England. She was very precocious, publishing a volume of verse at the age of fifteen. She married Captain Hemans in 1812, and, after an unhappy union, was separated from him six years later. She lived most of her life in Wales, removing thence to Liverpool and Dublin. Her work was wholly in verse, and very voluminous.

HOLMES, OLIVER WENDELL (1809–1894). Born at Cambridge, Massachusetts. He studied medicine and practised in his native town until appointed Professor of Anatomy and Physiology at Dartmouth College. Later he occupied a similar chair at Harvard University. Until 1857 he did little literary work, but in that year he became the principal contributor to the *Atlantic Monthly*. In this magazine appeared his best known works, *The Autocrat of the Breakfast Table*, *The Professor at the Breakfast Table*, and *The Poet at the Breakfast Table*. The best of his poems are embodied in these books.

William Morton Payne, in his *Little Leaders*, says of Holmes: "We have no other so expert in personal and occasional verse, no other who could so distill the very quintessence of Yankee humor, or of the other and finer qualities of the New England intellect, into the most limpid of song. And when he was entirely serious, how exquisite was his touch, how pure his pathos, how clear his ethical sense! Let 'The Voiceless,' 'Under the Violets,' and 'The Chambered Nautilus' bear witness."

HOOD, THOMAS (1799–1845). Born at London, England. His father being a bookseller Hood was from the first interested in books and thrown in contact with literary people. His first publication, *Odes and Addresses to Great People*, 1825, was a great success, and encouraged he wrote several other works humorous and serious. He is best known to-day for his serious, pathetic poems, of which "The Song of the Shirt" and "The Bridge of Sighs" are the best examples.

HOWE, JULIA (WARD) (1819–1910). Born in New York City. She received an excellent education, becoming proficient in ancient and modern languages and in music. At the age of seventeen she began her literary career with contributions to the *New York Magazine*.

At the age of twenty-four she married Samuel G. Howe, the philanthropist; after a trip abroad they settled in Boston, where their home became a centre of culture and good works. She has written several volumes of verse. Her most noted poem is "The Battle Hymn of the Republic," which was written in beleaguered Washington in the dark days of 1861, and published in the *Atlantic Monthly* in February, 1862, the air being the one to which the Union soldiers had marched to the front — "John Brown's Body," or, "Glory, Glory, Hallelujah!"

HUNT, JAMES HENRY LEIGH (1784–1859). Born at Southgate, England. Educated at Christ's Hospital School. He early became a contributor to the magazines, and so slipped into the editorial profession. He was one of the most voluminous writers of his times, treating of a wide variety of subjects in light, discursive style. It is, however, in his poems that he achieved his most lasting success.

JOYCE, JOHN ALEXANDER (1842). Born at Shraugh, Ireland. Reared and educated in Kentucky. Served in Union army during the Civil War. After war practised law. Author of a number of books in prose and verse.

KEATS, JOHN (1795–1821). Born in London. He was sent to school at Enfield, and having meantime become an orphan was in 1810 apprenticed to a surgeon. In 1815 he went to London to walk the hospitals; he was not, however, at all enthusiastic in his profession, and having become acquainted with Leigh Hunt, Hazlitt, Shelley, and others he gave himself more and more to literature. His first work — some sonnets — came out in 1817. *Endy-*

[421]

mion appeared in 1818 and was savagely attacked by the reviews. In 1820 he published *Lamia and Other Poems*. His health had by this time completely given away and in 1821 he set out on a journey to Italy from which he never returned.

KEY, FRANCIS SCOTT (1780–1843). Born in Frederick County, Maryland. After his graduation from St. John's College, he studied law. He began practice in Fredericktown, Maryland, but soon removed to Washington, where he became District Attorney of the District of Columbia. He was known among his friends as a graceful and facile poet. During the War of 1812 he was a spectator from a vessel of the bombardment of Fort McHenry, one of the defences of Baltimore, by the British, and he immediately drafted the song "The Star-Spangled Banner." Sung to the tune of "Anacreon in Heaven" it became popular at once, and has since become the rival of "America" as the national hymn of the country.

KIPLING, R. (1865). Born in Bombay, India, and educated in England. When but seventeen he returned to India and took up rough and ready journalistic work. He turned out a number of short stories and poems, *Barrack-Room Ballads*, *Departmental Ditties*, *Soldiers Three*, which were quickly caught up by the press, followed by several novels, notably *Captains Courageous* (1897), and two wonderful series of animal fables, *The Jungle Books*, which placed him in the front rank of English novelists and poets of the present day.

KNOX, WILLIAM (1789–1825). Born at Firth, Roxburghshire, Scotland. Failing as a farmer, he went to Edinburgh, and became a journalist. He wrote several books of verse.

LAMB, CHARLES (1775–1834). Born in London, England, and educated there in Christ's Hospital School. At the age of twenty-three he contributed to a volume of verse by S. T. Coleridge, Charles Lloyd, and himself. In 1802 he published *John Woodvil*, a drama. It was as an essayist, however, that he achieved his greatest fame, his *Essays of Elia* being one of the world's greatest works in this form of literature.

LONGFELLOW, HENRY WADSWORTH (1807–1882). Born at Portland, Maine. Was educated at Bowdoin College, where, upon graduation, he was appointed to the chair of modern languages. Later he accepted a similar chair at Harvard. He travelled extensively abroad, being received with honor after he had gained recognition as a poet. Longfellow was essentially American, choosing the legends and scenes of his native country for the subjects of his poems. Besides his shorter lyrical poems and sonnets he is known as the author of *The Golden Legend*, *Hiawatha*, *Evangeline*, and *The Courtship of Miles Standish*. His work was greatly beloved in England, where he was almost the only American poet known to the common people. Yet he was essentially American. As Prof. Brander Matthews says: "He had acquired the culture of all lands, but he understood also the message of his own country. He was a true American, not only in his stalwart patriotism in the hour of trial, but in his loving acceptance of the doctrine of human equality, and in his belief and trust in his fellow man."

LOWELL, JAMES RUSSELL (1819–1891). Born at Cambridge, Massachusetts. He was educated at Harvard, and began active life as a lawyer, but soon abandoned business and devoted himself to literature. In 1841 he published a volume of poems, *A Year's Life*, and in 1843 a second book of verses appeared. Other volumes followed and in 1855 he was appointed Professor of Modern Languages at Harvard. In 1877 he was appointed United States Minister to Spain and held a similar appointment in England in 1880–1885.

LUDLOW, FITZ–HUGH (1836–1870). Born in New York and educated at Union College. Admitted to the bar, he shortly returned to journalism, becoming well known as a writer of short stories, poems, and dramatic, musical, and art criticism. He wrote several books, the most noted being *The Hasheesh Eater* and *The Opium Habit*.

LYTLE, W. H. (1826–1863). Born in Cincinnati, Ohio. Studied law and began practice. He volunteered at the beginning of the Mexican War and served through the war. At the beginning of the Civil War he was commissioned colonel of the 10th Ohio Regiment. He served with distinction, and was killed leading a charge of his brigade at Chickamauga. General Lytle was a poet of much merit, but no collection of his verses has been published.

McCALLUM, DANIEL CRAIG (1815–1878). Born in Johnstown, Renfrewshire, Scotland. His parents settled in Rochester, New York, while he was young and there he became architect and builder. In 1862 was appointed military director and superintendent of railroads in the United States, with the rank of colonel, and "for faithful and meritorious service" was brevetted brigadier-general and major-general of volunteers.

MALONE, WALTER (1866). Born in De Soto County, Mississippi, and educated at the University of

[424]

Mississippi. After practising law for several years at Memphis, Tennessee, he went to New York and engaged in authorship, his work chiefly consisting of poetical contributions to the magazines. Later he returned to his law practice in Memphis.

MARKHAM, EDWIN (1852). Born at Oregon City, Oregon. His parents removed, during his childhood, to California. By working at farm labor, blacksmithing, and herding, he earned his way through normal school and Santa Rosa College, and prepared himself as a teacher. He contributed poetry to the best Eastern magazines, and finally, in 1898, received world-wide recognition as a poet of the first order with his "The Man with the Hoe." In 1899 he removed to New York City and devoted himself to literature.

Mr. Markham's poem on "Lincoln" is thought by some superior to his "The Man with the Hoe." It is here presented, specially revised by the author.

MASSEY, GERALD (1828–1907). Born near Tring, Herts, England. When he was fifteen he came to London, where he was taken up by Maurice and Kingsley. A selection from his poems was published in 1889 under the title "My Lyrical Life." Later he wrote and lectured on spiritualism.

MILTON, JOHN (1608–1674). Born in London, the son of a scrivener and teacher and composer of music, who destined Milton from his youth to become a man of letters, sending him to St. Paul's School, and afterward to Cambridge. For six years after leaving the university Milton devoted himself to study in his father's house, and then travelled for fifteen months on the continent, being everywhere received with honor for his scholarship by noblemen and authors. Returning to London in 1639 he began teaching. He took active part in the ecclesiastical controversies of the time, supporting the Puritan side. In 1643 he married Mary Powell; the union was unhappy, and they separated, but became reconciled in 1645. In 1649 Milton was appointed Latin Secretary in Cromwell's government. He became blind one year later. In 1652 his wife died; four years later he married Catherine Woodcock; she died in 1658, and in 1663 he married Elizabeth Minshull, who survived him. During the Restoration he was imprisoned for treasonable publications, but was shortly released. He died in 1674 in London and was buried in St. Giles's Churchyard.

Milton's fame rests on *Paradise Lost*, the greatest by far of English epic poems. Nevertheless, had he not written it, his sonnets and lyrics would entitle him to a high place among poets. Said George William Curtis: "While yet a youth he wrote those minor poems which have the simple perfection of productions of nature; and in the ripeness of his wisdom and power he turned his blind eyes to heaven, and sang the lofty song which has given him a twin glory with Shakespeare in English renown."

MOORE, CLEMENT CLARKE (1779–1863). Born in New York City. He prepared for the ministry, but was never ordained, preferring to devote himself to the study of Hebrew and the classics. The *Hebrew-English Lexicon* (1809) gave him title to be considered the pioneer American lexicographer. He wrote much on religious subjects, and became Professor of Oriental and Greek Literature in the General Theological Seminary of New York. He published a volume of poems, of which "A Visit from St. Nicholas" is the most famous.

MOORE, THOMAS (1779–1852). Born in Dublin, Ireland. Educated at Trinity College, Dublin. Law student at Middle Temple, London. Appointed to a government position in Bermuda, which he held for eight months; then, leaving the office in charge of a deputy, he travelled in the United States, after which he returned to England and began contributing to the *Edinburgh Review*. He wrote many books of verse, the first under the pseudonym of Thomas Little. He also wrote a *History of Ireland*, and translated and imitated Anacreon. His songs were set to exquisite melodies, and this combined with the intrinsic merit of his verse to render him the favorite poet of his generation. In the height of his fame he received the following encomium of Edgar A. Poe; "A vivid fancy, an epigrammatic spirit, a fine taste, vivacity, dexterity, and a musical ear have made him what he is, the most popular poet now living, if not the most popular that ever lived."

MORRIS, GEORGE POPE (1802–1864). Born at Philadelphia. Entering into journalism he established with Samuel Woodworth the *New York Mirror* in 1823, and, on its discontinuance, with N. P. Willis the *New Mirror* in 1843, this shortly afterwards taking the name of the *Evening Mirror*. In 1845 he founded the *Home Journal*, which he edited jointly with Willis till shortly before his death. He wrote one novel, *Briarcliff*, and edited two collections of American verse. He is best known by his two poems, "My Mother's Bible" and "Woodman, Spare that Tree."

NAIRNE, BARONESS (CAROLINA OLIPHANT) (1766–1845). Born at Gask, Perthshire, Scotland. Married at the age of forty Major (subsequently Lord) Nairne.

[427]

They settled at Edinburgh. Upon her husband's death Lady Nairne removed to Ireland, and afterwards to the continent. Of her eighty-seven songs, four at least are immortal: "The Land o' the Leal," "Caller Herrin," "The Laird o' Cockpen," and "The Auld House."

NORTON, CAROLINE ELIZABETH SARAH (SHERIDAN), LADY STIRLING–MAXWELL (1808–1877). Born in London, the daughter of Richard Brinsley Sheridan, the dramatist. She displayed precocious literary ability. She wrote books upon the position of women, especially in relation to marriage, several novels, and a number of volumes of verse.

O'HARA, THEODORE (1822–1867). Born at Danville, Kentucky, of Irish parentage. Educated at St. Joseph's College, Bardstown, Kentucky. He enlisted in the army during the Mexican War, and was brevetted major for gallant service. Subsequently he fought for the liberation of Cuba, and went with Walker on his filibustering expedition to Central America. Returning, he embarked in journalism, becoming noted as one of the most brilliant of Southern editors. At the outbreak of the Civil War he joined the Confederacy and performed efficient service as staff officer under Gen. A. S. Johnston and Gen. John C. Breckinridge. He wrote very little; however, his *Bivouac of the Dead* is sufficient to immortalize his name. It was written to commemorate his comrades who fell in the Mexican War and who were buried in a lot set apart for them in the Frankfort, Kentucky, cemetery, where his own body now lies among them.

PAYNE, JOHN HOWARD (1792–1852). Born at New York. He appeared on the New York stage at the age of seventeen and played abroad as well as throughout America, being known as "The American Juvenile Wonder." He retired from the stage in 1832 and devoted himself to playwriting, being the author and adapter of more than sixty plays and operas. He was American Consul in Tunis from 1843 to 1845, and from 1851 to his death in 1852. He lives in fame as the author of "Home, Sweet Home," a song in his opera "Clari, the Maid of Milan." The melody he adapted from the song of an unknown Italian street singer.

PIERPONT, JOHN (1785–1866). Born in Litchfield, Connecticut. Educated at Yale. After studying law he went into business in Baltimore. Becoming bankrupt, he studied theology at Harvard and was ordained as a Congregational pastor in Boston; later he became a Unitarian. He wrote a volume of verse entitled *Airs of Palestine* and a number of patriotic lyrics, which, says James L. Onderdonk, in his *History of American Verse*, are "among the best and most spirited in our literature."

POE, EDGAR ALLAN (1809–1849). Born at Boston, of theatrical parentage. Being left an orphan at an early age, he was adopted by a Mr. Allan of Virginia. He received a broken, unfinished education at the University of Virginia and West Point. Poe is known as a short-story writer, poet, and literary critic, his work in each branch being memorable. His first volume of poems appeared in 1829; others followed in 1831 and 1845. He had a morbid mind, prone to dwell on the horrors of death and insanity. Afflicted with poverty, and grieved by the death of his young wife (in Fordham, near New York, 1847), he resorted in the last years of his life to drink, and death came to him, as the result of a

[429]

debauch, in Baltimore, as he was returning to New York from a visit to his old home in Richmond, Virginia.

PROCTER, ADELAIDE ANNE (1825–1864). Born in London, the daughter of Bryan Waller Procter (Barry Cornwall), the poet. As a young woman she contributed poems to Charles Dickens' magazine, *Household Words*, under the pseudonym of Mary Berwick. She became a Roman Catholic and engaged in charitable work, writing a volume, *A Chaplet of Verses*, for the benefit of homeless women in London. Her best known poem, "A Lost Chord," was set to music by Sir Arthur Sullivan.

RILEY, JAMES WHITCOMB (1853). Born at Greenfield, Indiana, and educated in the common schools. Since 1873 his work has been appearing, at first in magazines, then in book form. He is popularly known as the "Hoosier Poet," his verse being for the most part in that dialect. Among his best known poems are "The Old Swimmin' Hole," "An Old Sweetheart of Mine," and "Out to Old Aunt Mary's."

ROGERS, SAMUEL (1763–1855). Born at Stoke-Newington, England. He was educated there and at Hackney. He entered his father's bank at the age of twelve, and succeeding his father, continued in this business until his death; travel, the pursuit of literature, and the study of the fine arts being his recreations. He wrote several volumes of verse, the chief being *Pleasures of Memory* and a book of *Recollections* published after his death.

RYAN, ABRAM JOSEPH (1839–1886). Born at Norfolk, Virginia. A Roman Catholic, he entered the priesthood, and served as chaplain in the Confederate army. Shortly after Lee's surrender he wrote a poem entitled "The Conquered Banner," which was received with praise in the North as well as in the South. He published three volumes of verse. At the time of his death, which took place in Louisville, Kentucky, he was engaged on a *Life of Christ*.

SANGSTER, MARGARET ELIZABETH (MUNSON) (1838). Born in New Rochelle, New York, and educated privately in New York City. Soon after her marriage to George Sangster in 1858, she began contributing to the magazines. She has held a number of editorial positions, and published quite an array of volumes in both prose and verse. Her muse is religious and domestic, causing her to be one of the most popular household poets of the day in America.

SAXE, JOHN GODFREY (1816–1887). Born in Highgate, Vermont; educated at Wesleyan University and Middlebury. He practised law with success, but his fondness for literature led him into journalism and in 1850 he purchased the *Burlington Sentinel*. Settling in New York he devoted himself to literature and lectured until 1872, when he moved to Albany and became editor of the *Evening Journal*. He contributed to the leading magazines of his day and achieved great reputation by his poetry, numerous collections of which have been published.

SCOTT, SIR WALTER (1771–1832). Born in Edinburgh, Scotland; was connected through both parents with several old border families. As a child he began to follow the irresistible bent which ultimately led to such brilliant results in a course of insatiable reading of ballads

[431]

and romances. He studied for the bar, to which he was called in 1792. The year 1802 saw the publication of Scott's first work of real importance, *The Minstrelsy of the Scottish Border*. In 1805 he produced his first great original work, *The Lay of the Last Minstrel*, which was received with great favor, and decided that literature was thenceforth to be the main work of his life. The *Waverley Novels* were published between 1814 and 1831, and on these his chief fame rests. Scott was ruined by the failure of the Ballantynes in 1826 and devoted the rest of his life to clearing off his debt. Scott's overworked body at last gave way and he died at Abbotsford in 1832.

SILL, EDWARD ROWLAND (1841–1887). Born in Windsor, Connecticut. He was educated at Yale. He studied for the ministry, but shortly abandoned his purpose and engaged in teaching, marrying and settling in Brooklyn, New York. In 1871 he went to California and, in 1874, became Professor of English Literature in the University of California, doing much for the development of original literature in that State. In 1883 he returned East and devoted himself until his death exclusively to writing.

SMITH, SAMUEL FRANCIS (1808–1905). Born in Boston. He attended the Boston Latin School and was graduated at Harvard and at Andover Theological Seminary. He was ordained to the ministry of the Baptist Church in 1834.

Dr. Smith has done a large amount of literary work, mainly in the line of hymnology, his most noted poem being the national hymn, which was written while he was a theological student and first sung at a children's celebration in the Park Street Church, Boston, July 4, 1832.

[432]

SOUTHEY, CAROLINE ANNE (BOWLES) (1787–1854). Born in Hampshire, England, the daughter of a retired officer. She remained at home till her literary work, consisting of poems, tales, and sketches, published in the magazines, brought her into public notice. She formed a warm personal friendship with Robert Southey, the Poet Laureate, and married him two years after the death of his wife. They wrote a number of poems in collaboration.

STANTON, FRANK LEBBY (1857). Born in Charleston, South Carolina. Educated in the common schools; he served an apprenticeship as a printer, thence rising into the plane of journalism. He is now connected with the *Atlanta Constitution*, in which his songs appear almost daily, being quoted by the newspapers all over the country. He has gathered the choicest of his verse into several volumes.

STEDMAN, EDMUND CLARENCE (1833–1908). Born in Hartford, Connecticut. Educated at Yale, from which he was dismissed for a boyish prank, although he afterward received his degree from his Alma Mater, proud of his reputation as a man of letters. He entered journalism and, during the Civil War, served as war-correspondent for the *New York World*. After the war he became a Wall Street broker, holding a position upon the exchange until 1900. He wrote a number of books upon poetry and edited, with Ellen M. Hutchinson, a large anthology of American literature. At the time of his death he was regarded as the "Dean of American Letters."

STEVENSON, ROBERT LOUIS (1850–1894). Born at Edinburgh, coming from a distinguished family

[433]

of Scotch engineers. His delicate health made a thorough education impossible. He read extensively and so fitted himself for a literary career. This he began in 1871 with contributions to various magazines. He reached distinction as a short-story writer, novelist, essayist, and poet. Among his works may be especially noted *The Merry Men* — a collection of short stories, *The Strange Case of Dr. Jekyll and Mr. Hyde*, *Treasure Island*, and *Kidnapped*. His poetical works are *A Child's Garden of Verse*, 1885, and *Underwoods*, 1887. He died in Samoa in the South Seas, where he had settled in a vain attempt to regain his health.

SWINBURNE, ALGERNON CHARLES (1837–1909). Born in London, England. Received his early education in France and was at Eton and Oxford, where he attracted the attention of Jowett. In his earlier days Swinburne was closely associated with the Rossettis, Meredith, and Burne-Jones.

His first two plays, *The Queen Mother* and *Rosamund*, made no impression on the public, but the appearance in 1865 of *Atalanta in Calydon* led to his immediate recognition as a poet of the first order. *Poems and Ballads*, published in 1866, created a profound sensation alike among the critics and the general body of readers by its daring departure from recognized standards. As a master of metre Swinburne's is hardly excelled by any of our poets.

TAYLOR, BAYARD (1825–1878). Born in Pennsylvania, of Quaker descent. He began to write by the time he was twelve. He travelled extensively in Europe. After his return joined the staff of the *New York Tribune* and published several books on travel and poetry, among which are *Views Afoot* (1846). His translation of

Goethe's *Faust* is perhaps his best work. He was appointed to the German Embassy and died in Berlin in 1879.

TENNYSON, ALFRED BARON) TENNYSON OF ALDWORTH) (1809–1892). Born at Somersby, Lincolnshire, England, the son of the rector of the parish. His education, which was completed at Trinity College, Cambridge, brought him in contact with many gifted men whose influence was most valuable. Although his first volume of poems had appeared in 1827, he received no general recognition until 1842, when his fourth collection of poems appeared. From this time on his fame grew apace. His greatest poem is the elegy on the death of his dear friend Arthur Hallam, *In Memoriam*, which appeared in 1850. This same year, on the death of Wordsworth, he succeeded to the Laureateship. Tennyson also turned his attention to the drama, achieving some success, especially with *Becket*, 1884. He was raised to the peerage in that year. The poet's life, which had been tranquil and uneventful, received a great shock at the death of his younger son, and from this blow he never recovered. He died in his eighty-fourth year, and receiving a public funeral, was buried in Westminster Abbey.

"Truly," said Sir Edwin Arnold, "the echoes of Lord Tennyson's song will live forever and forever, and roll from soul to soul. Beyond all dispute he is the representative singer of the great reign of Victoria."

THACKERAY, WILLIAM MAKEPEACE (1811–1863). Born at Calcutta, India. At the age of five, on the death of his father, he came to London to receive his education at Charterhouse School. He was intended for the law, but, having no liking for that profession, turned his attention to journalism, in which business he lost his fortune. He studied art, but finding his talent limited, turned to literature as a means of livelihood. Thackeray is best known as a novelist, his greatest works being *Henry Esmond* (1832) and *Vanity Fair* (1848). He also achieved success as an essayist. He wrote but little verse, and that largely in light and humorous vein.

TUBBS, ARTHUR LEWIS (1867). Born at Glens Falls, New York, and educated there in the high school. Studied music, entered into journalism. He is now the dramatic and musical critic of the *Philadelphia Evening Bulletin*. He has written a number of plays and many poems and short stories.

WEBSTER, DANIEL (1782–1852). Born at Waterford, New Hampshire, of old New England stock. Studied law and was a member of the United States Senate and Secretary of State. He was one of the greatest orators America has produced. His place in literature rests on his published speeches.

WHITTIER, JOHN GREENLEAF (1807–1892). Born at Haverhill, Massachusetts, coming of Quaker stock. His youth was passed on a farm; later he became interested in journalism. He was active in local politics, being a strong champion of the anti-slavery cause. In 1836 he began to publish his poems, many volumes appearing in the following years.

Edmund Gosse, the English critic, said of Whittier: "He is filled with moral enthusiasm as a trumpet is filled with the breath of him who blows it. His Quaker quietism concentrates itself until it breaks into a real passion-storm of humanity, and when Whittier is roused he sings with the thrilling sweetness of a woodthrush."

WITHER, GEORGE (1588–1667). Born at Bentworth, Hants, England. Entered Oxford, but left it after three years, and studied law at Lincoln's Inn, London. In the Civil War he served as a major-general on the Parliamentary side. His writings are many, consisting for the greater part of poems and political tracts.

WOLFE, CHARLES (1791–1823). Born in Dublin, Ireland. Educated at Dublin University. He became an Anglican clergyman. He suffered from ill-health during his last years, and died at the age of thirty-two. His most famous poem is *The Burial of Sir John Moore*, which gave title to his only volume of verse.

WOODWORTH, SAMUEL (1785–1842). Born at Scituate, Massachusetts. He received a scant education in the miserable common schools of the day and region, but some juvenile verses that he wrote attracted the attention of the village clergyman, who taught him the classics. In 1823 he and George P. Morris founded the *New York Mirror*. He wrote operatic pieces and a number of popular songs, of which "The Old Oaken Bucket" is by far the best.

WORDSWORTH, WILLIAM (1770–1850). Born at Cockermouth, Cumberland, England. Educated at Cambridge. He travelled abroad and then returned to live with his sister. They resided in various parts of England, finally settling at Grasmere, among the Cumberland lakes. Wordsworth was the centre of a group of poets, including Coleridge and Southey, and called the

[437]

"Lake Poets." Wordsworth succeeded Southey as Poet Laureate. With the exception of a few books descriptive of natural scenery, Wordsworth's works are poetical.

By some of the greatest minds of the age Wordsworth is revered as the greatest English poet since Shakespeare and Milton. John Burroughs, the naturalist, gives the following reason for this worship: "He stands for a particular phase of human thought and experience and his service to certain minds is like an initiation into a new order of mysteries. He is not, and can never be, the world's poet, but the poet of those who love solitude and solitary communion with nature."

INDEX OF TITLES

[440]

[441]

[442]

[445]

INDEX OF FIRST LINES

[447]

POETICAL FAVORITES